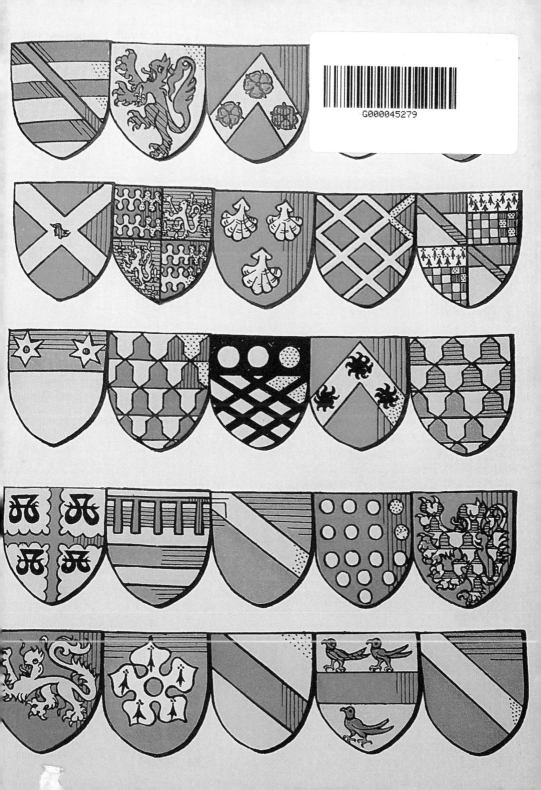

TINY CASTLES
DIXE WILLS

TINY
CASTLES

DIXE
WILLS

Published by AA Media Limited, whose registered office is
Grove House, Lutyens Close, Basingstoke, Hampshire RG24 8AG

First published in 2019

A CIP catalogue record for this book is available from the British Library.

ISBN: 978-0-7495-8197-8

Publisher: Phil Carroll
Editor: Donna Wood
Art Director: James Tims
Designer: Tracey Freestone

Printed and bound in Dubai by Oriental Press.

A05695

For Canadian Jess

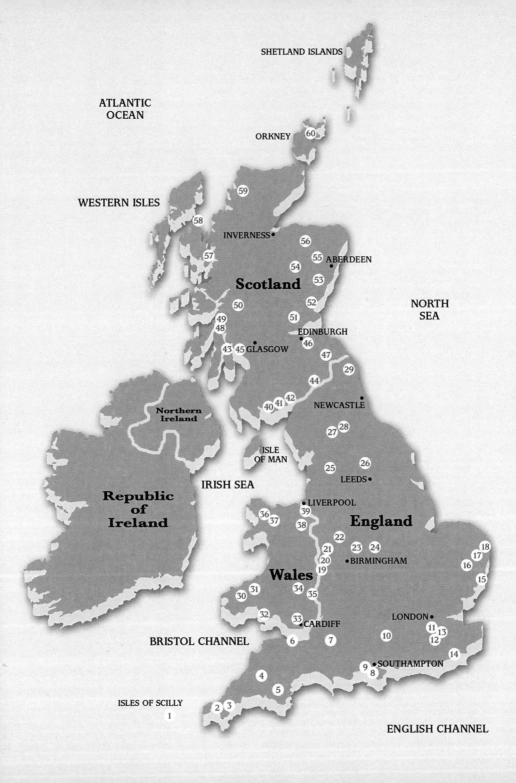

CONTENTS

INTRODUCTION

et's be honest here: all castles, even the smallest ones, are monumental buildings. It's just that some are rather more monumental than others. I've simply searched the length and breadth of the land for the best castles that are tiny in comparison with what (for want of a better word) might be termed a 'normal' castle.

Thankfully, it turns out that there are some crackers amongst the nation's more diminutive strongholds, many of them hidden away and visited by only the most persistent of off-piste trippers and castle cognoscenti. Indeed, Britain is such a treasure trove of castles – Wales has more per square mile than any other country on the planet – that the difficult task was whittling down the contenders to a book-sized number.

There's also plenty of variety on offer, as you might expect from an island that consists of three very different nations, each harbouring a plethora of distinct cultures and ways of doing things.

It means that the Scottish county of Dumfries and Galloway, for example, is represented by three wildly contrasting fortresses. There's **Orchardton Tower** (page 207), which rather resembles a sail-less windmill; **MacLellan's Castle** (page 202), a tower house completely at home in its modern urban environment (well, as modern as Kirkcudbright gets); and **Caerlaverock Castle** (page 214),

the only triangular fortress ever built in Britain. Extraordinarily, despite them being geographically close, the histories of these three barely overlap.

Meanwhile, in North Wales, the castles that Edward I erected to oppress his newly conquered subjects tend to be on the larger side (we're looking at you Conwy, Caernarfon, Harlech et al). However, a lot of the strongholds constructed by the Welsh themselves are a good deal more modest but no less fascinating. For instance, on the edge of the Snowdonian town of Llanberis you'll find picturesque **Dolbadarn Castle** (page 179), which for 22 years became a prison holding just one inmate. His crime? A disagreement with his younger brother. There's a lesson to be learned there somewhere.

That's not to say the Anglo-Normans couldn't throw up a little castle in Wales if they wanted to. And the fabulous incompetence displayed in the 'improvements' made to one such – **Pennard Castle** (page 156) on the Gower – were only matched by its ultimate destruction at the hands of… a sand dune.

Many people assume that **Castell Coch** (page 163), just outside Cardiff, is merely a Victorian folly. And although it certainly has the air of one, it's actually a rebuilding of a 13th-century castle (you can still see the join) by perhaps the greatest and most eccentric architect of

his age – aided and abetted by one of the world's richest men.

And so to England, where even a man's home is reputedly his castle (though presumably less so when he's appealing against an excessive council tax banding). Here we have everything from **Cromwell's Castle** (page 12), a Civil War anti-naval blockhouse on the gorgeous Scillonian isle of Tresco, to the late 14th-century **Preston Tower** (page 140) in Northumberland, thrown up as a safe house from the lawless border reivers. There's Hampshire's **Calshot Castle** (page 48), built by Henry VIII to prevent a French invasion and yet still able to take an active part in World War II, and **Hopton Castle** (page 94) in Shropshire, whose grisly secrets even Sir Tony Robinson's* *Time Team* could not uncover.

There's truly something for everyone. And just because they are small, it's a mistake to imagine that these castles have been unimportant. Name a battle from the Middle Ages and one of them is likely to have been involved in some way. Name a medieval monarch and there'll be a connection to one of these bijou fortresses.

Whether you use this book as a guide for your own travels or as a chance to do some armchair exploring, I do hope you enjoy reading it as much as I have enjoyed writing it. Indeed, more so, because I hate writing.

Yours and oblig,

Dife

*Yes, he's a sir.

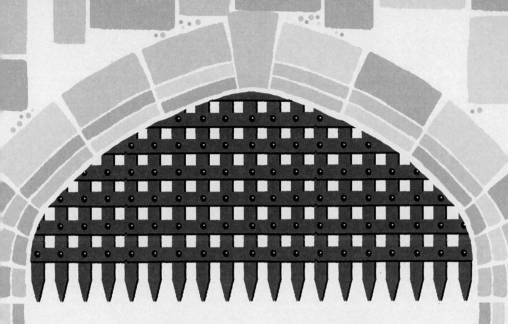

ENGLAND

CROMWELL'S CASTLE
ISLES OF SCILLY, CORNWALL

One of Britain's most far-flung castles occupies one of its most glorious locations

LOCATION
Tresco, Isles of Scilly,
Cornwall TR24 0QE

GRID REFERENCE
SV 881 159

PUBLIC TRANSPORT
From Penzance – the
terminus of the railway line
that heads out to the sunny
southwest – you can catch
the *Scillonian III* ferry
(islesofscilly-travel.co.uk;
01736 334220) to St Mary's,
the main island of the Isles
of Scilly. From there, a boat
operated by the Scilly
Boatmen's Association
(scillyboating.co.uk; 01720
423999) will take you across
to the little island of Tresco.
The castle is on its
northwestern shore.

WHEN TO VISIT
Open any reasonable time
during daylight hours.

ADMISSION CHARGE
Free

WEBSITE
english-heritage.org.uk

TELEPHONE
0370 333 1181

ourney to the far southwest corner of Britain and you'll find on the edge of a little island a distillation of the English Civil War in castle form.

On Tresco's shore, strong and strategically located, stands Cromwell's Castle. Up above, poorly sited and stripped of much of its stone for use in the fortress below, stands (or rather slumps) King Charles' Castle. The two rivals also serve to remind us of a little-known fact: that a full two years after the execution of Charles I, the Isles of Scilly remained in Royalist hands.

Though the second-largest of Scilly's islands, Tresco is still rather small – an area just a little over a square mile. It supports a population of 175 and earns its keep almost exclusively through tourism. However, what one might consider to be one of the nation's more obscure outposts was in fact of some strategic importance back in the 1650s. It formed part of an archipelago that could operate as a secure naval base just off the British coast, and would thus have proved a highly useful acquisition to any of the nation's seafaring enemies.

The castle is set upon a rocky promontory that pokes a toe into the shallow anchorage separating the isle of Tresco from neighbouring Bryher (so shallow indeed that at some extremely low tides it's possible to walk between the two). It's just north of New Grimsby, one of the twin settlements that between them straddle the island.

To a large degree, the castle owes its existence to the Dutch. In March 1651, a fleet from the Dutch Republic – no friend of England at that time – arrived at Scilly with a demand for reparation. Their complaint was that Dutch ships had been waylaid by Royalist pirates (or 'privateers', as the English preferred to call them euphemistically) who had used the islands as a base. The English parliament, concerned lest the islands fall under Dutch influence or be used as a staging post for an invasion by Royalist-supporting troops from Ireland, determined to launch their own assault on Scilly.

The richly talented Admiral Robert Blake was quickly dispatched to win the islands for England, which he did with his usual aplomb. One of the measures he put in place to safeguard the archipelago from a counter-invasion was the building of Cromwell's Castle. As such, it is one of the very few surviving strongholds built during the interregnum – the period that began in

1649 with the execution of Charles I and ended with the restoration to the throne of his son, Charles II.

Blake wisely refrained from attempting to repair the existing King Charles' Castle. Despite its name, this had actually been constructed during the reign of Edward VI to avert a French invasion and was originally simply called the Castell of Tresco. As soon as it had been finished in the early 1550s, it had been discovered that, being 130ft above sea level, its guns would have to be aimed downwards in order to hit enemy ships in the channel below. However, this would cause the cannonball inside to roll out before it could be fired. The oversight effectively rendered the castle all but useless. A blockhouse at just above sea level was hurriedly thrown up soon afterwards. When Blake and his troops showed up a century later, the Scillonian Royalists severely damaged the castle with explosives to deny them the rather dubious privilege of using it.

Blake chose the location of the Tudor blockhouse for his own fortification. He named it after the Lord Protector of England, Oliver Cromwell, artfully snubbing the Carolean-monikered castle above, whose stone he also quarried for re-use in the lower stronghold. The gun platform on top of the new 50ft-high circular tower served a triple purpose – it protected the harbour at nearby New Grimsby; sealed off the channel that

provided one of the main entrances to the Isles of Scilly; and guarded against the landing of troops along the western side of Tresco.

The castle was still operational in 1739, albeit reportedly in need of new cannonry, when one of the more curiously named international conflicts erupted. The War of Jenkins' Ear was a largely naval affair fought by Britain and Spain. The former belatedly used a possibly spurious incident that took place eight years beforehand – the removal of an ear from a British smuggler's head by the crew of a Spanish patrol vessel – as an excuse to go to war. Cromwell's Castle was hastily re-armed and Master Gunner Abraham Tovey improved the fort's fire-power by adding a second gun platform. However, just 13 years later, the castle was reported as being in a state of decay.

Visit today and you'll find the castle in remarkably good condition, the main victim of the years being the floors between each storey, which have disappeared. Access is gained through a door installed by Tovey on the level of his new gun platform (the original entrance was via an exterior wooden staircase to an upper storey). Just inside are a guard room and a latrine, both also added by Tovey. A spiral staircase leads right up to the roof, where Blake's original gun platform was installed, the six cannons ranged in a semicircle for maximum coverage of the channel below. As might be imagined, the views of the sea and across to Bryher from this vantage point are superlative.

While you're on Tresco, do take the opportunity to seek out its other military remains. Aside from the polygonal King Charles' Castle, there's the Old Blockhouse which was built at the same time to defend Old Grimsby harbour. Head south for another of Admiral Blake's defensive works: Oliver's Battery.

In the end, Tresco fell to neither the French nor the Dutch. Ironically, the only successful invasion of the island during this period was by a less likely enemy, the English.

PENGERSICK CASTLE
PRAA SANDS, CORNWALL

A fortified manor house whose owner plunged England into an international incident involving its oldest ally

LOCATION
Pengersick Lane, Praa Sands, Cornwall TR20 9SJ
NB The Praa in Praa Sands is pronounced *pray*, which you may find helpful when buying a bus ticket.

GRID REFERENCE
SW 581 284

PUBLIC TRANSPORT
From stand E4, outside Penzance railway station, take the U4 bus (firstgroup.com; 0345 646 0707) to Pengersick Lane in Praa Sands. The castle is a two-minute walk north along Pengersick Lane.

WHEN TO VISIT
Pengersick offers private guided tours and self-guided visits (when the castle is not being hired out for weddings and other events) for small groups and individuals but these must be booked beforehand.

ADMISSION CHARGE
Yes

WEBSITE
pengersickcastle.com

TELEPHONE
01736 763973

If the stories about them are even half true, it's fair to say that the Pengersicks of old were a bit of a rum bunch. For generations, the men of the family were disposed to make what might be generously described as interesting life choices. One managed to get himself excommunicated by assaulting a clergyman, while another caused the valuable contents of a ship belonging to a Portuguese king to 'disappear'. The ill wind that caused the king's ship to run aground certainly did the Pengersicks no harm. Perhaps predictably, given this tendency towards anarchic behaviour, Pengersick has been saddled in recent times by spurious stories of a murder and sightings of various ghosts (including those of rats, which is at least a little different from the normal run of such tales).

The tower, which is by far the most salient feature left to us, is a fine example of Tudor craftsmanship. Its design treads a line between the need to create a stronghold that would give some security in the face of coastal raids launched by England's enemies, and a fashionable manor house fit for a member of the *nouveax riches*.

The history of the manor at Pengersick (the stress falls on the *ger*) stretches back to a time well before the

building of the current castle. We know it can trace its roots at least as far back as the end of the 12th century because it is mentioned in passing in a document titled the Feet of Fines which was written in 1199 (it recorded a disagreement over the ownership of some land). The current castle was by no means the first building to occupy this site. Archaeological remains suggest that a hall house stood there in the 13th century, where the adjacent wood now grows.

Legend has it that the tower was built by a man from Bridestowe in Devon named Millaton (his surname suffers a number of spellings from source to source). The story goes that he killed a man and fled into Cornwall. Arriving at Pengersick he is said to have built a tower to defend himself against anyone who might either seek to bring him to trial or attempt to administer justice on the spot.

You'll find none of this hokum in the brief but informative guide to the castle published by the Pengersick Historic and Education Trust. Their booklet attributes the building of a fortified manor house at Pengersick – considerably upgrading the derelict hall house on the site – to Elizabeth and John Milliton, sometime in the first decade of the 1500s. The Millitons, far from being killers on the run, were both from wealthy and influential families. Their son (also John) rose even higher in society, becoming Governor of

St Michael's Mount in 1521 and eventually High Sheriff of Cornwall. This latter post doubtless made him unpopular with a lot of locals since he took a lead role in putting down the Prayer Book Rebellion of 1549, when the (largely Catholic) Cornish population revolted against the imposition of the Book of Common Prayer. Thousands were killed or executed in a series of pitched battles ending with the bloodbath that was the Battle of Sampford Courtenay in Devon.

Ironically, it was this same John Milliton who was involved in the disappearance of the contents of King John III of Portugal's carrack *St Anthony* that ran aground at nearby Gunwalloe. When the king demanded the return of his goods, Henry VIII established a Court of Star Chamber to investigate the incident. Along with two other local landowners, Milliton was acquitted of purloining the flagship's cargo, which was valued at £18,800 – a colossal sum at the time. Improvements and refurbishment at Pengersick, which occurred in the aftermath of the 1527 shipwreck, have been attributed to the looting of the royal vessel.

Of that grand fortified manor house, little more than the tower remains, but what a wonderfully well-preserved tower it is. Arrow loops pierce the walls of the ground floor, while an unusually wide stone spiral staircase connects it with

In recent years those grounds have been diligently laid out with a woodland walk and a number of discrete gardens. These latter demonstrate the variety of gardens that are likely to have been created at Pengersick through the ages. Thus the visitor may stroll from a pleasure garden to a ladies' herber, from an apothecarist's garden to a knot garden, travelling in time from the early Middle Ages to the age of the Tudors. The original apothecarist's garden, dating from the 14th century, was established by the Benedictine monks who lived here prior to the building of the present castle. An orchard has also been planted and features mulberry, medlar, quince and cobnut trees, all of which would have been typical in the Middle Ages.

And if you fancy getting married and haven't plumped for a venue yet, you can become a Pengersick for the day, hiring out the tower and gardens for your wedding. However, it's probably a good idea not to assault any clergymen who may turn up to officiate – it's not a great start to married life to find yourself excommunicated.

the three floors above, all of which are largely taken up by a single generously proportioned room. Each one – the gun room, drawing room, solar and bedroom – has now been tastefully decorated and furnished. Open fireplaces, woven wall-hangings, suits of armour, ancient weaponry and venerable furniture made from oak and leather all conspire to give an impression of the graceful life lived by previous generations. A small door at the top leads onto the roof from where there are excellent views of the grounds far below.

3 ST MAWES CASTLE
ST MAWES, CORNWALL

A most singular castle built by Henry VIII to defend southern England

LOCATION
Castle Drive, St Mawes, Nr Truro, Cornwall TR2 5DE

GRID REFERENCE
SW 841 327

PUBLIC TRANSPORT
Given the castle's seaward-looking stance, it's appropriate that the easiest way to arrive there by public transport is on a boat. Once you get off the train at Penmere station in Falmouth, walk to the Prince of Wales Pier, where you may board the handsome ferry for the 20-minute crossing to St Mawes. Alternatively, if you happen to be on the Roseland Peninsula, you can take the tiny and rather wonderful ferry (both falriver.co.uk; 01326 741194) from Place to St Mawes (sails spring to autumn). Whichever you take, it's a pleasant half-mile walk west around the coast to the castle.

WHEN TO VISIT
Open April to September daily 10am–5pm. Opening days and times variable in other months – see the website for details.

ADMISSION CHARGE
Yes (free to EH members)

WEBSITE
english-heritage.org.uk

TELEPHONE
01326 270526

We are apt to think of castles as fossilised remains – fragments of medieval history that became redundant as more modern methods of waging war developed. It seems unconscionable, therefore, that a castle built by Henry VIII to defend against an enemy arriving in ships made of oak and pine could find itself pressed into service by Neville Chamberlain to defend against a foe employing planes that could fly at speeds of over 300mph. However, that is precisely what happened in the case of St Mawes, a castle out of the common mould.

This is arguably the finest surviving example of the 30 castles and forts Henry built to defend the southern English shore between 1539 and 1545. Combined with Pendennis Castle – which is sited on the western side of the Fal Estuary – St Mawes provided protection to Carrick Roads, the wide channel whose shores were viewed as a potential landing place for an invading army. Two additional blockhouses at sea level completed the defences. The attempted invasion, when it came in 1545, saw the French endeavouring to obtain a foothold at Portsmouth. St Mawes was thus spared from action (see page 50 for more about the farce that this invasion became).

St Mawes is almost as far removed from the traditional medieval castle as it is possible to imagine. There is no vast keep behind a curtain wall pierced with arrow slits and topped by battlements. Instead we see a short round tower pockmarked with gunports. It pokes its head cautiously above three lower circular towers tightly packed around it in the form of a clover leaf. These in turn are afforded a measure of protection by a relatively low wall at the base of the mound on which the fortress sits. The whole edifice is designed as an artillery platform, and so is less concerned with its own defence than going on the attack against hostile shipping while offering a small target at which to aim. The castle bristled with 19 artillery pieces including heavy guns designed to deal such severe blows that they would not just kill enemy sailors but sink the very ships beneath their feet. Remarkably, the castle at St Mawes today is little different to the one you would have seen had you visited shortly after it was completed, so we have a very precise idea of what its capabilities were.

Despite the outright hostility between England and Spain which was maintained throughout the remainder of the 16th century and translated itself into a state of war in 1585, those capabilities went untested. St Mawes was kept garrisoned,

but the gunners and militiamen whose numbers rose (to a maximum of about 15) and fell as emergencies came and went lived charmed lives. In 1574, Spanish ships were said to be forming into a fleet to head for England, but nothing came of it; while 14 years later the fabled Armada simply sailed past to its doom. When, in 1595, the Spaniards did at last raid Cornwall, they did so much further to the west; and in the following two years a second Armada was stymied by the weather.

It was only in the 17th century that the castle began to see some action, and the defenders instantly regretted it. During the Civil War, Cornwall was staunchly Royalist. Carrick Roads became an important base for King Charles' ships, which carried out guerrilla-like actions against Parliamentarian vessels in the Channel. While the castle was a formidable challenge if attacked from the sea, it was extremely vulnerable to an assault on its landward side. In 1646, a strong Roundhead force led by Colonel John Arundell marched towards St Mawes. The colonel generously offered the castle's captain, Major Hannibal Bonithon, the option of decamping to the more easily defendable Pendennis Castle just across the water. Bonithon turned the proposal down, but rather than fight to try to save the fort, he waved the white flag. Along with the castle, Arundell took

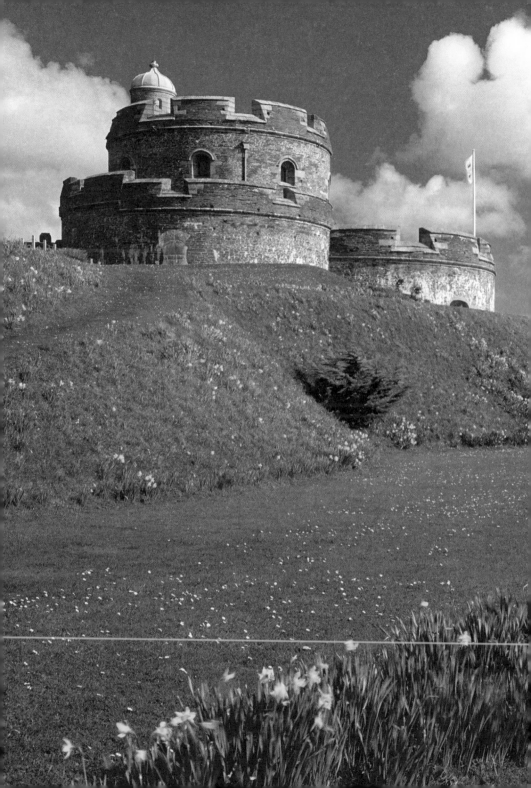

possession of a great quantity of his enemy's artillery pieces and small arms, which he duly used in his siege and eventual capture of Pendennis.

In the latter part of the following century, the threat of invasion from France began to loom again. Once more, the garrison was put on high alert. All through the Napoleonic Wars at the start of the 19th century – when the south and east coasts of England were braced for what seemed an inevitable invasion – the little force at St Mawes scanned the seas in vain. In the 1850s, renewed fears of attack from across the Channel led to a significant upgrading in the castle's firepower. The Grand Sea Battery and a sunken magazine replaced the ageing shoreline fortifications and were equipped with modern 8-inch guns. As the century wore on, these were updated with 64-pounder weapons, to which were added smaller rapid-action guns for use against a whole new threat: the torpedo boat, a vessel that was adopted by many navies around the world in the 1890s. Unfortunately, the location of the battery was not ideal and another one had to be installed above the castle at the turn of the century.

Though used as a barracks in World War I, the castle's last preparations for invasion came in 1939, when Britain again declared war on Germany. Two years later, a new battery was built to accommodate 6-pounder guns with an anti-aircraft Bofors gun positioned next to the castle. By then, a garrison of 115 was required for the defences to work at full capacity. The days of living-in at the castle were well and truly over – the servicemen and women posted here were lodged in a nearby Nissen hut or billeted in the town.

There's a great deal to see inside the castle today. Alongside the impressive range of artillery weapons and exhibitions on castle life, there are some original inscriptions in Latin extolling the supposed virtues of Henry VIII and Edward VI.

After visiting St Mawes, take the ferry across to Falmouth to see Pendennis Castle. Perched on top of a narrow headland, it is a very different structure – a circular fort defended by a system of ramparts created by one of Henry's successors, his daughter Elizabeth I.

4 LYDFORD CASTLE

LYDFORD, DEVON

A curiosity of a castle that held a medieval member of parliament captive within its walls and inspired a change in the law that endures today

LOCATION
School Lane, Lydford,
Okehampton, Devon
EX20 4BH

GRID REFERENCE
SX 509 847

PUBLIC TRANSPORT
From Gunnislake railway
station, take the 79 bus
(plymouthbus.co.uk; 01752
662271) to the bus station at
Tavistock, from where you
can pick up a number 118
(dartline-coaches.co.uk;
01392 872900) to Lydford.
The castle is on the main
road next to the Castle Inn.

WHEN TO VISIT
Open any reasonable time
during daylight hours.

ADMISSION CHARGE
Free

WEBSITE
english-heritage.org.uk

TELEPHONE
0370 333 1181

We all know the punchline to that hoary old joke, 'When is a door not a door?' However, what about the riddle, 'When is a castle not a castle?' Or to be more precise, 'When is a castle not a castle and yet is felt to be so like a castle that it becomes accepted as a castle to generations of its neighbours and the wider world beyond?' The answer, you'll perhaps be unsurprised to learn, is 'When it's Lydford Castle.'

The austere stone building in the Devonshire village certainly looks like a castle. It's also located on top of a previous castle. Furthermore, it is delineated on maps, information boards, books and websites as a castle. Even the owners – English Heritage – call it a castle. And yet, despite all this, it was only ever a prison. It was such an unconscionably awful prison to be held in, by all accounts, that many an inmate must have wished that they had been confined in a castle dungeon instead.

Lydford may be only a small village today but in Saxon times it grew to some prominence, having made itself wealthy through local tin mining. It is situated above the River Lyd in an easily defensible position. Two sides of its triangle of land are protected by a steep natural drop to river valleys, while the third was safeguarded by a long rampart made of earth, which is still in evidence today and helped ward off a Viking attack in 997.

By the late 12th century, Lydford had reached giddy heights. The whole forest of Dartmoor was administered from the village. The 'forest' in this sense was a classification established by the Crown. All business (hunting, building, the exploitation of natural resources, etc) within its borders was subject to strict regulations and taxes. Lydford also controlled all of Devon's stannaries (tin-mining districts), which further added to its importance. In order to be able to imprison those accused and convicted of breaking forest or stannary laws, a two-storey tower was commissioned in 1194 by Richard I's younger brother John (later King John I). This housed both a court and a gaol.

It was rare in England at that time to build a prison – castles usually fulfilled that purpose – which is perhaps why the tower, which was so like a castle, was accorded that epithet. When Richard, Earl of Cornwall, was granted Lydford and all its powers by Henry III, he played on that theme. He added a couple of storeys to the tower and buried the ground floor under a mass of earth. The result was a building that looked like a motte-and-bailey castle, the Norman construction that had become emblematic of unyielding dominance. The creation of the 'motte' also meant that the former ground floor was now entirely underground, making it a perfect place in which to deposit particularly undesirable prisoners.

In 1300, on the death of Richard's son Edmund, the castle passed back to the Crown. In 1337, Lydford and Dartmoor were handed to the Duchy of Cornwall, currently presided over by Prince Charles.

The castle's most famous prisoner was Plymouth MP Richard Strode. A tin-miner, in 1510 he brought to light the fact that his fellow tinners were dumping spoil and other detritus in Dartmoor's rivers. As a consequence of these actions, Plymouth harbour was silting up, and he moved that a law be brought in to halt the practice. A rival tinner took Strode to Lydford Castle's Stannary Court and the

parliamentarian was fined the then vast sum of £160. He had become another victim of the once notorious 'Lydford Law'. The phrase was used for centuries in England as a synonym for rough justice. It was encapsulated in a piece of doggerel composed by William Browne in 1644:

> I oft have heard of Lydford Law,
> How in the morn they hang and draw,
> And sit in judgment after:
> At first I wondered at it much;
> But since, I find the reason such,
> As it deserves no laughter.

Strode refused to pay his fine and was duly imprisoned at the castle. He was released three weeks later after the intervention of the exchequer. He complained that he had been half-starved on a diet of bread and water, kept in leg-irons (until a bribe facilitated their removal) and consigned to a deep pit. His one-star review of the castle didn't pull any punches. He declared it 'One of the most annoious, contagious and detestable places wythin this realme.'

Strode's experience spurred him to introduce the Privilege of Parliament Act, which was passed in 1512. This gave MPs immunity from prosecution for carrying out parliamentary business (which meant that his own fine was rescinded). 'Strode's Act', as it is still known, most frequently hits the news with regard to its establishment of parliamentary privilege – the principle that no member of the Commons or Lords can be prosecuted for anything said inside either House.

The annoious, contagious and detestable place (Lydford Castle, not parliament) was still serving as a prison when Royalists used it to confine captured Roundheads during the Civil War. It returned to its traditional function afterwards and, though dilapidated, was only finally abandoned in 1833.

There is actually a real castle to see at Lydford. Or at least a remnant of a very early Norman castle. About 150yds to the southwest, on the other side of St Petroc's church, lie the ringworks of (Old) Lydford Castle. Built around 1068, it stood on what was probably the site of an earlier Saxon fortification. It was a very humble affair indeed, consisting of just five wooden buildings (probably granaries) defended by a wood and earthen rampart. Ælfthryth, Queen of Wessex, was born in a castle at Lydford around 945, so it is more than likely that the Normans built theirs on top of that one rather than choosing a whole new site. It seems to have been abandoned after just a few decades and is now owned by the National Trust.

TOTNES CASTLE
TOTNES, DEVON

Involved in wars from the Normans to World War II, this diminutive fortress always escaped attack

LOCATION
Castle Street, Totnes, Devon
TQ9 5NU

GRID REFERENCE
SX 800 604

PUBLIC TRANSPORT
Totnes railway station is
about 500yds from the
castle, along Castle Street.

WHEN TO VISIT
Open April to September
daily 10am–6pm; October
to early November daily
10am–5pm; November to
March weekends only
10am–4pm. Closed 24–26
December and New Year's
Day. Last entry 30 minutes
before closing.

ADMISSION CHARGE
Yes

WEBSITE
english-heritage.org.uk

TELEPHONE
01803 864406

oday, Totnes has a reputation as a town populated by free-thinkers, creative types and those seeking out alternative lifestyles to the ones generally on offer in Britain. Back in Saxon times, the port town on the Dart became prosperous through its craftspeople, who drew traders from far and wide who sailed up the river or used the road network the Romans had built towards the east. For a while it even ran to its own mint. A further measure of its standing came in 907 when King Edward the Elder ordered that Totnes be fortified – a rare honour for a town in the southwest of England.

By the time of the Norman Conquest, the town's fortunes appear to have ebbed somewhat, but it was still considered a major settlement in the region. So when the Normans headed out this way in 1067–8 in order to quell a rebellion organised from Exeter by the late King Harold II's mother, Gytha Thorkelsdóttir, the capture of Totnes was one of their priorities. They seized Exeter after an 18-day siege, and soon after took possession of the smaller town. A knight from Brittany called Juhel (other spellings include Judhael and Judhellus) was given command of Totnes by King William.

It's not known exactly when the new Norman overlord built a castle in Totnes, though it's likely that work began soon after the town's Saxon defenders capitulated. It was certainly finished before 1087, the proof of which is given in an undated charter that mentions the castle

31

in passing and also offers up prayers for King William's health (in 1087 the monarch's death would have made such appeals to the Divinity redundant). As with so many other Norman constructions, the castle's purpose was to cow the local populace into subservience, thus negating the chances of a further rebellion. Juhel also founded a Benedictine priory in the vicinity as a further measure to embed Norman rule.

As might be expected, the style of castle chosen to keep the plucky locals in their place was a motte-and-bailey. The height of the mound and its timber keep served as a physical representation of the dominance of the new masters, not least because several houses and part of the town defences disappeared below the motte. It also meant that an eye could be kept on comings and goings along the Dart, a little to the east. This original keep's stone foundations are still in evidence today and show us that it was square in outline and rather small.

The castle's inner bailey was protected by the usual palisade made of wood. A moat was dug between the inner and outer baileys, and was traversed by a drawbridge. This moat still exists, though now it is covered with wild flowers and makes a location for a very pleasant stroll. The inner moat, at the foot of the motte, has long since been covered over.

Juhel became exceedingly rich and controlled scores of manors, but made Totnes his seat of operations. However, he was injudicious enough to rebel against William's successor to the throne, William II, and only saved his own skin by fleeing the country. The new king granted Totnes to one Roger de Nonant. This began the process suffered by so many English castles – that of being handed to one family or another on the whim or well-thought-out strategy of the monarch of the day. In 1205, it came into the hands of William de Braose, who may have been a descendant of Juhel's (and certainly averred that he was).

The following year, King John granted Totnes a royal charter, making it a free town. Despite this, it appears that de Braose was less than unswerving in his devotion to the Crown, and John stripped him of the castle, handing it to the Earl of Cornwall. Not many years later, Totnes Castle was returned to the de Braose family, with William's son Reginald taking charge. Sometime in 1219 or shortly afterwards, he was responsible for pulling down the timber tower and creating a stone shell keep. Unfortunately, this was something of a shoddy affair and barely lasted 30 years before it had become a ruin.

It is the de la Zouch family – best known for appending their name to the small town of Ashby in Leicestershire –

that had previously taken place in the latter. The town's slow downward spiral was mirrored by its castle. By the time of the Civil War in the 17th century, it was in a state of decrepitude, albeit that the keep was still largely intact. A small Royalist force did occupy the stronghold at one stage but, on hearing the news that a Roundhead force was on its way, they prudently took to their heels. It was the last time the castle played any significant role in public life.

Not only can the keep be enjoyed today, but the curtain wall that climbs the motte to the summit is also extant, a state of affairs that is most unusual for an English motte-and-bailey castle. However, don't be fooled by the stone steps up the motte, which are an early 20th-century confection. The 20th century was a peculiar time for the castle. First, the inner bailey sprouted a tennis court and tearoom. Then, during World War II, evacuees were temporarily housed here. Italian prisoners of war from the same conflict were also brought to the castle and given conservation work to carry out. When you visit, do take time to seek out a dead tree in the inner bailey. On its decaying trunk you can still see the names those prisoners carved there, along with the dates of their incarceration.

that we have to thank for the fine stonework we can see today. Indeed, without them, it is unlikely that there would be much left of the castle at all. As it is, Totnes ranks among the best preserved motte-and-bailey fortresses in England. The de la Zouch family took control of the castle in the late 13th century and, following the orders of Edward II, started bringing it back to its former (modest) glories in 1326.

However, the rise of Dartmouth in the following centuries led to the decline of Totnes. Located on the coast, the former hoovered up much of the trade

6 DAWS CASTLE
WATCHET, SOMERSET

A clifftop stronghold built to protect the coast from Viking raids that saw more action than it would have liked

LOCATION
B3191, near Watchet,
Somerset TA23 0JP

GRID REFERENCE
ST 062 433

PUBLIC TRANSPORT
For a treat, take the train to Taunton, then catch one of the frequent number 28 buses (firstgroup.com; 0345

646 0707) that runs from the station directly to Bishops Lydeard station, followed by a steam train to Watchet on Britain's lengthiest preserved railway line (west-somerset-railway.co.uk; 01643 704996). From Watchet head west along the South West Coast Path for half a mile out of the village to the Daws Castle enclosure.

WHEN TO VISIT
Open any reasonable time during daylight hours

ADMISSION CHARGE
Free

WEBSITE
english-heritage.org.uk

TELEPHONE
0370 333 1181

Were you able to travel back in time to the days of Alfred the Great you'd be able to witness a deadly game of cat and mouse taking place on the Bristol Channel. This was a time of Viking raids on the British Isles and the north coast of Wessex had become a favourite hunting ground. To counter them, the king of the Anglo-Saxons had ordered the construction of a string of *buhrs* (fortified towns), fortresses and look-out stations along the Wessex coast. These outposts reported sightings of Viking longships to army commanders. The herepath – a road specifically laid as an anti-incursion measure – allowed Alfred's forces to travel swiftly enough to mirror the movements of the would-be

marauders and perhaps dissuade them from landing or meet them with sharpened blades and missiles if they did.

One of the fortifications designed by the king to protect his people was Daws Castle. At least, the cake-burning monarch – who reigned as King of the Anglo-Saxons from *c.*886 to 899 – is the most likely candidate to have built it. Standing at the top of 260ft cliffs, just to the northeast of Exmoor, it was constructed towards the end of the 9th century. Regrettably, there's not a great deal left of it to see, beyond an impressive curved bank that stretches for about 200yds and runs roughly east–west. The lack of remains is largely due to the fact that the grand stone structures we

generally associate with castles belonged to a later era than this. The chief Saxon building material was timber, which rarely leaves behind much evidence of its existence. At least the stunning setting at Daws, with its panoramic view over the Bristol Channel, is just the thing to bring its defenders back to its walls again, if only in the imagination.

From excavations carried out at the site in 1982, archaeologists have concluded that there were two distinct building phases here. The first was a very simple affair – a bank and a mortared stone wall to form an enclosure – and this is believed to have been Alfred's work, carried out between 871 and 899 (though intriguingly, radiocarbon testing of

material within the defences gave a date of 730 plus or minus 140 years). The second phase has been attributed to either Edward the Elder (899–924) or Æthelred II (978–1013 and 104–16) and was carried out in the 10th century, again to guard against Viking raiders. With so little time between the two phases, it's unsurprising that no great evolutionary leap had taken place with regards to castle design. However, the later wall is larger and sturdier, the bank behind it broader, and a ditch was dug in front of it.

Though you'll often see it claimed that Daws was established on the site of an Iron Age or Roman fort, no evidence has been found to suggest that this is the case. What is true is that the area enclosed by the defences used to be larger than it is today. The encroaching sea has chewed off the northern portion of the castle, leaving a 5-acre site. Limestone workings, lime kilns and a tramway; a now defunct golf course; and farming activities (this last as recently as 1982) have all helped to obliterate other sections of the enclosure. However, you may spot a small stretch of bank 300yds to the east, just by the road, which suggests that the defences may have reached at least that far.

The castle has had its name rather messed about with as well. While the generally accepted term today is Daws (sometimes spelt Daw's), that certainly wasn't what it was called when it was active and there's disagreement as to how it received the new moniker. Some sources claim that it came by it because the land in which the castle lies was owned by one Thomas Dawe in the 16th century. Others point to early Ordnance Survey maps that mark this spot as Dart's Castle, and suggest Daws/Daw's is a 20th-century corruption. Still others point to a time when it was actually called Dane's Castle. Alfred, on the other hand, probably knew it as Weced. This is the name first recorded in the Burghal Hidage, a list compiled in 919 that documented the *buhrs* created to stave off the Vikings. Watchet, the small town half a mile from the fortress, doubtless derived its name from this ancient appellation.

The castle is also name-checked in the Anglo-Saxon Chronicle, that treasure trove of the eponymous people's doings. It recalls a famous victory for the soldiers defending Daws. They managed not only to see off a Viking party that landed in 914 but also killed a great many of the raiders. The chronicler writes that 'few of them

came away, except those only who swam out to the ships'. The Norsemen appear to have had more joy here in 987 and 997, on both occasions leaving a trail of death and destruction in their wake.

There were happier – or at least more prosperous – times for locals as well though. For one thing, Daws was blessed with its own mint, which is a sure sign of the community's importance (just ask the good people of Llantrisant). Again, there is debate surrounding the date of its establishment. Some opt for 1035, while others believe that coins bearing the name of Æthelred II were minted here. What is certain is that it was one of very few mints in Somerset from that era. Furthermore, no coins were struck here between 1056 and 1080. Given that the Domesday Book makes no reference to a castle at Weced, it has been suggested that the fortress was forsaken in the wake of the Norman Conquest and that the mint was eventually pressed into action once more in the nearby town of Watchet.

What remains of that clifftop fortress today is an atmospheric reminder of troubling times, an era when the sight of a foreign sail heading up the Bristol Channel was often a harbinger of violence, ruination and mayhem.

NUNNEY CASTLE
NUNNEY, SOMERSET

An exquisitely small castle undone by advances in technology

LOCATION
Castle Street, Nunney, Somerset BA11 4LW

GRID REFERENCE
ST 736 457

PUBLIC TRANSPORT
Take yourself along the Bristol to Weymouth line to Frome railway station. From there make your way to the Market Place in the centre of town whence a 162 bus (patsofwinsley.co.uk; 01373 471474) will whisk you the 3.5 miles to Nunney in 12 minutes. Alternatively, take the 31 bus (libratravelltd.com; 01373 812255) from the railway station to the Esso Garage at Nunney Catch and walk three-quarters of a mile along Catch Road and the High Street to the castle.

WHEN TO VISIT
Open any reasonable time during daylight hours.

ADMISSION CHARGE
Free

WEBSITE
english-heritage.org.uk

TELEPHONE
0370 333 1181

For a demonstration of the sheer havoc that could be caused by artillery in the mid-17th century, you could do a lot worse than visiting Nunney Castle. In September 1645, a single shot was fired by a cannon from the top of a low hill overlooking the fortress. The cannonball blew such a large hole in the first floor of the northwest wall that its owner surrendered the castle before the army posted at its gates could take another potshot at it. The rest of the wall would not come tumbling down for another 265 years, which testifies both to the robustness of the structure and to the impressive force it must have taken to punch a great hole through it.

Nowadays, that missing wall is the only reminder of the most violent episode in the castle's history. The rest is peace, harmony and that certain tranquillity that only exists in bucolic settings. The little-known castle stands by a brook on the edge of a village in Somerset, just to the east of the Mendip Hills. Amid lawns and graceful trees, with views of woods beyond, the compact and partially ruined stronghold is a very pleasing sight indeed.

However, as you approach it, you'll begin to notice a couple of rather curious details. In the vast majority of moated castles, the moat is merely a water-filled ditch circling the walls. Nunney, on the other hand, looks more like a castle that has squeezed itself onto a tiny island in the middle of a large pond. The domestic appearance of the little lake turns out to be misleading – it is deep and steeply shelving (the drawbridge that once spanned it has been replaced today by a simple wooden footbridge). Furthermore, although the round towers that protect each of the four corners of the stronghold seem conventional at first glance, it soon becomes apparent that at both ends the towers are built so close to each other that they're almost in danger of overlapping. Even the walls on the longer sides of the castle are of no great span. The overall effect is one of a toy castle with aspirations.

Nunney Castle would probably not have existed at all had it not been for the Hundred Years' War, the 116-year on-and-off conflict between England and France that eventually ground to a halt in 1453. The local lord of the manor (and later Sheriff of Somerset), Sir John de la Mare, went off to fight alongside Edward the Black Prince, King Edward III's oldest son. Sir John enjoyed a successful campaign during which he helped to capture various members of the French nobility for whom large ransoms were subsequently paid. Flush with this honourably acquired pelf, he petitioned the king for permission to crenellate his manor house at Nunney and implement other adaptations that would turn it into a castle.

In the event, de la Mare (sometimes spelt de la Mere) decided to build a whole new fortified manor house more or less next door to the one he already owned at the foot of a hillock. This 1373 construction was the first incarnation of Nunney Castle. It was not a building that had any pretensions to being a stronghold, but was more a statement about the sort of dwelling de la Mare thought fit for a victorious knight back from the wars. The nobleman used the king's own architect and had that exceptionally generous moat dug (it was at least 10ft deep) after the manor house was completed. A mighty 12ft-high wall was constructed forming three sides of a good-sized bailey, with Nunney Brook acting as the fourth.

Come the 16th century, the castle was given a sprucing up. It was purchased around 1560 by a wealthy Londoner named Prater who made wholesale improvements. The floors and ceilings were ripped out and rebuilt at different levels, windows were enlarged, a splendid spiral staircase was installed, and the moat was pushed back a little from the walls, creating the attractive terrace that is still in evidence today.

But then came the only action Nunney Castle ever saw. Its brush with organised violence turned out to be calamitous. The fortress had been passed down the generations and in the 1640s

was in the ownership of Richard Prater, a staunch Catholic and arch Royalist. The castle, which was garrisoned by Irish mercenaries, was besieged by Parliamentarian troops under Sir Thomas Fairfax in September 1645. The siege lasted just three days. On the third, the Parliamentarians fired off that single devastating cannon shot and Prater hurriedly waved the white flag. Following Oliver Cromwell's orders, Fairfax had the roof ripped out and the floors taken apart so that the castle could not be re-occupied by Royalists (though Richard Prater's son George did manage to reclaim the building on the restoration of the monarchy in 1660). Many of the fixtures and fittings found their way into the homes of villagers in Nunney, and some cottages today still boast a fireplace, wooden beams or some artefact from the castle.

The great breach – that testament to Nunney Castle's brief yet unfortunate moment in the limelight – remained until Christmas Day 1910 when virtually the whole of the northwest wall collapsed. Almost as soon as it had been slighted, the castle had become overgrown with ivy, choked with weeds and shrubs and undermined by the roots of trees that grew up around it. Even so, it became a tourist attraction in the late 19th century, with visitors paying a small fee to poke about in the ruins and undergrowth. Thankfully, no one appears to have been doing so when the disaster occurred.

In 1950, the castle was auctioned off to Robert Walker for £600. Walker, who lived in Nunney, was not without means, being the heir to the Johnnie Walker whisky fortune (some of which went to financing his own Formula One team). The castle is still in private hands today but the building is in the care of English Heritage and open to the public. The rather lovely 18th-century manor house that stands near the castle is also privately owned but is sadly not open to visitors.

Despite Nunney's treatment at the hands of the Roundheads, the castle continues to play an important role in village life. Once a year the miniature fortress gets a chance to shine. On the first Saturday in August the Nunney Community Association holds a bustling daytime street market and fair. The castle plays its part by acting as a romantic backdrop to the musical artistes who perform as part of the festivities.

8 YARMOUTH CASTLE

YARMOUTH, ISLE OF WIGHT

A seemingly unimportant little stronghold on an English island blazed a trail for British fortresses for hundreds of years

LOCATION
Quay Street, Yarmouth,
Isle of Wight, Hampshire
PO41 0PB

GRID REFERENCE
SZ 353 897

PUBLIC TRANSPORT
The simplest route from
the mainland involves a
train to Lymington Pier
and a 40-minute ferry
crossing over the Solent
(wightlink.co.uk; 0333 999
7333) to Yarmouth
(with great views of the
fortress). The castle is right
next to the ferry terminal.

WHEN TO VISIT
Open April to September
daily 10am–4pm.

ADMISSION CHARGE
Yes (free to EH members)

WEBSITE
english-heritage.org.uk

TELEPHONE
01983 760678

ake the ferry across to Yarmouth on the Isle of Wight and, right next to the terminal, you'll come across an unassuming little fortress with a cracking view of the mainland across the Solent. It might be tempting to imagine that it is an unimportant affair, especially when the much larger and more famous Carisbrooke Castle – one-time prison to Charles I – is less than 10 miles away. However, Yarmouth can claim to be a stronghold of some significance, for it was the pioneer of a whole new type of defence system that would become integral to British fortress design over the following three centuries.

The castle came into being at a time of extraordinary political tension. In 1538, two of the great powers of Europe, France and Spain, had ceased hostilities by signing the Truce of Nice. Henry was no friend to either party, thanks to his previous invasion of the former and his divorce from the Spanish princess Catherine of Aragon. Freed from the inconvenience and cost of having to fight a war against each other, the two nations could afford to turn their attentions to England. Fearing invasion, Henry VIII began an immense programme of fort building along the south coast of England in 1539 (see page 21 and page 48). The expense of this ambitious venture was met

by the royal coffers, which had been swelled considerably by the plundered wealth of the many monasteries, convents and other religious establishments the king had dissolved.

Henry was often favoured with good luck throughout his reign and he was the beneficiary of a major slice now: year after year passed before an attempted invasion materialised, by which time the majority of his coastal fortifications were ready and waiting. In July 1545, French ships filled with more than 30,000 troops sailed across the English Channel. A much larger force than the Spanish Armada of 1588, it set course for Portsmouth, hoping to secure the city as a base from which to conquer England. Due to poor leadership and debatable tactics, all the invaders managed were a few brief incursions onto the Isle of Wight before being chased off.

However, it was clear that the area was potentially vulnerable and Henry ordered a fortress to be built at Yarmouth, near the narrow western entrance to the Solent and at an important communications centre between the island and the mainland. It would also serve to plug a gap in the Isle of Wight's defences – a French landing seems to have taken place here in 1543. The castle was constructed with impressive speed, taking just six months to its completion in November 1547. Its builder was George Mills, working under the orders of the

Captain of the Island, Richard Worsley. King Henry himself never got to see it, having died in January that year.

Unlike previous Henrician forts, Yarmouth came with a major defensive upgrade. The angle bastion (or 'arrow head') was a leap forward in castle design in Britain. It had been in use for 50 years or more in Italy and had proved its value, so Henry had been keen to incorporate it in his new forts. Unlike his concentric castles such as St Mawes (page 21), which were found to have blind spots that could be exploited by an attacker, the angle bastion allowed guns to cover every scrap of ground in front of a fort, which was of particular value for coastal strongholds on their often vulnerable landward side. The system was adopted by fortress builders into the Victorian era.

The garrison, in common with most of Henry's forts, was small: just 17 soldiers, a master gunner and a porter were required to man the six cannons and a dozen less powerful weapons. Their first commander was Richard Udall, who had a residence in the castle itself (the garrison lived in houses nearby). He was later executed by the Catholic Queen Mary for having supported her rival to the throne, the Protestant Lady Jane Grey.

Richard Worsley's career also waxed and waned according to the religion of the monarch of the day. Sacked as Captain of the Isle of Wight by Mary, he was reinstated by her successor Elizabeth, a confirmed Protestant. By this time, Spain had replaced France as the likely aggressor and Elizabeth called upon Worsley to make improvements at Yarmouth. Out of his own pocket, he had half the castle area filled in to create an artillery platform. The master gunner's residence, which has survived more or less intact, is probably also his work. Further improvements were made around 30 years later, before and after the coming of the Armada, including a second artillery platform based outside the castle. The destruction of the Spanish fleet before it could effect an invasion meant that these enhancements were never tested.

The fort's strategic importance was recognised by Charles I, who ordered its restoration and modernisation from its half-ruinous state. However, when the moment of truth came, Yarmouth was found wanting: Parliamentary forces received the castle's surrender in 1642 from its governor, Captain Barnaby Burley, without firing a shot.

The restoration of the monarchy brought in more changes. The Captain of the Island, Robert Holmes, built another new battery, filled in the moat and swept away the exterior platform. He also constructed a fine house for himself next door, to which Charles II was a visitor on several occasions. The castle remained more or less active during the following century and some minor enhancements were made to the building during the Napoleonic Wars, with the French reprising their role as potential invader. Yarmouth was eventually abandoned as a military stronghold in 1885. By then, the Victorians had set up a whole string of batteries and a couple of forts along the coast of Wight to the west of the castle, making it redundant.

Its relative lack of action has left Yarmouth Castle extremely well preserved. None of the successive improvements completely obliterated the previous incarnations of the fortress, leaving a fascinating jigsaw whose pieces all fit together but hail from quite different eras. Satisfyingly, the walls forming both the basic square outline of the castle and that all-important angle bastion are original. The stone you see may in fact have come from the much older Quarr Abbey, closed down by Henry a decade or so beforehand. Inside, there's a fascinating, if sobering, exhibition covering the catastrophic loss of shipping that has occurred in this strip of the Solent over the centuries. Doubtless, many of these shipwrecks will have been witnessed from the castle by helpless onlookers.

9 CALSHOT CASTLE

CALSHOT, HAMPSHIRE

A castle that mastered the fine art of participating in many wars without becoming their victim

LOCATION
Calshot Spit, Fawley, Hampshire SO45 1BR

GRID REFERENCE
SU 489 025

PUBLIC TRANSPORT
From Southampton Central railway station, walk the very short distance to Wyndham Place from where a number 8 bus (bluestarbus.co.uk; 01202 338421) will take you to Calshot. From there it's a little over a mile's walk out along the spit to the castle.

WHEN TO VISIT
Open April to September daily 10.30am–4.30pm (closed for half an hour at lunchtime).

ADMISSION CHARGE
Yes (free to EH members)

WEBSITE
english-heritage.org.uk

TELEPHONE
02380 892023
(02380 892077 when castle is closed)

Calshot Castle can have few English rivals when it comes to the sheer number of wars with which it has found itself entangled. And yet, miraculously, it has remained obscure, its name barely known beyond the New Forest. More miraculously still, the little hexadecagonal tower on the Solent has survived for over four and a half centuries with barely a scratch on it – the greatest indignities inflicted upon it have come from a peacetime fire and from those who have adapted the castle to the military needs of each successive age.

It began life as one of Henry VIII's Device Forts. Along with St Mawes (page 21), Weymouth, Yarmouth (page 44), Deal and others, it formed a line of defence along the south coast of England which was organised by the king between 1539 and 1547 in preparation for a French invasion. Not since the Roman occupation had England experienced such an extensive programme of coastal defence. Calshot was one of the earlier constructions and was completed in 1540.

Henry himself was to blame for the fact that the Device Forts had to be built at all. His scandalous divorce of Catherine of Aragon had angered her nephew, Charles V of Spain. The Pope, of whom Henry had made an enemy by separating the English Church from Roman Catholicism, had ordered the Spanish monarch to join forces with Francis I of France and invade England in order to haul the English

apostate from his throne. Henry had countered this by forming an alliance with Charles against their common enemy, France. He subsequently invaded his Gallic neighbour in 1544 with a 38,000-strong army. When Charles unexpectedly signed a peace treaty with France, a possible invasion of England was back on the cards. Indeed, on 3 January 1545, Francis declared to the world that he would invade England to 'liberate the English from the Protestant tyranny that Henry VIII had imposed on them'.

Calshot's part in the defence of the realm would be to protect the important port of Southampton from a spit that juts out into Southampton Water at its confluence with the Solent. When the French invasion came in July that year, the huge fleet – much larger than the Spanish Armada – concentrated its efforts on capturing nearby Portsmouth. Although they vastly outnumbered the English fleet, the enterprise was something of a fiasco. The French troops were reduced to invading the sparsely populated Isle of Wight, withdrawing just over a week later to return to France with their tails between their legs.

The episode set the tone for much of Calshot's existence up until the 20th century: it would be readied for an expected invasion but then not called into action. In 1584, the fort was repaired (127 New Forest trees had to be felled for the task) in the wake of a disastrous fire to ward off an expected Spanish invasion. This materialised four years later in the form of the Spanish Armada, which was defeated by the weather and a dash of Sir Francis Drake's military nous, and never troubled the Solent.

Calshot was in Parliamentarian hands for the duration of the English Civil War. Deemed of strategic value on account of its ability to protect Southampton and control the Solent, its 15-strong garrison was kept well armed throughout the hostilities. The War of Spanish Succession (1701–14), in which Britain entered a Grand Alliance with the Holy Roman Empire, the Dutch Republic and Habsburg Spain, saw re-armament – possibly with as many as 25 guns – but no action.

The castle then experienced a lull until the other end of the century. Despite improvements made in the 1770s, it had fallen on hard times. Its armaments were poorly maintained and its aged commander was clearly no longer up to the job. Britain's entry into the French Revolutionary Wars in 1793 meant that once again the fortress was brought up to scratch, though never had to fire a shot in anger.

However, three years after British involvement ceased in 1800, the Napoleonic Wars erupted and with them came the threat of a possible French invasion. Calshot found itself aiding a

prototype Home Guard, acting as a munitions dump for a flotilla of volunteer-crewed armed fishing boats called the Sea Fencibles. Come the 1890s, Britain was again looking fearfully across the Channel. To guard against possible French attacks, a boom was built across Southampton Water, protected by a battery installed beside the castle, with searchlights positioned on the walls.

And so it went on. Calshot's location – facing the Continent and overlooking the entrance to one of England's most significant ports – guaranteed it an almost permanent position on the front line.

The castle truly entered the modern era in 1913, when its grounds played host to a Royal Naval Air Station controlling a dozen seaplanes (an astonishing thought when you consider that the Wright brothers' first flight had happened just 10 years beforehand). The base saw considerable action during World War I, with its planes flying thousands of hours to participate in sorties on the lookout for German submarines. The castle itself was topped with a small observation hut.

Strange times indeed for a Henrician fortress, still with water in its moat and walls built from stone probably filched from the dissolved abbeys at Beaulieu and Netley. It had been constructed in an age when the bow and arrow was still an effective weapon in battle.

In World War II Calshot's boats participated in the evacuation of Dunkirk, and to counter the expected German invasion, the castle was fitted with 12-pounder guns. Remarkably, despite the terrible pasting Southampton and Portsmouth both took from the Luftwaffe, the castle got through the conflict unscathed, and three years after the war was able to send its Sunderland flying boats off to help with the Berlin airlift.

Its participation in the Cold War may well have brought the curtain down on Calshot's military service. The castle became a coastguard lookout tower in 1952 and a signal and radar station six years later, before its 43-year tenure as RAF Calshot came to an end in 1961.

The castle was handed to English Heritage in 1983. The organisation made the decision to revert the fortress to its 1914 incarnation, which involved tearing down the radar station among other measures. A visit today is thus a weird and wonderful amalgam of a trip back to Tudor times and an exploration of the dark days of the early 20th century.

10 ODIHAM CASTLE

NORTH WARNBOROUGH, HAMPSHIRE

One of the most deliciously odd-looking castle ruins in Britain is also a collector's item

LOCATION
Basingstoke Canal, near Mill Lane, North Warnborough, Hampshire RG29 1HQ

GRID REFERENCE
SU 725 518

PUBLIC TRANSPORT
Hook railway station is 2 miles from the castle. You can take the number 13 bus

(stagecoachbus.com; 0345 121 0190) to the outskirts of North Warnborough from where it's a gentle walk along the towpath of the Basingstoke Canal to the castle.

WHEN TO VISIT
Open all year daily 9am–5pm

ADMISSION CHARGE
Free

WEBSITE
visit-hampshire.co.uk

TELEPHONE
01252 370073

Known to locals as King John's Castle, Odiham sits between the bends of two waterways: the River Whitewater and the Basingstoke Canal. It's a peaceful, bucolic spot, so removed from the mainstream of life that it's difficult to believe that in its day this was not only an important royal castle, but also hosted parliament on occasion. Indeed, it found itself at the crucible of Anglo-Norman politics almost before the last of the lime mortar had dried in its walls.

As its informal name suggests, Odiham was built by King John. Posterity has made of the monarch something of a pantomime villain, particularly with regard to his fictional dealings with Robin Hood,

so it's surprising to learn that during his 17-year reign this apparent megalomaniac only got around to ordering the building of three castles. The location for Odiham is believed to have been chosen by the king himself in order to provide a handy place for him to rest up for the night when riding between his two mighty bastions at Windsor and Winchester.

Work began in 1207, with the castle and its protective ring of ditches being completed in 1214. Seven years may seem like rather a long time to devote to what was really quite a small castle, but before even the foundations could be dug, the Whitewater had to be diverted to create a semicircular defence to the north and west of the castle, complementing a square inner moat. A two-storey stone keep was erected along with what was known as a *domus regis* (king's house), which would provide a comfortable place for John to reside on his visits. When the castle came into the possession of his daughter Eleanor, she was quick to have a kitchen and further accommodation added. Unusually, both structures were built on bridges that spanned the inner moat. She also had a hall attached to the octagonal keep.

The ruins of the keep still exist today, along with some of the earthworks that helped guard it. They make for a curious sight. Rather than crumbling and collapsing in the manner of many ancient castles, Odiham seems almost to be melting away. Its walls, the colour of vanilla ice cream, are pockmarked with holes that once held joists in place and are riven with what were once arches for doors and windows. These latter perforations have taken on an altogether more organic shape, as if the wind had been trying its hand at a bit of sculpture. Also of note is an overgrown pond to the south of the canal – it is all that remains of the original moat.

Odiham bears no resemblance at all to Spofforth Castle (page 127), in faraway Yorkshire, or Tonbridge Castle (page 63) in Kent, but history has tied it to those two fortresses. Magna Carta is

said to have been drafted at Spofforth in 1215 and, on 15 June that same year, King John is believed to have ridden from Odiham to Runnymede to press his seal grudgingly into the hot wax dripped upon the barons' ultimatum. When civil war broke out just months later, King John captured Tonbridge Castle from one of the rebelling barons, but also suffered the capture of Odiham Castle himself. French knights over in England to support the barons besieged the fortress for a fortnight before the skeleton garrison – a mere 13 men – surrendered on 9 July 1216. Some considerable damage must have been done to the castle before the troops within

capitulated, because the keep had to be entirely rebuilt.

King John died of dysentery the same year and his infant son was crowned Henry III. Twenty years later, the monarch – who proved as unpopular as his father – granted Odiham to his sister, Eleanor, who was a wealthy and influential widow. Her second marriage was to a leading nobleman named Simon de Montfort, making Odiham the base for one of medieval England's great power couples. De Montfort was one of the leaders of the Second Barons' War, a revolt against his brother-in-law that broke out in 1264.

In defeating Henry's army and apprehending the king at the Battle of Lewes that year, de Montfort became England's de facto ruler. Much of his success was down to Eleanor, who made Odiham their tactical headquarters. She ran a network of communications that allowed her to feed her husband and sons valuable information as they attempted to vanquish the king's forces in various parts of the country. She also liaised with de Montfort's backers while keeping key royalist supporters imprisoned in the castle.

However, despite her efforts, she was not able to save her husband from falling into a trap laid for him by Prince Edward (later Edward I), who defeated him in battle at Evesham in 1265. De Montfort and the couple's eldest son were killed (another son apparently arrived on the scene to witness his father's head being paraded on the end of a spear) and Eleanor fled into exile, becoming a nun at Montargis Abbey in France. Odiham passed back into the hands of Henry III, whose freedom was won as a result of the events at Evesham.

Thenceforth, Odiham continued to punch above its weight when it came to political manoeuvrings. Parliament sat there in 1303; the Despenser family took over the castle and went on to have a whole war named after them (the Despenser War of 1321–22); and from 1346 to 1357 it became a prison for King David II of Scotland, who was kept in remarkable comfort there, with his own servants and cooks. However, the slide from proud castle to ruin had begun. It was downgraded from its role as sometime prison to hunting lodge the following century. The buildings were eventually abandoned and were reported to have become utterly derelict by the early 1600s.

The last time Odiham Castle's hard-earned rest was broken in any material way came in 1792, when the Basingstoke Canal was cut across the edge of the bailey, all but turning the keep and its defences into a tiny island. Its isolation from the outside world is now virtually complete. The time when this little castle was at the very centre of affairs of state is a memory that lives on only in its mouldering stone walls.

EYNSFORD CASTLE

EYNSFORD, KENT

A fortress fought over by the nation's two most powerful clergymen, one of whom was heading for a fall

LOCATION
Gibsons Place, off High Street, Eynsford, Kent DA4 0AA

GRID REFERENCE
TQ 541 658

PUBLIC TRANSPORT
The castle is a 0.75-mile (1.2km) walk from Eynsford railway station along Station Road to the High Street.

WHEN TO VISIT
Open April to September daily 10am–6pm; October to March daily 10am–4pm.

Closed 24–26 December and New Year's Day.

ADMISSION CHARGE
Free

WEBSITE
english-heritage.org.uk

TELEPHONE
0370 333 1181

There is arguably no more famous nor easily recognisable style of castle in Britain than the motte-and-bailey. The image of a circular mound topped by a keep above a compound protected by a wooden stockade has become so identified with the Normans that it's easy to forget that they ever built any other sort of stronghold. However, although few in number, there do survive instances of an altogether different class of Norman fortress: the enclosure castle. These did not have a motte at all and merely relied on a high stone curtain wall and (sometimes) towers to keep those within from harm. Eynsford is an extraordinary example of just such a castle. The fact that the majority of its wall (it never had any

towers) has somehow made it into the 21st century at its full height – despite the rigours of age and a dispute that led to a shocking incident of medieval vandalism – makes it a rare gem indeed.

Eynsford began life like many a post-Conquest Norman castle: on the site of a pre-existing Saxon structure. In this case it was a manor and *burh* (fortified settlement) on the River Darent. Since the construction of a bridge of any great size was an expensive affair in the Middle Ages, and ferries were few and far between, places where one might effect a river crossing without facing the prospect of being swept away to an untimely death were much rarer than they are today. As such, they tended to be sedulously controlled by the powers that be, as was notably the case at Tonbridge (page 63). The location of this particular Saxon fortification was determined by the presence of a ford across the Darent, a river that has its genesis near Westerham in Kent and flows into the Thames close to Dartford.

The Normans recognised the strategic value of the site and took advantage of the terrace that had been thrown up there, along with a rampart and ditch. Unusually, the Saxon manor house was built of stone, a sign of the wealth of Christ Church in Canterbury, which appears to have possessed the manor until the advent of the Normans. It stayed within the church, since its new owner was Odo, the Bishop of Bayeux, who was made Earl of Kent by his half-brother William the Conqueror. The cleric evinced no great distaste for Mammon, amassing estates in 23 English counties and becoming the most powerful person in the land besides the king.

A considerable rivalry existed between Odo and Lanfranc, an Italian monk who was invested Archbishop of Canterbury in 1070. A debate arose between them concerning the manor (which was not yet called Eynsford), with the archbishop claiming it on the grounds that it lay within territory that he largely controlled. Happily for Lanfranc, Odo overstepped himself politically and experienced an almighty fall from grace. In 1082, he was caught planning a private military excursion to Italy (possibly with the aim of making himself Pope) without William's permission or knowledge. He was arrested, stripped of his earldom and English estates, and thrown into prison. Lanfranc seized the manor by the Darent and put a knight named Ralph de Eynsford in charge.

Ralph's son William had inherited the post by the time Lanfranc decided to improve the fortifications of the *burh*. During the years 1085–87 de Eynsford built an encircling curtain wall, turning the manor into a bona fide castle. It was now ready for any return to power Odo might engineer from his prison cell. As it happened, the disgraced churchman was released the same year but never regained his English title or possessions. He died 10 years later in Palermo in Sicily en route to the Holy Land with the First Crusade. William, meanwhile, was the first of seven consecutive William de Eynsfords to hold the castle on behalf of the archbishopric.

The only major improvements to the fortress came around 1130, when a gatehouse was built to protect the entrance; the Saxon hall was replaced with a new one; and the height of the curtain wall increased. The enclosure is so small, and the wall around it so high, that one can't help feeling that to live at Eynsford must have been a trial for anyone given to claustrophobia.

About a century later – during William VI's tenure – the hall went up in flames and had to be rebuilt. Look at the fireplace in the undercroft solar and you'll see tiles taken from local Roman villas. But it was in 1261, when the Eynsford male line ceased with the death of William VII, that trouble really started brewing. The two families that inherited the estate – the Heringauds and the de Criols – were both descendants of William V.

Things were complicated by the Second Barons' War, which saw both families enter on the side of the rebels and the empty castle seized by a royal official named Ralph de Farningham. He handed it over to a judge, Ralph de Sandwich, who forced the Heringauds into ceding him their share of the castle and then sold it on to another judge, William Inge.

Inge began to exercise his right to the half share in the castle he had bought, a move that angered the de Criols. In 1312, three de Criol brothers staged a raid on the castle they half-owned, shattering windows, smashing down doors, breaking whatever was breakable and letting cattle run wild. The damage was so extensive that the castle was never habitable from that day onwards.

Over the centuries the castle passed between families of varying degrees of nobility and it gradually withered away. By the 1750s, the ruin was being used as a stables and kennels. Hunting hounds were still being accommodated within Eynsford's walls in 1835 when some sort of decorum was at last returned to the ailing fortress. The dogs were turned out, and the stables and kennels were stripped out. Sadly, this turned out to be but a temporary reprieve, and Eynsford continued its decline. It was saved for the nation by local man E D Till and, after his death, by Agnes Lady Fountain, who bought the castle and later handed it into the care of the state. A visit today is a fine reminder of how, when it came to castle design, the Normans were more than a one-trick pony.

12 TONBRIDGE CASTLE

TONBRIDGE, KENT

A seat of constant rebellion on the Medway that played its part in the defence against Hitler

LOCATION
Castle Street, Tonbridge,
Kent TN9 1BG

GRID REFERENCE
TQ 589 465

PUBLIC TRANSPORT
It's a five-minute walk along
the High Street from
Tonbridge railway station
to the castle.

WHEN TO VISIT
Open Monday to Saturday
9am–5pm, Sunday and bank
holidays 10.30am–4.30pm.
Closed Christmas and New
Year's Day. Grounds open
daily 8am to dusk.

ADMISSION CHARGE
Yes (but entrance to the
grounds is free)

WEBSITE
tonbridgecastle.org

TELEPHONE
01732 770929

In their defence, the de Clare family lived hundreds of years before philosophers Edmund Burke and George Santayana pointed out the folly of ignoring or refusing to learn from history. However, it is true to say that the early period of the de Clares' occupation of Tonbridge Castle consists almost entirely of loops of time that follow precisely the same format. They rebel against the king of the day; the castle is captured by said monarch; the castle is returned to them sometime later, usually by a king they hadn't yet rebelled against. They rebel against this new king...

Their story starts by the bank of a river in Kent. The Medway famously divides the county between the Men and Maids of Kent (to the east of the river) and the Kentish Men and Maids (to the west). At the time of the Norman Conquest the bridges that spanned the river tended to be infrequent, and so controlling them was vital to anyone who wanted to exert their dominance over the populace. Therefore, when William the Conqueror granted vast tracts of Kent to Richard FitzGilbert, the Norman knight wasted no time in establishing a castle at one of his new acquisitions, Tonbridge, the site of an important river crossing.

As was the Norman way, FitzGilbert employed earth and timber to build a motte-and-bailey fortress beside the river. He arranged for two baileys to be created

– one to protect dwellings and other key structures, and another to which less important outbuildings were consigned.

It's one of those quirks of history that the first attack upon the castle that we know about came not from oppressed Saxons but a Norman king. William II (otherwise known as William Rufus) had ascended to the English throne on the death of his father. However, his brother Robert had inherited Normandy, the other part of William the Conqueror's kingdom. This sparked a revolt against William Rufus by the most powerful Norman oligarchs, who felt their lives would be unnecessarily complicated by this two-headed arrangement. On learning that FitzGilbert (now called de Clare) had joined the rebellion, William had Tonbridge Castle besieged and then, on its surrender, burnt down. Magnanimously, the king chose not to execute the insurgent but let him end his days in obscurity as a monk.

Eventually, the de Clare family managed to ingratiate themselves sufficiently with the crown to have Tonbridge Castle restored to them. A stone keep was built by Gilbert de Clare, 1st Earl of Hertford, who also diverted river water to fill a couple of dry moats. He then chose to rebel against King Stephen and was consequently imprisoned until he handed over all his castles to the crown. After a

rapprochement with Stephen later on, Gilbert recovered his possessions, and Tonbridge was back in de Clare hands.

A wall around the inner bailey, constructed in the 12th century, gave the castle such an air of affluence that the saintly Thomas Becket, Archbishop of Canterbury, fell foul of the tenth commandment and began coveting his neighbour's stronghold. Roger de Clare, the neighbour in question at the time, refused the cleric's demand that he pay homage or hand over the castle. Indeed, he went rather further, forcing the ecclesiastical messenger who brought the diktat to eat it in front of him, 'parchment, seals and all'.

The next attempt on Tonbridge came at the hands of King John in 1215. A man given to rage, he fumed at having been coerced by a cabal of barons to put his seal to Magna Carta (see page 116). He was even more incensed that one of its provisions (the infamous 'clause 61') established grave repercussions if he broke faith with the charter, and so he quickly engineered what would become known as the First Barons' War. John's forces captured Tonbridge Castle from Richard de Clare, one of the barons who had been holding the king to account. Richard had to wait until John was replaced by Henry III before he got his castle back, along with a licence to fortify it. In 1259, de Clare began the building of the towers and the impressive gatehouse. Three years later, at the age of 39, he could be found lying in a tomb at Tewkesbury Abbey, reputedly the victim of a deliberate poisoning. His likeness in stone can be seen at the castle.

In 1264, Richard's son Gilbert de Clare supported the rebels in the Second Barons' War (and instigated a massacre of Jews at Canterbury). Despite the brand new defences, he lost Tonbridge Castle to the king. In a new low for the de Clares, he also lost his wife Alice, whom Henry's forces captured at the same time (the king ordered her release later because she was his half-niece). Gilbert got his own back by being on the winning side at the Battle of Lewes (at which Henry himself was taken prisoner) only to fight for the king the following year at the Battle of Evesham. This last successful engagement not only secured Henry's freedom but also the return of Tonbridge Castle to the de Clares.

The cycle of rebellion/loss of castle/ recovery of castle ended with the death at the Battle of Bannockburn of the 7th Earl of Hertford, another Gilbert, which put an end to the de Clare line. The castle subsequently changed hands between various ennobled families until, by the outbreak of the Civil War in 1642, it was held by a commoner called Thomas Weller. Being a civil servant in the pay of parliament, it is unsurprising that he declared the castle for the Roundheads.

The following year, the fortress at last managed to see off an attack and never fell under Royalist control. However, that didn't save it from a Cromwellian order to make it untenable as a stronghold. Thankfully, although the gatehouse was damaged, it was by no means destroyed.

The castle suffered most at the hands of those who would recycle it. In 1741, when the Medway was canalised, bridges and locks were made from Tonbridge Castle stone. Fifty years later, the mansion (now used for offices) that stands beside the gatehouse was created using the same raw material. Tonbridge Urban District Council bought the castle in 1898, little knowing that it had not quite completed its military service. During World War II, the castle was to become part of a fortified line designed to defend against a German advance in the event of an invasion. A pair of pillboxes were built into the walls, and machine-gun emplacements and tank traps installed.

In the 1990s, the gatehouse underwent major reconstruction, restoring it to something akin to its original state. Today's keepers of the castle describe the audio tour of the gatehouse as 'an interactive recreation of medieval life' and it certainly does its best to immerse visitors in the doings of that distant epoch. The castle also plays host to food festivals, music festivals and carnivals – all of which the medieval lords of the castle would no doubt have heartily approved of, shortly before heading off to take part in another rebellion...

13 ST LEONARD'S TOWER

WEST MALLING, KENT

Not just a castle – or perhaps not even a castle – but a riddle, wrapped in a mystery, inside an enigma

LOCATION
St Leonard's Street, West Malling, Kent ME19 6PD

GRID REFERENCE
TQ 675 570

PUBLIC TRANSPORT
The castle is just over a mile from West Malling railway station, outside the southwestern outskirts of the village.

WHEN TO VISIT
Open any reasonable time during daylight hours.

ADMISSION CHARGE
Free

WEBSITE
english-heritage.org.uk

TELEPHONE
0370 333 1181

Who doesn't love a mystery? That patch of impenetrable darkness that lies in the midst of our existence can spark the imagination and remind us that, for all humankind's supposed cleverness, there is much that we seem unable to fathom. For a good old stare into this well of unknowing, make for a spot just southwest of the ancient market town of West Malling. There you'll find St Leonard's Tower standing apart from the thrum and prickle of life, enigmatic and inscrutable.

Not only is very little known about the history of this fortification in the Kent countryside, there have also been questions raised over what it actually is. Naturally enough, there's a debate over who was responsible for the construction

of the 72ft three-storey tower as well. One theory holds that it was once part of a castle built between 1077 and 1108 by Gundulf, a Norman monk who became Bishop of Rochester. Around 1090, the cleric founded the (now ruinous) Malling Abbey, a house for Benedictine nuns established half a mile away. Thus, it's certainly possible that he built some sort of fortification at St Leonard's.

Another take on the tower is that it was raised by William the Conqueror's half-brother Odo, Bishop of Bayeux (see also page 59). It's true that Odo held title to land at West Malling (ostensibly in the name of the church), which would therefore put him in the frame for the St Leonard's work. However, the estate was merely one of very many across the

country to which he laid claim, and this was by no means one of the more important ones, so ordering some sort of construction here is unlikely to have been a priority for him.

A third hypothesis – once quite popular – holds that it was built by Gundulf but as a bell tower for an adjacent church called St Leonard's, which was demolished in the 18th century. However, there are a couple of problems with this notion. If it had been a bell tower, it was out of proportion to the very much smaller church it was supposed to have served, and the architectural style bears a striking similarity to Norman keeps of that period rather than Norman bell towers.

All things taken into consideration, even though it's impossible to make any conclusive claims today as to who the originator was and precisely when the tower was constructed, it seems that Gundulf's was the more likely hand behind St Leonard's, that 1077–1108 is the most probable timeframe, and that the structure was not a bell tower.

Worthy of note are the materials used for the tower's construction. Its thick walls are built of rag-stone – a hard and relatively rare type of limestone transported from a quarry near Maidstone. Meanwhile, the spiral staircases that would prove to be the tower's salvation are mostly composed of tufa, a porous rock of calcium carbonate.

Another intriguing feature is the lack of evidence of the basic facilities one would expect in a building intended to accommodate a garrison or to be used as a fortified residence. For instance, there is nothing to suggest the presence of latrines or garderobes, or even fireplaces. While some have taken this as an indication that the tower's primary role was as a keep to which defenders could take refuge in times of danger, for others it points to the possibility that it functioned as a headquarters for the overseeing of local estates held by the church.

For more than half a millennium the story of St Leonard's Tower is a blank page. It is only when it is put out of action for good that we read something of its tale. From 1621 to 1660, the tower was in the hands of a Royalist supporter called Sir John Rayney of Wrotham Place. He owned a large estate that also included Malling Abbey, which had been dissolved by Henry VIII the previous century.

At the end of May 1648, a Parliamentarian army led by Sir Thomas Fairfax passed through West Malling on its way to Maidstone. There it would engage and defeat Royalist forces that included Sir John and his followers. It was probably at some point the following year – with Charles I beheaded and the Royalists vanquished – that parliament ordered St Leonard's Tower to be slighted. Archaeological investigations have revealed that there was a ham-fisted attempt to destroy the building completely by blowing up the stair turret at ground level. The venture was foiled by the extremely unusual (indeed, possibly unique) design of the staircase. This consisted of a vaulted tunnel which used very much more stone than would have been the case in a normal medieval spiral staircase and was thus very much more resilient.

Wisely deciding not to give the gunpowder another go and possibly perish in the endeavour, whoever had been handed the task of disabling the tower (possibly the owner himself) appears to have dismantled the top storey with some care, and then taken out each floor, working downwards, until all of them had been removed. This left the castle without a roof and thus prey to the further debilitating effects of the weather. Given that, it's remarkable that it has remained as intact as it has, and was not quarried for stone in later years, as happened to the church next to it.

The slighting reduced the tower's height from three storeys to two, lowering the structure to 59ft. However, the fine views of the surrounding countryside that would have been enjoyed from the top of St Leonard's confirm the suggestion that it would have made an excellent Royalist lookout tower in its day.

We may conclude that some of that countryside was given over to the production of hops because the last known use of the tower – as recorded by Edward Hasted in 1782 – was as a storage facility for that particular crop. Since St Leonard's had long since lost its roof by then, it seems likely that the tower served as a very temporary staging post for the hops before they were whisked away to be turned into good Kentish beer.

14 YPRES TOWER
RYE, EAST SUSSEX

Residence, courthouse, mortuary and museum are just some of its many guises

LOCATION
3 East Street, Rye, East Sussex TN31 7JY

GRID REFERENCE
TQ 922 202

PUBLIC TRANSPORT
Rye railway station, on the Marshlink line between Ashford and Hastings, is a 500yd walk from the tower,

heading southeast through the town.

WHEN TO VISIT
Open April to October daily (weather permitting) 10.30am–5pm (last entry 4.30pm) November to March 10.30am–3.30pm (last entry 3pm). Closed Christmas Eve and Christmas Day.

ADMISSION CHARGE
Yes

WEBSITE
ryemuseum.co.uk

TELEPHONE
01797 226728

Many castles have an air of mystique about them. There are copious instances where we do not know precisely when a certain castle was built or by whom, and there's many a fortress whose history resembles a book almost entirely composed of blank pages. But there can be few castles in the land that can match Ypres Tower when it comes to the sheer inscrutability of its origins. Not only do we not know when it was constructed or who was responsible, we don't even know exactly what it was meant to be. All we can be really sure about is the bewildering array of uses to which the edifice was subsequently put.

Some guides confidently declare that Ypres Tower (which, to add to the confusion, is often referred to as Rye

Castle) was built in 1249. However, that was merely the year in which a grant was made to the Constable of the Cinque Ports, Peter of Savoy, 'to fortify the castles of Hastings and la Rye', which suggests that a castle was already largely in existence by that time and merely required some finishing touches. There is a record as far back as 1226 of Henry III's desire to have a castle erected at 'Ria' (as Rye was known), which would seem to give further credence to the theory that Ypres Tower was already around in some form before 1249. Unfortunately, the waters are muddied further by the fact that one would expect contemporary documents to mention the castle but instead we are met with an unerring silence. This has led some historians to posit that there were plans to build a castle here but that no one ever got around to it, or perhaps that 'Rye Castle' was not a castle at all but merely one element of the town's defences.

If that were not confusing enough, the structure – whatever it was – was not called Ypres Tower until later. The earliest name it went by appears to have been Baddings (sometimes spelled Baddyngs) Tower, a reference to the ward of Rye in which it stands.

In the 13th century, Rye was still defended by ramparts but had no stone walls behind which to shelter. A grant to build the first ones was given in 1329. Unusually, the walls had a double function:

to guard against raiders from across the Channel and from flooding by the Channel itself. At that time Rye was a coastal town whereas today the sea is 2.5 miles away, though still connected to the town by the River Rother. Both raiders and waters did their best to put the little settlement out of business. The French sacked it in 1339 and 1377; while in 1348 the sea is reported to have encroached so far inland as to have made of Rye an island in imminent danger of being overwhelmed. It seems probable that Baddings Tower came into being at some point after 1329, in tandem with the town walls which, despite the obvious dangers facing the

community, were slow to go up (a full circle had still not been built by 1385).

We do know that the tower was in position to fail to keep those French raiders of 1377 at bay. The attackers overran the town and laid waste to the courthouse. The tower was hurriedly pressed into use as a substitute court and may also have served as a prison as well. These were the first among many different functions that the building would serve over its long life.

Evidently, some other venue in which to hold and try local miscreants had been found by 1430, because in that year it came into the ownership of John de Iprys (to whom the tower owes its name). He used it as a residence, probably in conjunction with other adjacent buildings. However, he held it on the understanding that should it be required again to safeguard the town against attack, he would have to hand it back.

The 1500s did in fact see Ypres Tower return to public service, again functioning as a courthouse and prison. At some unknown juncture it was stripped of its judicial duties and turned into a dedicated jail. Clearly, it was well suited to such a role because it remained a prison for

several centuries. More cells were added in the early 1800s, followed by an exercise yard, which later also found use as a soup kitchen. A second tower was built alongside Ypres in 1837 to accommodate female convicts. It was the arrival of a police station in Rye in 1891 that finally brought Ypres' custodial career to a close.

Once again the tower proved its versatility – going from housing those serving time to housing those whose time was up, the basement becoming the town's mortuary. However, it was not always a place where the dead could rest in peace. Caught up in an air raid in 1942, the tower's pyramidal tile roof was lost.

Extraordinarily, Ypres Tower's most recent incarnation as a museum overlapped its use as a morgue. Rye Castle Museum opened on the ground and upper floors in 1954 and took over the basement when the mortuary closed five years later. The former women's prison in the neighbouring tower is now also part of the museum (there's a rather good audio-visual presentation in which a former inmate tells her story), while the former exercise yard has been transformed into a re-creation of a medieval herb garden. To give more space for its burgeoning collection, the museum has added a second site in the town at a former brewer's bottling factory.

The erstwhile castle (or defensive building of some sort) has been a residence, courthouse, prison (with sometime soup kitchen attached), mortuary and museum. Regardless of why, when and by whom it was built, there can be no denying that the former Baddings Tower has led a colourful and useful existence, albeit that it wasn't great at defending the town from the French. Its history suggests that someday the museum will move on and Ypres will be free to don yet another disguise. Haberdasher? Camera obscura? Fall-out shelter? Only time will tell.

15 ORFORD CASTLE
ORFORD, SUFFOLK

A truly impressive fortress whose octagonal keep makes it unique in Britain

LOCATION
Orford, Woodbridge,
Suffolk IP12 2ND

GRID REFERENCE
TM 419 498

PUBLIC TRANSPORT
The nearest railway station
is Wickham Market which is

8 miles (13km) from Orford
but there is no bus service.

WHEN TO VISIT
Open April to September
daily 10am–6pm; variable
opening the rest of the year
– see website for details.
Last entry 30 minutes
before closing.

ADMISSION CHARGE
Yes (free to EH members)

WEBSITE
english-heritage.org.uk and
orfordmuseum.org.uk

TELEPHONE
01394 450472

There are many reasons why some castles have survived into the 21st century more or less intact while others have become ghosts, their existence reduced to an insignificant pile of stones or a grid of faint lines traced across a grassy field. Orford Castle owes its continued existence not to any great strategic value it once had or because it became a stately home but on account of its value to sailors. Back in the early 19th century, when navigation was often a hit-and-miss affair, the castle at Orford provided mariners with a useful landmark by which they could orientate themselves, and its utility proved its saving grace.

The fact that the castle was built at all, two miles from a stretch of Suffolk coast known principally for its wildlife and eerie landscape, is down to two men: Hugh Bigod and Henry II. The Bigods were the

Earls of Norfolk and held sway over vast swathes of East Anglia in the 12th century. Such was their influence that they posed a threat to any king of England with whom they were not on good terms. In an attempt to neutralise this danger, Henry initially expropriated Hugh Bigod's four castles, including Bungay (see page 85). In 1165, he decided on a different tack, restoring two of Bigod's castles to him but beginning the building of his own royal fortress near the Suffolk coast.

At that time, Orford was a very small village, albeit one with a market, whose population probably earned its living through fishing. The castle there took eight years to complete. Its layout could barely have been simpler: a single keep surrounded by a curtain wall. However, the design chosen was rather extraordinary. No one knows just why Henry elected to

have an octagonal keep built at Orford, though clearly such an unusual style – believed to have been influenced by Byzantine architecture – would certainly have impressed anyone who saw it. Its function, however, was obvious: it would act as a bulwark against the Bigod dynasty and a none-too-subtle reminder of who was king and who subject. The royal castle also had a dramatic effect on the village. Orford's economy was given a powerful boost by the wide range of services required by its new addition and the population grew swiftly. (By the start of the following century, its port was even busier than that of the prosperous trading town of Ipswich, just to the south.)

No fewer than 20 loyal knights swelled the garrison at Orford during the revolt against Henry II in 1173–74 (see page 87–88). The Bigods, who had been heavily involved in the failed uprising, were dealt a devastating blow, losing mighty Framlingham Castle permanently. Ironically, the downfall of the Bigods also sealed Orford Castle's fate. With the sudden absence of a potential adversary in the region, the royal stronghold and propaganda tool lost much of its *raison d'être*.

It's a surprise then to find the castle suddenly in the thick of things again not all that long afterwards. From 1199, when he came to the throne, the castle belonged to King John, who was not one of England's most beloved monarchs. The First Barons' War broke out in 1215, and the following year Prince Louis of France was invited by rebel nobles to invade England. Orford Castle was one of the many royal fortresses that fell briefly to the insurgents but does not seem to have been badly damaged.

The stronghold was then passed from governor to governor – holding it for the monarch of the day – until Edward III granted it in perpetuity to Robert de Ufford, the Earl of Suffolk. This ushered in a new and uneventful chapter of Orford's life in which the castle passed through the hands of several of East Anglia's leading families and went into a slow spiral of decline, one effect of which was the loss of most of its curtain wall.

It is not often that a castle is affected by the movement of the landscape around it, but this is just what happened in Orford's case. North Sea currents deposited silt which clogged up the mouth of the Ore Estuary and caused the shingle spit of Orford Ness to grow, forcing shipping to sail up a long and narrow channel in order to reach the harbour. With its port growing increasingly unpopular, the town of Orford withered, dragging its expensively built octagonal fortress down with it.

By 1805, the castle was in a poor condition and its owner, the 2nd Marquess of Hertford, wanted to tear it down.

Thankfully, the government intervened, forbidding the destruction on the grounds that mariners used the castle to judge the whereabouts of dangerous sandbanks just off the coast. Instead, some attempts at conserving the keep were made, though not the curtain wall, which disappeared completely, its stone recycled.

Nowadays, the tall slim keep is cared for by English Heritage and is in excellent shape. Visitors can climb its circular staircase from the ground floor to the fourth floor and even up onto the roof, from where there are sumptuous views across the lunar-like landscape of Orford Ness and the mysterious-looking military radar installation mouldering upon it. Though space inside the castle is naturally constrained, there is just enough room for the admirable Orford Museum, which tells the history of the area through local finds.

One most unusual story recounted there is that of the Wild Man of Orford. The curious events surrounding the unfortunate creature were chronicled by Ralph of Coggeshall. He reported that local fishermen caught a naked man in their nets one day in 1167. This strangest of strangers, who was apparently extremely hairy, was locked up in the castle while attempts were made to question him. Since the prisoner behaved like a feral animal and did not speak, these attempts proved fruitless, even when backed up by torture. After six months he effected his escape, never to be captured again.

So if you are in the area and happen to see a hairy naked man acting like a wild animal, it's probably wise simply to wish him good day and move on.

16 EYE CASTLE
EYE, SUFFOLK

Perched high above a town in rural Suffolk, this fortress is not what it seems

LOCATION
Access via a gate in Castle Hill, off Castle Street, Eye, Suffolk IP23 7AP

GRID REFERENCE
TM 147 737

PUBLIC TRANSPORT
From Diss railway station walk the short distance to Victoria Road to catch the 112 bus (travel-galloway. com; 01449 766323) to Eye.

WHEN TO VISIT
Open Easter to October daily 9am–7pm (or dusk, if earlier); November to Easter weekends only 9am–7pm (or dusk, if earlier). If locked during these hours, a list of key-holders is posted by the gate.

ADMISSION CHARGE
Free

WEBSITE
n/a

TELEPHONE
01449 724639

It's fitting that what you see when you look at the castle at Eye is in fact a trick of the eye. Climb to the top of the Norman motte to look more closely at the stone keep at its summit and you'll discover that it is not at all what it appears to be from below. Indeed, there can hardly be a motte in the whole of England that has had such a strange afterlife since the destruction of its castle keep.

The history of Eye Castle begins rather routinely. In 1066, the land in those parts was in the hands of a Saxon named Edric of Laxfield. Two years after Harold II's defeat near Hastings, Edric had his possessions confiscated and handed to one of those who fought alongside William the Conqueror – in this case, a certain William Mallet, Lord of Graville. The knight – who claimed Anglo-Norman ancestry – promptly had a motte-and-bailey castle constructed, one of scores that had begun to dot the English countryside since the invasion. The area was predominantly marshland, which acted like a vast moat around the 40ft-high island motte. In flat countryside, the castle must have been an awe-inspiring spectacle for the defeated Saxons.

However, there was one man in the region who refused to be awed: Hereward the Wake. His East Anglian rebellion caused no end of trouble to the new Norman king. William Malet himself was killed in the uprising in 1071, and Eye Castle was inherited by his son Robert. Clearly a man with a head for business, he

took the unusual step of founding a market here. The Domesday Book, collated in 1086, records only two castles that made their owners any income. One is Chepstow (it collected tolls from those crossing a wooden bridge across the Wye) and the other is Eye, on account of its market. It must have been a reasonably sizeable affair because the Bishop of Norwich complained that it had taken custom from his own market at Hoxne, three miles away to the northeast.

As it was for many a Norman motte-and-bailey castle, the 12th century would prove the making or breaking of Eye. After the death of William the Conqueror, the Anglo-Norman kingdom was split between two monarchs, one reigning over England, the other Normandy. In 1106, when Henry I was ruling over the English part of the kingdom, he invaded Normandy. Robert Malet, who had been sent into exile by Henry (but who was still in possession of Eye), aligned himself with the Duke of Normandy, Robert Curthose. When the two armies clashed at Tinchebray on 28 September 1106, Malet was killed. His lands were forfeited and Eye became the property of the Crown. Seven years later, Henry handed it to his favourite nephew, Stephen of Blois, who would seize the throne in 1135.

The terrible and prolonged civil war that broke out during Stephen's 19-year reign saw one major change at Eye – the

castle was passed to William of Ypres, a nobleman who had been landless when he joined the king's household in 1133 but who became one of his most important military leaders. Stephen later transferred the keeping of Eye to his son-in-law, Hervey Brito, and then to his own son, William. Between them, the three successfully held Eye for the king during his lifetime, only for William to be coerced into relinquishing it to the next king, Henry II, when the new monarch moved to secure his position against the country's powerful nobles in 1157.

It's surprising to learn that, a century after it had been built, the castle was still reported to have an outer stockade made of timber rather than stone. Despite this, the king's garrison managed to resist an attack made on it in 1173 by Hugh Bigod, the Earl of Norfolk (see page 87–88) during a revolt led by Henry II's sons. Nevertheless, the castle appears to have sustained some sort of damage because two years later we read of repairs and improvements being carried out. By the end of the century its inner bailey was the possessor of two new square towers.

A stronghold in a region of the country where the monarch was often threatened by powerful and headstrong noblemen, Eye Castle became an important royal outpost, despite its modest size (especially when compared with nearby Framlingham). Successive kings kept it well garrisoned and fortified until 1265, when disaster struck. An attack made on it that year during the Second Barons' War overwhelmed the defenders and the castle was sacked. Although the outer wall does seem to have been built in stone at some juncture

after this, the castle never recovered from this calamity.

However, it was at this point that it began its curious second life. Though much ruined, in the 14th century it was being used as a prison, a function it performed until 1603. By that time, a windmill had adorned the summit of the motte for 40 years, taking advantage of this rare elevated position in the landscape. It was later replaced by a newer model. The 1830s saw a workhouse and school added to the mix, both erected in the bailey.

But it was in1844 that the *trompe l'œil* we see today was begun. Sir Edward Kerrison, then owner of the castle, tore down the windmill and in its place built a house of flint for his batman to thank him for saving his life during the Battle of Waterloo. In a nod to the past, Kerrison had the residence resemble a Norman shell keep (see Tamworth Castle on page 112). Eventually abandoned, it braved the elements until 1965 when a storm brought about its partial demise. A further collapse occurred in 1979, perhaps in response to events elsewhere. Perversely, this newly acquired derelict look rendered the former house even more like a ruined Norman keep, and the illusion was complete.

But now the castle has added yet another role to its roster: that of theatre. Medieval pageants and open-air productions take place here every summer.

BUNGAY CASTLE

BUNGAY, SUFFOLK

'Old and ruinous, and worth nothing a year'

LOCATION
Enter through Jesters Café, 10 Castle Orchard, Bungay, Suffolk NR35 1DD

GRID REFERENCE
TM 335 897

PUBLIC TRANSPORT
From Beccles railway station, walk to the Old Market Place to pick up the number 581 bus (simonds.co.uk; 01379 647300) for the half-hour journey to Bungay. The castle is in the centre of town, but well hidden.

WHEN TO VISIT
Open during the Jesters Café hours: Monday to Saturday 9.30am–5pm; Sunday 10am–4pm.

ADMISSION CHARGE
Free (donations welcome)

WEBSITE
n/a

TELEPHONE
01986 896485 (Jesters Café)

It's a state with which anyone over 40 is likely to be able to empathise. In 1382, the words 'Old and ruinous, and worth nothing a year' were used in an official document to describe Bungay Castle. What gives the report even greater pathos is that the fortress had sunk to this pitiable condition less than a hundred years after reaching its zenith. Its owner, Sir Roger Bigod, had invested a large amount of money to rejuvenate the castle, then obtained a royal licence to crenellate it. Aside from installing battlements, he built a fine twin-towered gatehouse, curtain walls that surrounded the castle's (possibly by then ruined) keep, and probably a tower as well. Unfortunately, he died in 1297, about three years after his magnum opus was completed. Since he had no heir, the castle became the property of the Crown. The Crown had little use for the place, forsaking it completely around 1365, and so it was lost.

With a population of 5,127 at the last census, Bungay (pronounced *bun-ghee*) isn't a large settlement by any means and has no skyscrapers save the tower of the priory church, and yet it does a good job of hiding its premier attraction. The two circular towers of the gatehouse and the various sections of wall that make up the castle today do not attempt to impose themselves on the attention of the passer-by. Indeed, it's perfectly possible to head through the little town and over the river into Norfolk without realising that this was once home to a formidable (if compact) stronghold held by one of the nation's leading families.

The first Roger Bigod to hold sway over Bungay was an obscure Norman knight who hit the big time through his support of William the Conqueror's invasion of England. Rewarded by the king with all manner of estates across East Anglia, he began a programme of castle building, eventually establishing Bungay in around 1100. The location was chosen to make full use of a bend in the River Waveney, which almost doubles back on itself here and thus helps serve as a defence.

Roger Bigod's eldest son William inherited the castle but was drowned in the infamous *White Ship* disaster of 1120. The eponymous vessel was the *Titanic* of its day with the over-confident captain striking a rock in the English Channel just off the French coast. Swathes of Norman royalty and nobility were wiped out at a stroke. William's younger brother Hugh inherited Bungay and quickly set about using it as a foundation from which to flex his muscles. When civil war broke out – the period of English history so chaotic that it is simply called the Anarchy – the charismatic Bigod aligned himself with the usurper King Stephen against Empress Matilda. In 1136, with rumours spreading that the king was as good as on his deathbed, Bigod turned against him and

took the royal castle of Norwich, though lost it again soon afterwards. Four years later, Stephen was in a strong enough position to turn his attentions to Bungay, and duly captured the castle.

In order to win his former ally around, Stephen made Bigod Earl of Suffolk. The newly ennobled warrior's loyalty lasted about a year before he began attacking the king again. He was made Earl of Norfolk by Matilda, but rather than being spurred on to greater deeds on her behalf, he sat out most of the rest of the war.

It was the reign of the following king, Henry II, that arguably had the greatest effect on the castle. Henry was crowned in 1154 and immediately confiscated

Bungay and Bigod's other possessions (including the mighty Framlingham Castle, also in Suffolk). The following decade, the king saw fit to return them in the belief that the earl was now too weak to pose a threat. Hugh Bigod began the first great work at Bungay, building a tall square keep with walls that were a colossal 16–23ft thick.

This evidently gave him a false sense of invulnerability because, in 1173, at the age of 78, he rebelled against the king, joining up with the Earl of Leicester to capture the royal castle at Haughley. Riled and keen to teach Bigod a lesson, Henry marched against him. The earl met the king at Syleham, close to Diss, and is

reputed to have made up a bit of doggerel in a show of bravado:

> *Were I in my Castle*
> *Upon the River Waveney,*
> *I wouldne give a button*
> *For the king of Cockney*

There are two competing stories about what happened next. One avers that Bigod's 'castle upon the River Waveney' was besieged and a mine gallery dug beneath the keep to cause its collapse.

When Bigod surrendered, the castle was further slighted. The other version, which is more in keeping with the sense of the ditty, is that Bigod surrendered at Syleham. The king then had the castle undermined but Bigod intervened, handing over a thousand marks and thus preserving the keep.

Precisely 101 years after it had been declared 'old and ruinous, and worth nothing a year', the castle came into the hands of the Dukes of Norfolk, who would oversee its gentle decay well into the 20th century. Perhaps the most notable event over this period was the penning by local author Elizabeth Bonhôte of the gothic novel *Bungay Castle*. Published in 1796, it describes the discovery by two sisters of a horrifying secret hidden with the fortress and is notable for being well ahead of its time in terms of its feminist slant.

A scheme to restore the castle was instigated in 1934 by a Dr Cane, the town reeve (an office that has existed in Bungay since Saxon times and continues today). In 1987, the former stronghold was handed over to the town and a trust was set up to care for it. Over six centuries after it was dismissed as 'old and ruinous', Bungay Castle is obviously even older and probably even more ruinous. But worth nothing? Any visitor will tell you that that's certainly not true.

18 BURGH CASTLE
BURGH CASTLE, NORFOLK

A small Roman fort surrounded by a very large and impressive Roman wall

LOCATION
Butt Lane, Burgh Castle,
Great Yarmouth, Norfolk
NR31 9QB

GRID REFERENCE
TG 474 045

PUBLIC TRANSPORT
From Great Yarmouth
railway station walk to the
Town Hall on Regent Street
to pick up the number X11
bus (firstgroup.com; 0345

646 0707) to Belton. From
there it's a pleasant 2-mile
(3.2km) walk along the
Angles Way long-distance
footpath to the castle.
Alternatively, you can pick
up the Angles Way from
Great Yarmouth station and
follow it all along the
southern shore of Breydon
Water to the castle, a
distance of just under
5 miles (8km).

WHEN TO VISIT
Open any reasonable time
during daylight hours.

ADMISSION CHARGE
Free

WEBSITE
english-heritage.org.uk

TELEPHONE
0370 333 1181

I t's not every fortress that finds
itself converted into a
monastery by a bona fide saint.
But then not every fortress is able to boast
origins that can be traced right back to the
third century either.

Burgh appears a bit of an oddity
today. It peers out over the final stretch
of the River Waveney as it pours into the
southern tip of Breydon Water – best
known today as an expansive yet shallow
playground for yachts and pleasure
cruisers. This location could suggest a
peculiar regard for a slightly obscure
corner of the British river system.
However, this misapprehension is largely
due to the presence of Great Yarmouth to

the east, which disguises the fact that
Burgh would once have guarded what is
actually an important estuary, for Breydon
Water is fed by not only the Waveney but
also the Yare, Ant and Bure, making it an
important gateway to the area.
Furthermore, on its 6-acre patch of
relatively high ground, the fort would also
have offered a clear view out to sea.

Burgh was part of a complex
defensive arrangement of coastal forts that
protected this stretch of the Roman
Empire from enemy shipping. They gave it
the name Saxon Shore. From the Wash to
the Solent on one side and from Calais to
Nantes on the other, the Romans
employed more than a score of forts to

keep vigil over the English Channel. The defensive system was administrated by a high-ranking Roman soldier known as the Count of the Saxon Shore. Burgh is one of the best preserved of these ancient strongholds and housed a cavalry unit that stood ready to be deployed against Saxon raiders landing along that section of coast. It complemented the fort at Caister, 5 miles to the northeast, which has also survived and which continues to look dutifully across its former Roman town and out to sea.

It's not clear by what name its builders and defenders would have known Burgh. In *Notitia Dignitatum*, a list of Roman army strongholds produced around AD 400, there is a mention of a fort called Gariannonum along this part of the coast. It is the only record we have of the name and, unfortunately, no one can be sure if it refers instead to the fort at Caister. And so the fortress on the Waveney has had to settle for the rather prosaic 'Burgh', which is derived from the Old English *burh* meaning 'fortified settlement' or simply 'fortification'. There is archaeological evidence of a large fortified settlement (known to the Romans as a *vicus*) immediately outside the walls.

Sadly, the buildings of neither *vicus* nor fort have survived. However, the fine

Roman defensive wall is in excellent shape and runs continuously around three sides, but for a couple of missing sections in the southern flank, the reason for which we shall come to in a moment. Only the western wall is missing, having toppled down the slope and sunk into the marsh below (though in Roman times this would have been water, since the estuary ran right beneath the fort). The wall is made of flint with seams of russet-coloured brick or tile running through it. Spaced out along it are six pear-shaped turrets (one of which has lived up to its shape and collapsed) – these would have given the garrison the ability to fire upon the flanks of any attacking force that had reached the foot of the wall.

The fort was set out on a trapezoidal rather than a rectangular plan, with the corners artfully rounded off rather than squared. These two subtleties of design, combined with the attractive stripes created by the knapped flint, brick and tile, give the structure a certain élan. They bear witness to a people who clearly considered themselves cultured, a cut above the barbarians they sought to civilise (or, failing that, cow into submission).

For 70 years or more, from its construction in the late third century, Burgh carried out its duties with a fair degree of efficacy. Then, in AD 367, the Saxons, Scots and Picts coordinated their assaults on the Roman occupiers, taking several forts, including Burgh, and even managing to slay the Count of the Saxon Shore. However, going by the pottery and coinage discovered at the site, it would appear that the Romans were able to recover possession of Burgh and hang onto it for another 40 years or so.

Sometime around AD 630, the missionary saint Fursey arrived in southern England, accompanied by two priests and his brothers Foillan and Ultan (both also future saints). Crossing the country by Roman road, they received a warm welcome from Sigeberht, king of the East Angles, who was already a Christian. The monarch gave the monk a place recorded as Cnobheresburg. Although there is some debate about it among historians, it is likely that Cnobheresburg was Burgh. Fursey transformed the fort into the first Irish monastery that southern England would ever have seen. From this base the group was successful in converting many of the East Angles to Christianity. However, after 10 years or so, Fursey found himself called to preach the gospel to the Franks. He sailed across the Channel and died on the road, sometime around 650.

Precisely how long the saint's monastery on the Norfolk coast survived after his departure is a matter for conjecture but coinage and pottery finds suggest that it kept going until some point in the ninth century (always assuming, of course, that Cnobheresburg and Burgh are one and the same). It was the Normans who breathed new life into the site, creating the eponymous castle. They used the remains of the Roman wall as a ready-made outer bailey, erected an inner bailey, threw up a motte in the southwest corner, and surrounded it with a ditch that, for reasons best known to themselves, ploughed a furrow straight through the south wall. Archaeologists discovered evidence of a timber keep but the motte it once crowned was flattened in 1839. It was not the final indignity perpetrated on the fort. The uneven ground on the open western side of the site is the result of 19th-century quarrying to supply a brickworks close by. An overgrown wharf bears witness to this incursion into the camp.

Should you come for a visit, on your way home, do take a look at the round-towered church of St Peter and St Paul in the neighbouring village (also called Burgh Castle). Examine its medieval flint walls and you will see Roman brickwork. There are no prizes for guessing where that might have come from.

HOPTON CASTLE
HOPTON CASTLE, SHROPSHIRE

The scene of a cold-blooded massacre that refuses to give up its secrets

LOCATION
Hopton Castle, Shropshire
SY7 0QF

GRID REFERENCE
SO 366 779

PUBLIC TRANSPORT
Hopton Heath railway
station is a request stop on
the charming Heart of Wales
line and is about a mile from
the castle.

WHEN TO VISIT
Open any reasonable time
during daylight hours.

ADMISSION CHARGE
Free

WEBSITE
hoptoncastle.org.uk

TELEPHONE
01547 530696
(Secretary, Hopton Castle
Preservation Trust)

 mystery surrounds Hopton Castle. It is a mystery so profound that even television's Sir Tony Robinson has not been able to fathom it. The puzzle surrounds an event that took place in early March 1644 in the aftermath of some intense and bloody fighting that cost over a hundred men their lives. It was very well publicised soon after it occurred and quickly became notorious throughout the land – a notably shameful episode in what was often a dirty and malicious conflict. The episode took place either in 'a cellar unfinished wherein was stinking water' or in a deep ditch. Or, on the other hand, perhaps it didn't take place at all.

At the beginning of the Civil War, Hopton was an anomaly: the only Roundhead-held castle in southern Shropshire. The sole Parliamentarian-supporting stronghold locally was over the Herefordshire border at Brampton Bryan Castle (held by the perfectly monikered Lady Brilliana Harley and, after her death in 1643, the Harley family doctor, Lieutenant Wright).

Furthermore, the Roundhead soldiers had been asked to hold a Norman-built castle that had become more of a residential complex than a stronghold. A very large brick mansion had been built below the low motte, one of many houses that clogged the bailey, making the castle difficult to defend. To make matters worse, the squat two-storey keep had been punctured by windows in the ground floor – a modification that was to prove disastrous. Given all this, it's extraordinary that a tiny garrison held out for so long against a Royalist force of hundreds of men.

It was Lt Wright of Brampton Bryan who took the decision to instal a small garrison at Hopton in a bid to deter Royalists from occupying it. Hopton was owned by a steadfast republican called Robert Wallop (who would later sit as a judge at the trial of Charles I), while the man asked to defend it was Samuel More, later a colonel in Cromwell's army.

In February 1644, a Royalist force under the command of Sir Michael Woodhouse launched an assault on the castle. The Roundheads, armed with muskets, prevented any major breach of the walls, though the attackers did set light to one of the many houses in the bailey.

A demand for the defenders to surrender the castle was tersely dismissed by More, who was no doubt buoyed by his troops' success. The attackers then withdrew temporarily to support Prince Rupert's main forces elsewhere.

During this lull, reinforcements arrived from Brampton Bryan, increasing the garrison at Hopton from 15 to 31. The men worked feverishly to throw up a makeshift stockade. In early March, the Cavaliers returned, and again Samuel More turned down a call to hand over the castle peacefully. This sparked a second assault involving hundreds of soldiers (More claimed 500 but this may well be an

exaggeration). The Royalist troops breached the curtain wall and poured through a burnt-out building only to find themselves trapped in a killing zone. This was probably a constricted channel created inadvertently by the houses in the bailey, which exposed them to fire from positions both in the keep and on other high ground. Anything up to 200 soldiers were slaughtered. Woodhouse withdrew again.

For their third attack, the Royalists brought up three very large cannons. Once again, Woodhouse demanded that the garrison surrender, this time warning that if they did not do so, the usual rules

of war would not apply. Once again, More turned him down flat. In a single eight-hour period, 96 cannonballs were fired at the defences. More houses were set alight; the Roundheads recorded their first losses; and the entire garrison retreated to the upper floor of the keep. The attacking troops eventually forced entry into the ground floor of the building through a window.

The garrison had held off this third assault for two weeks but now they were exhausted and feared being blown to smithereens by charges laid by their enemies below. Samuel More offered to surrender if they could be allowed to leave with their weapons. It was now his turn to have his offer rejected out of hand and he was forced to surrender unconditionally. The commander was taken away for questioning while his men were imprisoned.

What happened next is the subject of some debate among historians. More's published journal of the siege claims that a Royalist lieutenant called Aldersea taunted him afterwards with the news that the entire garrison had been put to death. Another report, written by a man named Davis who was a member of the garrison at nearby Brampton Bryan, claimed that the Roundheads were 'driven into a cellar unfinished wherein was stinking water, the house being on fire over them, and they were every man of them presently

massacred'. Just a few weeks after the event, a newspaper article stated: '[The Royalist victors] caused a deep pit to be digged (sic) and throwing them all in together they buried some alive.' Other reports have the men being stoned or drowned, or having their hands hacked off prior to death.

Unfortunately, none of these accounts comes from an impartial source, and it's quite possible that the tale was nothing more than an exercise in propaganda. When Tony Robinson and his Channel 4 *Time Team* visited the site for a 2010 broadcast, they found plenty of evidence to back up the accounts of the terrible struggle for the castle. However, they were unable to locate the remains of the supposed victims, and the only evidence they unearthed that supported the massacre story was the existence of a cellar. That is not to say, of course, that mass murder did not occur at Hopton Castle back in March 1644, but that no guilty verdict passed on the alleged perpetrators today could be deemed safe.

What we can say is that the fierce mêlée fought over Hopton Castle proved its undoing. With its surrounding houses destroyed and the keep battered, it's surprising to learn that the place remained habitable for another 50 years or so after the siege.

This small and obscure late Norman castle – held for most of its life by families on the sidelines of history – might well have crumbled away completely had it not been for the sterling work of the Hopton Castle Preservation Trust, which purchased it in 2006. The question as to whether they bought up a gravesite as well as an ancient monument is yet to be resolved.

20 STOKESAY CASTLE
CRAVEN ARMS, SHROPSHIRE

A reminder that beauty and fortifications are not always mutually exclusive

LOCATION
Stokesay, Craven Arms,
Shropshire SY7 9AH

GRID REFERENCE
SO 435 816

PUBLIC TRANSPORT
Craven Arms railway station
is just over a mile from
Stokesay Castle. For much of
the walk, it is possible to
follow the Shropshire Way
long-distance footpath.

WHEN TO VISIT
Open April to September
10am–6pm; October to
early November daily
10am–5pm; variable
opening the remainder of
the year (see website for
details). Last entry 30
minutes before closing.

ADMISSION CHARGE
Yes

WEBSITE
english-heritage.org.uk

TELEPHONE
01588 672544

nglish Heritage, who have looked after Stokesay Castle since 1986, call it 'the finest and best-preserved fortified medieval manor house in England'. Though the owners of fine buildings are apt to be a little overblown in their praise for them, in this case it's a claim that few would dispute. Not only is Stokesay an astonishing piece of architecture, it also appears to have been preserved in aspic since the Middle Ages. With the exception of the gatehouse, almost everything is much as it was when the lavish house was built in the late 13th century. Such is its authenticity that you almost expect to see some falconer's boy cross the courtyard to ask the local apothecary about a herbal remedy for his mother, 'who has been sore

afflicted with the ague since last Michaelmas-tide, sire'.

The brains and the money behind all this sumptuousness in the valley of the River Onny was Laurence of Ludlow, who had become one of England's wealthiest men through the simple device of trading wool, England's chief export at the time. He purchased the manor here in 1281 and from 1285 used his riches to create an opulent residence. Six years later he received a royal licence to crenellate the house, at which point he began to mould it into the vision on view today.

But Mother Nature is no respecter of wealth, however great (and Laurence was so rich he even loaned money to the king). On 26 November 1294, while the magnate was en route to Flanders in

one of a flotilla of ships crammed with cargoes of wool, a storm struck in the North Sea just off the coast of Suffolk. The majority of the ships were able to see the tempest out, but Laurence's sank, and he was drowned.

News of his death was met with delight by sheep farmers. Not long beforehand, Laurence had persuaded Edward I that if the king needed to fill his coffers to fund a war against France, he should raise taxes that would hit the producers of wool rather than those who traded in it. His demise was thus interpreted by the farmers as the act of

a righteous and avenging God. The castle, which Laurence had had very little time to enjoy, was passed down through succeeding generations of his family for the next two centuries until the male line ran out.

Although Laurence's son probably put the finishing touches to his father's plans, later descendants clearly did not feel the need to make many improvements to the home they inherited, which remained one of the most impressive in the country. Many an English fortified manor house offered but a cursory nod in the direction of fortifications – perhaps sporting the odd battlement or a gun loop or two. Stokesay, on the other hand, bore more of a resemblance to a castle than a manor house, particularly if viewed from an angle that emphasised the lofty south tower and moat. However, this is largely artifice, a showy display of strength from Laurence, playing at being a knight in a fine castle. Likewise, the addition of a gatehouse in 1640–41 by later owner William Craven might seem to have been a wise precautionary measure with the storm clouds of a civil war about to burst. However, even though the castle was subsequently garrisoned by Royalist troops, the fact that it was surrendered without offering any show of resistance suggests that there was no real expectation that Stokesay could repel a serious attack. That said, as medieval fortified manors

go, it's among the most castle-like examples still in existence (and certainly one of the most handsome). And for the purpose that Laurence intended – to keep his wealth safe from the brigands, bandits and desperadoes that plagued the English border even after Edward I's victory over Wales in 1284 – it served his family admirably well.

Although Stokesay avoided being slighted by the victorious Parliamentarians after the Civil War (perhaps they felt it unnecessary given the castle's evident weakness), its fortunes declined over the following centuries. By the 1700s, it was being let out to tenant farmers who used many of the rooms as ad hoc agricultural buildings. A blacksmith's workshop was set up in one of the towers (and caused a serious fire in 1830), while the impressive great hall found service as a granary.

It was tourism that was largely responsible for saving the castle for the nation. Artists' representations of the ill-served and ramshackle building began to spark an interest in Stokesay and concern for the parlous state into which it had descended. In 1853, an artist named Frances Stackhouse Acton made an open appeal to owner Lord Craven to keep his possession from ruination. The move resulted in some remedial action being taken, but it was only in 1875, six years after the purchase of the estate by the glove tycoon John Derby Allcroft, that a thorough renovation took place. The Victorians are notorious for the often disastrous 'restoration' work they carried out on ancient churches, often mutilating the structures they were purporting to save. Blessedly, Allcroft proved an incredibly enlightened individual in such matters, and the repairs made to Stokesay were as inconspicuous as the conservation techniques of the time would allow.

It means that today everyone can enjoy the fabulous fortress residence that Laurence of Ludlow created. Highlights include the south tower, whose roof affords some wonderful views out over the Shropshire countryside; the great hall with its cruck roof; and the wood and plaster gatehouse, with its now famous mustard-yellow colouring. There are also frequent events at the property, many aimed at a young audience.

But it would be an act of negligence to leave Stokesay without paying tribute to those whose efforts were fundamental to the creation of the castle: the good sheep of the borderlands. Without their innumerable fleeces – whose extremely high quality made them much prized – Laurence of Ludlow could not have laid a single stone upon another.

21 ACTON BURNELL CASTLE

ACTON BURNELL, SHROPSHIRE

An important piece of the history of English democracy stands largely unnoticed in rural Shropshire

LOCATION
Acton Burnell, Shrewsbury,
Shropshire SY5 7PE

GRID REFERENCE
SJ 533 018

PUBLIC TRANSPORT
Both Church Stretton and
Shrewsbury railway stations
are 8 miles (12.9km) away.
Sadly, there are no viable
bus routes to and from
Acton Burnell.

WHEN TO VISIT
Open any reasonable time
during daylight hours.

ADMISSION CHARGE
Free

WEBSITE
english-heritage.org.uk

TELEPHONE
0370 333 1181

very dog, so they say, has its day; every horse its year; and, by some unspecified future date, every human their 15 minutes of fame. The same does not appear to be true of castles. While some remain significant for decades and even centuries, many others pass their entire existence in obscurity. However, there is the occasional member of this latter group that has its moment in the sunshine. Or in the case of Acton Burnell estate, two moments a couple of years apart. But what moments they were, and the fact that Acton Burnell is not acclaimed for its part in the formation of English democracy perhaps says something about England's relationship with its history.

Acton Burnell's story begins back in the 1180s, when the Burnell family acquired land in the area near the old Roman road of Watling Street. Generations lived and died there before the family's brightest star, Robert Burnell, was born. He worked his way up the pinguid pole of medieval politics by taking a humble job in the royal household, that of clerk to Prince Edward, the eldest child of Henry III. He clearly impressed in his role because preferment followed preferment, with Burnell becoming a firm friend and counsellor to Edward. When the prince became King Edward I in 1272, he installed Burnell as Chancellor of England and Bishop of Bath and Wells.

It may seem peculiar to our modern sensibilities that one man should hold two such high-flying posts at once when one is clearly secular and the other religious. However, in the Middle Ages, such distinctions were much more blurred. Indeed, clerical appointments tended to be politically inspired and often had little or nothing to do with the theology or faith of the appointee. For example, Thomas Becket's installation as Archbishop of Canterbury by Henry II was a purely political move by the monarch to try to gain control over the Church. Becket had held no ecclesiastical position previously and enjoyed a reputation in court as something of a bawdy young man. It was only because he appears to have had some kind of religious conversion while in situ that he began to exhibit some of the virtues expected of a clergyman, which in turn brought State and Church onto a collision course.

As is so often the way in human societies, with power and influence came wealth. Burnell not only became one of the most important figures at the court of Edward I, he became one of its most affluent. However, it was evidently Edward's close kinship with Burnell rather than any great luxuries the latter could offer that drew the king to Acton Burnell in 1283. The monarch who would eventually subdue the Welsh often found himself in Shropshire en route with an army to Wales. And so it was that, in the autumn of that year, he and his retinue visited Acton Burnell.

It's not clear exactly what stood on the estate at the time but there was a large tithe barn (so called because that's where the 'tithe' or tenth of peasant farmers' crops would be stored). It is believed that this was the building chosen for a parliament that would make history, albeit one that has largely been consigned to oblivion. For the first time in England, commoners were involved in the process of drawing up and agreeing a law. The one that came into being at the Acton Burnell parliament was called the Statute of Acton Burnell. It concerned itself with the protection of the rights of creditors, which had become a burning issue due to the recent expansion of trade.

In January the following year, the loyal bishop was granted a licence by his friend the king to fortify a manor house at Acton Burnell. He took the opportunity to build himself a whole new residence which was duly fortified and crenellated (i.e. provided with battlements). The structure was surprisingly modest – a rectangular three-storey building with four extremely small square towers at the corners which enclosed a staircase, garderobes, tiny chambers and a porch respectively.

A plan of the castle drawn up by English Heritage, which now looks after the site, shows just how authentic the ruins are to the late 13th-century vision Burnell had of a fortified manor house. Almost everything you can see of the extensive remains of the shell is from

the 1284–92 period in which it was constructed (Burnell himself died in 1292). The only alterations are a brace of arches knocked through the walls of the castle during the period in which it was treated as a folly and alterations to a couple of windows in the mid-18th century. Some features, such as the battlements across the top of the north wall, are very well preserved indeed. The glorious red sandstone castle, which once would have provided gracious accommodation for Burnell and his family, comprised a great hall, solars (upper bedrooms), a chapel, kitchens and offices.

Remnants of the tithe barn in which the momentous parliament was held have survived, though the ancillary structures have disappeared – only their foundations remain and they are hidden underground. These included the all-essential brewery, bakery and stables as well as the housing necessary for guests and a resident staff.

Edward I returned in 1285 and held a second parliament here, presumably in the castle's great hall. Acton Burnell was passed down various generations of Burnells but was eventually abandoned in 1420. It was never rehabilitated, so it entered the 21st century almost unaltered. Acton Burnell Hall, which stands nearby today, was constructed in the 18th century.

Burnell may not have spent much time carrying out his ecclesiastical duties in Bath and Wells but he did at least build a church at Acton Burnell (St Mary's, which you can visit) crafted in the Early English style. However, like his castle, which today is surrounded by woodland, his part in the evolution of English democracy remains largely hidden from view.

22 STAFFORD CASTLE
STAFFORD, STAFFORDSHIRE

The property of three generations of the Buckinghams, all of whom came to a sticky end

LOCATION
Newport Road, Stafford, Staffordshire ST16 1DJ

GRID REFERENCE
SJ 901 222

PUBLIC TRANSPORT
Stafford railway station, on the main line between Crewe and London, is 1.25 miles from the castle, along the Newport Road (A518). Alternatively, the number 5 bus (arrivabus.co.uk; 0344 800 4411) will take you from station to castle in (an advertised) three minutes.

WHEN TO VISIT
Open April to October Wednesday to Sunday and bank holidays 11am–4pm; November to March weekends only 11am–4pm.

ADMISSION CHARGE
Free

WEBSITE
staffordmuseums.co.uk

TELEPHONE
01785 257698

o arrive at Stafford Castle you must take a track uphill that burrows through a dense thicket of birch. Only when you begin to emerge at the top does a small stone fortress come into view, at the summit of a motte. One could be forgiven for thinking that it has been hidden away deliberately. Unlike many urban castles that are the centrepiece of their particular settlement, Stafford is parked right out on the far edge of town. It also appears to have gained two extra baileys beyond its own ancient boundaries. Today it is surrounded by an inner bailey of woodland and an outer bailey comprising a golf course and the M6. These ultra-modern enclosures turn out to be rather apposite because the castle is not quite as it appears.

The Normans were quick to see the advantages of placing a stronghold upon this high ground in territory whose people would not be put down easily. In 1069, local Mercians and Celts from Wales, led by cult hero Wild Eadric, banded together to attack the invaders. Such was the severity of the threat to his command that King William himself travelled up to crush the uprising. He won the resulting Battle of Stafford and terrorised the area in its aftermath. The following year (or thereabouts), William's fellow countryman Robert de Toeni raised up an earth and timber castle here, possibly on express orders from the king himself.

It is de Toeni's earthworks that really catch the eye at Stafford. The motte still rises imposingly into the sky, while the inner and outer baileys below it form a magnificent sweep of undulating greensward. Together they create an extremely pleasing Norman motte-and-bailey construction so it's little wonder that Stafford is considered one of the most impressive examples anywhere in the country. It's nigh on impossible to walk around it without imagining what was once here. And if your mind's eye needs a little help, there's an artist's impression of the castle during its Norman phase on one of the excellent information panels dotted along a walkway through the grounds.

It wasn't until 1347 that Stafford gained its first stone keep. It was built by Ralph de Stafford, who was made 1st Earl of Stafford in 1350 and whose other claim to fame was being a founder member of the Order of the Garter. Given the generous proportions of the Norman structure, the keep was surprisingly modest. While many similar castles were much enlarged throughout the Middle Ages in keeping with the dangers, aspirations and fashions of the passing ages, Stafford remained compact. Ralph's keep began with a discreet tower at each of the four corners, with a fifth tower added later.

The 15th century proved something of a rollercoaster for the Stafford line.

By 1444, the 41-year-old 6th Earl, Humphrey Stafford (the 'de' having been discarded), was declaring himself 'The Right Mighty Prince Humphrey Earl of Buckingham, Hereford, Stafford, Northampton and Perche, Lord of Brecknock and Holdernesse' to anyone who would listen for long enough. That year, he was raised to the dignity of a dukedom, becoming the 1st Duke of Buckingham, and three years later he was made the principal duke in the land, save for those in the royal family. Unfailingly loyal to the crown and a peacemaker between Henry VI and his many enemies, he died during the Wars of the Roses fighting for the king at the Battle of Northampton.

His son having already died of the plague, the title passed to Humphrey's

infant grandson, Henry, who became a ward of the new Yorkist king Edward IV. A bridegroom at 11 and later chief suspect in the case of the murders of the Princes in the Tower, Henry rebelled against Edward's successor, Richard III, and was executed without trial in 1483. Stafford Castle – along with all the other Buckingham possessions and the title itself – was forfeited, only to be returned to Henry's son Edward two years later when Henry VII ascended to the throne. Just like his father and grandfather before him, the 3rd Duke of Buckingham died a violent death: beheaded on spurious charges that he had plotted to murder the king (a trial dramatised in Shakespeare's co-written play *Henry VIII*). He was attainted posthumously in 1523, which meant that Stafford Castle and its deer parks came into the possession of the crown.

Although the castle was eventually returned to the Staffords, they never again hit the heights of those heady but dangerous days when they went by the title of Buckingham. The castle suffered accordingly and was a shadow of its former self by the time the Civil War broke out in 1642. The Staffords duly came out for Charles I. A Parliamentarian army, led by Colonel William Brereton, besieged and captured the town of Stafford on 23 May 1643 and then paid a visit to the castle, which was in the charge of Lady Isobel Stafford.

Lady Isobel refused to surrender the fortress to Brereton, who ordered the burning of the outhouses around the castle in a fruitless bid to soften her resolve. The ensuing siege (which is occasionally recreated here by a re-enactment society) was lifted a fortnight later by a force led by Colonel Hastings. Lady Isobel was prevailed upon to leave with them for her own safety. The skeleton garrison that remained abandoned the castle a few weeks later on hearing that siege cannons were being moved up to blast them out. The Roundheads seized the castle and, as was their wont, soon set about destroying it to keep it from falling back into Royalist hands. They made a thorough job of it. The diarist Celia Fiennes noted in 1698 that the castle was 'ruinated and there only remains on a hill the fortified trenches that are grown over green'.

In the normal run of things, we would simply have been left with de Toeni's excellent earthworks topped with a few bits of later medieval rubble. However, in an echo of the Stafford family's social climbing, Sir William Jerningham had the scant remains excavated in the 1790s. He believed the castle's restoration would help him secure the barony of Stafford, which had been attainted in 1680. In 1813, four years after his death, his son George had the fortress partially rebuilt to the same footprint as the original stone keep but in the popular Gothic Revival style. Some 11 years later, parliament agreed to reverse the attainder and George Jerningham was recognised as the 8th Baron Stafford.

The keep was occupied by the Stafford family and later by caretakers until it was abandoned in the 1950s. By then, the baronetcy had become extinct and the Staffords of Stafford Castle were no more.

23 TAMWORTH CASTLE
TAMWORTH, STAFFORDSHIRE

A mishmash of eras on show at a castle whose owners had a very singular royal duty

LOCATION
The Holloway, Tamworth,
Staffordshire B79 7NA

GRID REFERENCE
SK 206 039

PUBLIC TRANSPORT
It's a half-mile walk from
Tamworth railway station
– on the West Coast main
line – to Tamworth Castle

heading directly southwest
through the town.

WHEN TO VISIT
Open April to September
Tuesday–Sunday (and bank
holidays) 11.30am–4pm;
October to March weekends,
bank holidays and
Staffordshire school
holidays only 11.30am–3pm.
Closed from Christmas Eve

to the first Friday in January
inclusive.

ADMISSION CHARGE
Yes

WEBSITE
tamworthcastle.co.uk

TELEPHONE
01827 709626

he early history of Tamworth
Castle reveals a perhaps little
known and, to the modern
mind, bizarre medieval custom: the duty
of one chosen man to take on all comers
in combat at coronations. The Royal
Champion, as the post-holder was known,
was required to dress up in the king's
livery, mount the best war horse in the
royal stables, and then guard the crowning
ceremony to 'oppose himself against any
person who should gainsay the Royal
Champion'. Aside from the fact that this
puts a whole new slant on early medieval
coronations – who knew that a horse was
always present? – it also suggests that
these were occasions at which trouble was
expected. It's akin to organising a lovely
wedding in a nice church and having a

burly bouncer with an Alsatian stand
beside the happy couple and invite
members of the congregation to 'come
on up if you think you're hard enough'.
However, given the number of occasions
in English history that individuals with less
than solid claims to the throne have
somehow managed to get an archbishop
to lower a crown onto their head, it was
doubtless thought a sage move to have
some muscle on the door.

In 1114, Robert Marmion inherited
both Tamworth Castle and the estate at
Scrivelsby in Lincolnshire. With the latter
came the responsibility of being the Royal
Champion. The role was handed down
through generations of Marmions until
Philip, 8th Baron of Tamworth, died
without heir in 1291. When his widow

Lady Jane died, King Edward I decreed that the castle should pass to Sir Alexander de Frevile, her niece's husband. Sir Alexander was the last holder of Tamworth to perform the role, living long enough to oversee the crowning of Edward III in January 1327.

As it turned out, he needn't have gone to all the bother. During Edward III's long reign, the holders of the estate at Scrivelsby were so outraged that they were being denied the honour of taking a halberd in the eye for a king they may or may not particularly care for that they challenged the right of the lords of

Tamworth Castle to do so. They successfully argued that the post should rightfully go with ownership of Scrivelsby and thenceforth the duty reverted to the keeper of the Lincolnshire estate.

The history of Tamworth Castle also highlights just how patriarchal the Middle Ages were. The male line of successive controlling families failed, but rather than have the castle pass to the distaff side, time and again it was granted to a husband of a female relative. And so Tamworth was inherited by the de Frevile family, followed by the Ferrers, the Shirleys, the Comptons and the

Townshends, by which time it was 1751 and the stronghold had long since ceased to have any military purpose.

By then there had been a building of some importance above the confluence of the Rivers Tame and Anker for around a thousand years. Offa (of Dyke fame) built a palace here in the 8th century, making Tamworth the caput of his Mercian kingdom. As is suggested by the name of the town – which means 'fortified enclosure by the Tame' – he also built defences around the neighbouring settlement. It remained the capital of Mercia until 874 when it was given up to the Danes, who duly burnt it to the ground.

As a protection against said Danes, the Anglo-Saxons created a number of fortified towns (known as *burhs*) and Tamworth became one in 912. The *burh* was still around in 1066 when William the Conqueror invaded. It did not take long for the Normans to arrive at Tamworth and overwhelm the turf and timber defences. William granted the *burh* to one of his countrymen named Robert Despenser, who is believed to have been the builder of the new castle in the 1180s, replacing the wooden tower on the motte with a polygonal stone shell keep. The extraordinary section of 'herringbone' curtain wall which was thrown up at the same time is well worth looking out for.

Today's castle is a mishmash of piecemeal additions made over the centuries, all crammed together inside the confines of a stone shell whose diameter is just 106ft. There's the lower part of a 13th-century gatehouse, a 15th-century great hall, a Tudor warden's lodge, and a south wing and footbridge dating from the 17th century. Much of what visitors see is also the result of alterations that took place in 1783. As castles go, it's a real oddity. The interior of the fortress reflects the different epochs that have helped shape it, with rooms decorated and furnished accordingly. There's everything from a chamber devoted to the Norman occupation to a bedroom used by a late-Victorian housekeeper named

Annie Cooke – it's quite a romp through the ages.

It might have been very different had fortune not smiled twice on Tamworth Castle at key moments in its history. The first lucky escape came in 1215. England's barons were plotting what would become Magna Carta, the groundbreaking charter they would coerce King John into signing that year (see page 127). The monarch was furious with Sir Robert Marmion, the 5th Baron of Tamworth, whom he accused of treachery for having colluded with his fellow peers. To teach him a lesson, he ordered his troops to burn down the castle. However, it's not clear whether an attack was actually carried out. There is evidence of the shell keep walls having been substantially repaired at some point but the castle certainly did not succumb to the fate the king had wished for it.

The second occasion concerns that fanatical leveller of English strongholds, Oliver Cromwell. Tamworth began the Civil War in Cavalier hands but was captured by the Roundheads in 1643 following a two-day siege. The future Lord Protector of the Commonwealth of England, Scotland, and Ireland gave orders that the castle be razed. How Tamworth escaped the destruction that befell so many other fortresses caught up in that terrible internecine conflict is a detail we may never know. Perhaps it is better just to be thankful that it was so.

24 KIRBY MUXLOE CASTLE

KIRBY MUXLOE, LEICESTERSHIRE

A stunning fortified manor house that never grew to full size due to the abrupt and brutal demise of its creator

LOCATION
Off Oakcroft Avenue,
Kirby Muxloe, Leicestershire
LE9 2DH

GRID REFERENCE
SK 523 046

PUBLIC TRANSPORT
From Leicester railway
station walk to St Peter's

Lane to pick up a number
153 bus (arrivabus.co.uk;
0344 800 4411) to Kirby
Muxloe. The castle is half a
mile away along Main Street.

WHEN TO VISIT
Open May to August
weekends and bank holidays
10am–5pm. Last entry 30
minutes before closing.

ADMISSION CHARGE
Yes

WEBSITE
english-heritage.org.uk

TELEPHONE
01162 386886

illiam, Lord Hastings, was a man who seemed to have it all. Life in 1480s England tended to be exhausting, violent, painful and short, even if you were one of the lucky ones who made it into adulthood. And yet here was a man who had unexpectedly become a favourite of the king; whose station in life appeared to be on an ever-upward trajectory; who had grown remarkably powerful and unfathomably rich; who had a wife who had borne him half a dozen children; and who appeared to be well liked and respected by all and sundry. On top of all that, he had been granted permission to crenellate and otherwise fortify all his manor houses and add deer parks to each one if he had a care to do so.

There did not seem to be a single cloud in his sky. Even the death of his close friend Edward IV in 1483 did not presage misfortune. His precipitous fall from grace would come as if from nowhere. In the twinkling of an eye he would not only lose his life but play an unwitting role in the prologue to one of the most notorious events in the English Middle Ages: the killing of the Princes in the Tower.

But that was all to come. In October 1480, William put his steward, Roger Bowlott, in charge of his most ambitious project to date: the creation of one of the most lavish fortified residences in the country. It was to be a cutting-edge showpiece with no expense spared. Built on the site of his existing manor at Kirby

Muxloe, the rectangular castle would measure 245ft by 175ft, with towers at each of the four corners, a trio of towers on three sides with a grand gatehouse on the fourth.

The space within these buildings would form a gracious courtyard. A brook would be diverted to fill a moat surrounding the great house. A dozen gunports would be built into its walls and fitted out with the latest in artillery weapons (though these may have been more for show than protection). An elegant garden would be laid out beside the castle, with a 2,000-acre park beyond. To help achieve all this, a workshop was established that could produce a phenomenal 100,000 bricks per week, and up to 40 men were engaged on construction duties at any one time. Many of these were employed in fashioning large motifs on the walls by using bricks of different colours.

The fallout from Edward IV's death in April 1483 did not at first seem particularly tumultuous. Although the late king's son and heir (also called Edward) was only 12, he would come under the guiding hand of the Lord Protector until he was a little older, when he would take the throne. However, his mother Elizabeth Woodville, the Dowager Queen, was set on her son being crowned immediately. She no doubt sensed that

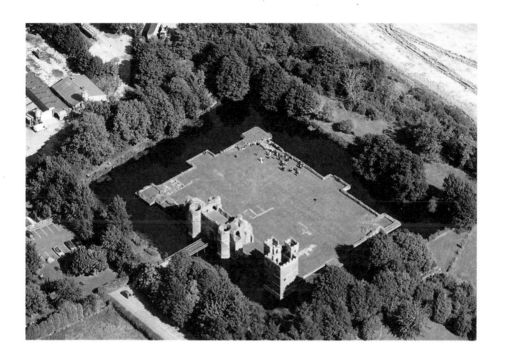

the man who would fulfil the role of guardian to Edward and his younger brother – their uncle Richard, Duke of Gloucester – was a dangerous individual who had designs on the throne himself.

William had always got on well with Gloucester. So when, on 13 June 1483 (a Friday, inauspiciously), he was invited by the duke to what he imagined was a run-of-the-mill council meeting at the Tower of London, he paid no heed to those who counselled him not to attend. He would have been wise to listen to them, because when he got to the Tower he faced a (probably spurious) accusation from Richard that he had been plotting against him with young Edward V's mother Elizabeth. William was frog-marched over to Tower Green and summarily beheaded. Needless to say, he had not been given the benefit of a trial.

The murder – for murder it was in all but name – had been planned by Gloucester because he knew that this powerful and popular man would stand four-square in the way of any attempt he might make to proclaim himself king in lieu of Edward. The 'execution' gave the murderous enterprise the thinnest veneer of respectability.

Of course, that still left the child Edward and his brother Richard in his path to the throne. Although there is some debate among historians over whether the Duke of Gloucester killed or ordered the killing of the Princes in the Tower, as has been widely believed for centuries, he was certainly the chief beneficiary of the disappearance of the two boys from the Tower of London (their bodies were never found and the manner and date of their deaths remain a mystery).

Richard III (as he became) has been reviled as something of a homicidal sociopath ever since Shakespeare's effective hit job on him in his eponymous play. However unfair that characterisation might be, the killing of William, Lord Hastings demonstrates that Richard was clearly a ruthless operator whose will to power was Macbethian in its scope.

It is not possible to say just how much of his dream home William had built by

the time of his untimely exit from the stage. However, we do know that, after a brief hiatus, his widow Katherine continued her late husband's work at Kirby Muxloe. When she called things to a halt, only one corner tower and some portion of the gatehouse had been completed, even though it's estimated that as many as 1.3 million bricks had been laid at the castle.

Although the partially built residence remained in the Hastings family until 1630, and appears to have been inhabited throughout, it was abandoned later that century and its bricks and stone quarried for other construction projects in the locality. Those parts that survived served as makeshift farm buildings – a terrible indignity for an edifice that once seemed destined to become the pride of the Midlands.

The castle was in a sorry state – ruinous and buried beneath foliage – when its owner, Major Richard Winstanley, called in the government's Commissioners of Works in 1911. Conservation work carried out over the next two years saved what was left of the castle from collapse. The moat was restored to its original state and a replacement bridge, in the style of its predecessor, thrown across it. Today the castle stands as a monument to thwarted ambition and provides an intriguing glimpse of what passed for the height of chic in 1480s English architecture.

25 CLITHEROE CASTLE
CLITHEROE, LANCASHIRE

The 'caput of the Honour of Clitheroe' still does the town proud today

LOCATION
Castle Hill, Castle Street,
Clitheroe, Lancashire
BB7 1BA

GRID REFERENCE
SD 742 416

PUBLIC TRANSPORT
The castle is easily
accessible by rail. Clitheroe
station is the Ribble Valley
line's northern terminus and
stands just a quarter
of a mile away from
the fortress.

WHEN TO VISIT
The castle and grounds are
open all the time. The
museum is open late March
to early November daily
11am–4pm; early November
to mid-February Friday to
Tuesday noon–4pm;
mid-February to late March
daily noon–4pm. Last entry
3.30pm all year. Closed
Christmas Day, Boxing Day
and New Year's Day.

ADMISSION CHARGE
Free (though there is a small
charge to visit the museum)

WEBSITE
lancashire.gov.uk

TELEPHONE
01200 424568

What building in its right mind would not wish to be known as the 'caput of the Honour of Clitheroe'? Once upon a time, the lucky edifice that went by that moniker was Clitheroe Castle. The 'honour' was the huge Norman demesne that spread itself out to the west of the Pennines. The 'caput' element merely indicated that the fortress was the seat of that estate, which belonged at that time to the de Lacy family. Sadly, the designation disappeared when the honour and the local earldom were amalgamated, later to form part of the Duchy of Lancaster.

This may be the second smallest surviving stone-built keep in England but it still manages to make an impact on the landscape by being perched on top of a rocky outcrop in the middle of the Ribble Valley. With its 360-degree views of the hills flanking the River Ribble, it's no wonder that this limestone mound was chosen as the site for a castle. Although the hillock is of no great height (128ft), any castle atop it effectively stopped up the valley, impeding the progress of anyone who might wish to use it as a convenient passageway southwest towards Preston or northeast to Settle and the Yorkshire Dales beyond – a route that had been important long before the Romans built a road along it.

Just who the first castle builder at Clitheroe was, and what sort of castle they built, are questions that may never be satisfactorily answered. It seems likely that a wooden structure existed prior to the arrival of the Normans, and we know that the invaders had raised up a citadel of some sort by 1102, because its name appears in documents from that year. By 1122, a charter mentions the presence of a chapel and bailey walls, indicating that this outpost was gaining in importance.

A further indication of its significance came in 1138, though in this case it does not seem to have been of much help to its owners. The Battle of Clitheroe that year was fought between a Scottish raiding army and English troops, the former coming away victorious.

But that was before the building of the stone castle keep we see today. Robert de Lacy is generally credited as having achieved that accomplishment at some point in the latter half of the 1100s (he died in 1193). A small garrison was maintained in the castle throughout the following century, with the keep also functioning as a prison and a courthouse.

By the early 14th century, Clitheroe was in the hands of the Earls of Lancaster. Thomas, the 2nd Earl, was in command in 1315 when a gentleman named Sir Adam Banastre led a successful raid on the castle to plunder it for weapons.

Various repairs were carried out and small additions made here and there over the next hundred years, as the castle continued to serve as the local court of justice (some of it undoubtedly rough) and to monitor comings and goings along the valley. However, at some point Clitheroe must have been deemed surplus to requirements, because an early 17th-century document lamented that it was in a 'very ruinous' state, partially collapsed.

And then came the Civil War, for so many castles both an opportunity for a last hurrah and the instrument that would bring about their calamitous demise. Such was the case with Clitheroe. It would be an exaggeration to say that it was ever a Royalist stronghold, but Cavalier troops deposited there by Prince Rupert did at least repair the gateway and then garrison the fortress for a brief period in 1644. Come the end of the war, it had escaped being slighted. Indeed, it found itself unexpectedly reoccupied, this time by Lancashire militiamen who had fought for Cromwell and who claimed to be owed wages for their labours. The new regime took a dim view of such demands and swiftly dislodged the rebels from their lair. To avoid any repeat of the occurrence, some of the castle was torn down, though it's not clear just how much. There was

certainly enough remaining in 1660 for it to be handed to the 1st Duke of Albemarle by a grateful Charles II, the duke having played a part in the king's restoration to the throne. Like so much else, the castle fell into the hands of the powerful Dukes of Buccleuch, who put up buildings in the bailey and, at some point around 1723, pulled down a good deal of what remained of the curtain wall.

It's somewhat surprising, therefore, to discover that the former fortress was still being used as the headquarters for the administration of the Blackburn Hundred (a subdivision of Lancashire) right up to 1822, the year a town hall was built in Clitheroe.

The fortress on the mound is a fine example of an enclosure castle. These were a relative rarity in England – only 126 are known to have been constructed throughout the entire Middle Ages – and relied on the outer curtain wall and whatever towers may have been built along it to provide the defence for the residence within. Some, like Clitheroe, added a keep of sorts, but these were never of any great strength and simply afforded the castle more dwelling space.

Clitheroe's keep once consisted of three storeys with a parapet above. Although its walls have maintained much of their original height, the keep is now a near-empty shell, a ground-floor fireplace the clearest and most complete detail. The roof long gone, the various nooks, crannies and niches have become favoured resting places for pigeons. There are a good many 19th-century buildings in the bailey but some parts of the medieval curtain wall survive, despite the efforts of Cromwell and Buccleuch. Unfortunately, the castle's chapel – dedicated to St Michael de Castro – has completely disappeared bar some subterranean remains. The views are as stunning as ever, though. The sentinel in the heart of the Ribble Valley not only commands the eponymous river but also offers a fine prospect of Pendle Hill to the east, Easington Fell to the north and Longridge Fell to the west.

After the Great War, the people of Clitheroe raised funds to buy the castle and park as a memorial to those who had given their lives in the conflict. The cenotaph and garden of remembrance established shortly afterwards can still be viewed today.

After visiting the keep, bend your steps to the castle museum, which sits just below it. Newly revamped galleries take visitors on a 350 million-year journey through local history, which, if nothing else, puts the eight centuries of the castle's existence into some perspective.

26 SPOFFORTH CASTLE
SPOFFORTH, YORKSHIRE

Where the most famous document in English history is said to have been drawn up

LOCATION
Castle Street, Spofforth, Harrogate, North Yorkshire HG3 1DA

GRID REFERENCE
SE 360 511

PUBLIC TRANSPORT
Pannal, just 4 miles away, is the nearest railway station to Spofforth. However, for a direct and frequent bus service, travel by train to Harrogate and pick up the X70 (connexionsbuses. com; 01423 339600) or the number 7 bus (harrogatebus.co.uk; 01423 566061) to the village. The castle is at the rear of the park on Castle Street.

WHEN TO VISIT
Open April to September daily 10am–6pm; October to March 10am–4pm. Closed 24–26 December and 1 January.

ADMISSION CHARGE
Free

WEBSITE
english-heritage.org.uk

TELEPHONE
0370 333 1181

It's fair to say that Magna Carta is probably cherished and misunderstood by the English in equal measure. There is not a charter in the land that rivals its facility for being misappropriated by charlatans and snake oil merchants bidding to further their own political agendas. The document did not, as is often claimed, protect personal liberties supposedly enjoyed by the ordinary inhabitants of Albion since time immemorial. Rather, it largely concerned itself with establishing the balance of power between the English monarch and the nation's barons. And tradition has it that it was here, at Spofforth Castle, that a cabal of those barons gathered in 1215 to draw up

Magna Carta and so rein in the despotic King John.

If it is true that the barons held their conclave at Spofforth, then they did so in the manor house built by William de Percy in the 11th century. De Percy was held in great esteem by his countryman William the Conqueror, which explains why the Norman nobleman was granted land at Spofforth and had the means to construct a manor house there. However, his residence has since disappeared, practically without trace. The ruins that stand in the village today are those of a later manor house erected on the same site. That one went on to be fortified in 1308 when Henry de Percy received a licence to crenellate the building, thus turning his home into a castle.

Henry also ensured that the de Percy family continued its long association with Spofforth. It would be the seat of their estate from the 11th until the late 14th century and there would be de Percys at Spofforth (with occasional brief lacunae) until the beginning of the 17th century. As one of the most powerful and influential clans in the north of England in the Middle Ages, they imbued the Yorkshire village with a rather greater significance than it enjoys today. Richard de Percy was one of the barons who drafted Magna Carta, so it is not unreasonable to imagine that he could have hosted the meeting of his peers as well.

The remains of the second of the Percy family's quarters at Spofforth have a decidedly odd look about them. Although they are at the top of a gentle grassy rise, the building appears to have slipped off the low rocky outcrop on which common sense decrees it should have been built. This is because only the west range still exists. In its pomp, another three ranges completed what was a fortified courtyard manor house that would have encircled the crest of the hillock.

We are fortunate that it is the west range that has survived because that was where the most important rooms could be found, including the great hall and chapel. Furthermore, today's visitors who descend the stairs from the former courtyard to the lower floor are in for a treat. From the hall undercroft the builders have burrowed into the rock, creating doorways and staircases, in the manner of Petra in Jordan, if on rather a humbler scale. This floor, with the one above, was the original early 1200s layout. It was extended towards the end of the century and, as we have seen, fortified in 1308.

A solar block reached by a spiral staircase from the ground floor increased the accommodation, but it was not until the 15th century that the castle began to spread its wings across the top of the rocky outcrop. Sadly, these north, east and south ranges were badly damaged during the 17th-century Civil War and now amount to nothing more than odd scraps of low wall and indentations in the ground. It's likely that during their construction the staircase that had been cut through the rock to join the lower floor with the great hall was closed off, which is a shame because it must have been quite a talking point.

The members of the de Percy line, for all their power, were not immune from backing the wrong horses when it came to politics and war. In 1377, Henry Percy (the 'de' having been dropped) was created Earl of Northumberland and, if such a thing were to exist, gained a form of posthumous immortality by becoming a major character in Shakespeare's *Henry IV*.

Unfortunately, he waged an unsuccessful revolt against that very monarch in 1408. Sir Thomas Rokeby, the High Sheriff of Yorkshire, masterminded Percy's defeat at the Battle of Bramham Moor. A grateful king seized all the earl's estates, including Spofforth, and handed them to his faithful sheriff. Percy did not live to suffer this ignominy. He was slain in the battle, and had his head cut off and placed on a spike on London Bridge.

The Percys managed to recover their lost possessions only to lose them again in 1461 when another Henry chose to side with the House of Lancaster in the Wars of the Roses. After the Battle of Towton – reckoned to be the bloodiest engagement ever fought on British soil – the victors from the House of York went on a prolonged and violent spree during which they set fire to Spofforth Castle and laid waste to the estate. The 3rd Earl of

Northumberland, like the 1st Earl before him, did not live to see the loss of his home, having been one of the tens of thousands slaughtered at Towton.

Once again, the Percys managed eventually to recover their battered possession and in 1559 the ruins were made habitable once more. However, it was no longer the family seat, which had been moved to Alnwick in Northumberland, and the Percy enthusiasm for their ancestral home had clearly cooled. A 1577 survey descibes it as 'almost utterly ruinated'. By 1604, it was occupied by just one person: Sampson Ingleby, the castle steward. When he died that year, Spofforth died with him.

27 PENDRAGON CASTLE
MALLERSTANG, CUMBRIA

A stronghold whose real history is more interesting than its mythical one

LOCATION
Mallerstang, Kirkby Stephen,
Cumbria CA17 4JT

GRID REFERENCE
NY 781 026

PUBLIC TRANSPORT
It is only 4 miles to the
castle from Kirkby Stephen
railway station but there is
no onward bus service.

WHEN TO VISIT
Open any reasonable time
during daylight hours.
Pendragon Castle stands on
private land and, although
access is allowed, do take
great care when visiting.
Do not approach
the walls, which are
potentially unstable.

ADMISSION CHARGE
Free

WEBSITE
n/a

TELEPHONE
n/a

There's nothing like a good legend to get the spine tingling when you visit a castle. These romantic ruins come with one that has an Arthurian connection, which sets it apart from your common or garden tall stories. It is said that the first castle on this site was built in the 5th century by Uther Pendragon, best known as the father of King Arthur. One story has Pendragon trying in vain to divert the course of the nearby River Eden so that it might serve as a moat. Several more have the mythical Celtic chieftain perishing here with a hundred of his men when the perfidious Anglo-Saxons – against whom he was leading a plucky resistance movement – poisoned the castle well.

Regrettably, there's not a shred of archaeological evidence to back any of these tales up: the very earliest workings here are from the 12th century. That's also bad news for the theory that, before even Pendragon's time, the Romans threw up a temporary fort on this site, filling a gap between their bastions at Bainbridge and Brough. Although this is more likely than the Uther Pendragon fables – particularly given that we know that the Romans existed – unless something truly compelling turns up to corroborate it, we must deposit the notion in the file marked 'conjecture'.

To be honest, this is one of those castles that really doesn't need a legend attached to it in order to work. Set on a low motte near the fledgling River Eden in

the glorious Vale of Mallerstang, the diminutive fortress is all but swallowed up by its setting, dwarfed by Mallerstang Edge to one side and Wild Boar Fell to the other. Fashioned with the attractive local stone that creates a jigsaw pattern of sandy browns and greys, Pendragon is the very definition of a craggy castle. Its uneven crumbling walls gnaw at the sky like a colossal set of decaying teeth. The remnants of its original 12th-century Norman keep are locked in an eternal slow dance with a 14th-century garderobe turret, while various oddities from the 17th century look awkwardly on. Doorways, arrow slits, windows in various styles, the lower steps of a spiral staircase optimistically heading into thin air – they all seem to have been placed haphazardly around the castle remains and they all give mute testimony to a former stronghold tested by the flames not once but twice.

More likely as not it was one Ranulf de Meschines who succeeded where the Romans (probably) and Uther Pendragon (unquestionably) failed. He built the castle during the brief reign of William Rufus at the tail end of the 12th century. A notable, indeed notorious, early lord of Pendragon was Sir Hugh de Morville. An Anglo-Norman knight in the time of Henry II, de Morville will be forever linked – and damned – for a single action he took at the other end of the country one winter's

night in 1170. Along with Richard le Breton, Reginald FitzUrse and William de Tracy, he set out from Normandy for Kent – borne along by words spoken in anger by the king – and slew Thomas Becket, the Archbishop of Canterbury, beside the altar of his own cathedral. For all that, de Morville's infamy did nothing to stop one of the peaks on Mallerstang Ridge, to the southeast of the castle, from being named Hugh Seat in his honour.

At length, Pendragon came into the hands of the powerful Clifford family, who also owned castles at Appleby and Brough. However, its location near the Scottish border left it vulnerable to raiding parties down from the north. In the early 1340s a Scottish army swept through here, attacking Pendragon and setting fire to it. The castle underwent reconstruction in 1360 but, 200 years after their first raid, the Scots were back to set fire to the fortress again, this time leaving it a complete wreck.

The castle might well have disappeared completely, disintegrating into the Cumbrian soil, had it not been for a timely intervention by Lady Anne Clifford. She celebrated the restoration of the monarchy in 1660 by rebuilding the castle and making it habitable once more. She made conditions at Pendragon more comfortable than they had ever been by the addition of a bakehouse, a brewhouse, a coach house and some stables. She stayed there often – for it became one of her most cherished castles – until she died in 1676 at 86, a quite extraordinary age for the times.

Lady Anne was the last of the Clifford family line and sadly her love of Pendragon Castle was not shared by the Earl of Thanet, who became its owner after her demise. He stripped it of all its valuables (including the expensive lead up on the roof) and left it to rot. A century later, most of the upper storeys of the building had toppled to the ground. Some remedial work has been undertaken in modern times in a bid to stop it from collapsing altogether, but the castle remains in a fragile state.

Two long-distance footpaths pass right by Pendragon Castle. One, the curiously named A Pennine Journey, roughly traces a route taken by the famous fell walker Alfred Wainwright. The other is a must for fans of Westmorland and Yorkshire castles. It's called Lady Anne's Way and is a trail that recreates the excursions she took between her various residences. It stretches 100 miles from Skipton Castle (where she was born) to Brougham Castle (where she died) and thence the short distance along the river to Penrith.

BOWES CASTLE
BOWES, CO. DURHAM

A rare hall keep ransacked by local peasants and finished off by Scottish raiders

LOCATION
Bowes Village, Co. Durham
DL12 9HP

GRID REFERENCE
NY 992 134

PUBLIC TRANSPORT
The castle is far from a railway station but can be reached from Bishop Auckland station by taking the B66 bus (jhcoaches.com; 0191 410 4107) to Bowes.

WHEN TO VISIT
Open any reasonable time during daylight hours.

ADMISSION CHARGE
Free

WEBSITE
english-heritage.org.uk

TELEPHONE
0370 333 1181

Don't let the entrance to this ancient fortress fool you. It may come with a modern ramp threading its way neatly through this large gap in the wall and be serviced by an arch high above – both of which are suggestive of a doorway – but this rough and ready portal is no such thing. What visitors to Bowes Castle walk through is an arrow slit. Admittedly, it is an arrow slit (or, more properly, loophole) that has been widened by, one imagines, the combined forces of human hands, weather and time, but it is one nonetheless. Any search for another ground-floor entrance will end in vain. The keep's real front door was accessed via a flight of steps (since disappeared) to the first floor on the eastern flank.

The Romans got here first. This is the site of a south-facing timber fortress they established called Lavatrae (or Lavatris). Anyone privy to the workings of the Roman mind might have guessed they would build themselves a stronghold around here. It is situated on a Roman road that connected Eboracum (York) and Luguvalium (Carlisle), and being on a high point it is perfectly placed to guard the eastern end of the Stainmore Pass and keep an eye on the River Greta at the same time. The fort was upgraded around 130 AD, when stone walls were erected to protect it. A small settlement also grew up on its northern side and a bathhouse added. Although it might seem unlikely, given the amount of water that would have been to hand in a bathhouse, excavations suggest that it was burnt down at some point and had to be rebuilt. Despite its remote location near the far reaches of

what was Roman Britain, Lavatrae was occupied for around 300 years from the early AD 70s when Petilius Cerealis first conquered the region for Rome.

The Stainmore Pass has been an important means of crossing the Pennines for over two millennia (the A66 trunk road runs along it today), providing a significant section of a main route between Scotland and England. Come the 12th century, Lavatrae's strategic location on the pass inevitably brought it to the attention of the Normans. The Count of Brittany, Alain de Bretagne, built a timber fort upon it, making use of whatever Roman

fortifications remained at the time. The building passed into the hands of his son Conan. When he died in 1171, Henry II took command of the fort, ordering a stone keep to replace the timber structure. This was completed in 1174, making Bowes a rare example in the region of a 12th-century royal castle.

Henry's interest in establishing a viable castle here was doubtless sparked by the Revolt of 1173–74. This was a rebellion led by the king's own wife, Eleanor of Aquitaine, and three of the couple's sons: Henry, Richard (later 'the Lionheart') and Geoffrey (confusingly, the second of the king's sons to be called Geoffrey, but the first legitimate one by that name). The rebels took exception to what they saw as the favouritism shown by the king to his youngest son, John (later King John), and to his probable complicity in the murder of Archbishop Thomas Becket at Canterbury Cathedral.

The Revolt lasted 18 months. Battles and skirmishes were fought, towns were razed to the ground and many lives were lost. The north of England and southern Scotland were swept up in the insurrection, and Bowes Castle played its part in securing the region for the king, particularly when the threat of an invasion from over the border came to pass. The castle sustained damage in 1173 from raiders led by William the Lion, king of Scotland. It was patched up in time for another of William's forays south the following year. This time the king besieged Bowes and a relieving force was duly raised by Geoffrey, Henry II's illegitimate son. Geoffrey was Bishop of Lincoln at the time, but clearly felt disinclined to turn his swords into ploughshares. His army's approach to Bowes pressed William into a hasty retreat.

Henry II's upstart family members were eventually forced to submit to his authority. Peace – or as near a thing as occurred in the kingdom at that time – reigned again.

At this, the castle's zenith, it comprised a stone three-storeyed hall keep – something of a rarity in England – which contained a basement for storage, a hall and solar (a chamber on an upper floor), a kitchen, spiral staircases and sundry smaller rooms. The walls were of such prodigious thickness that passages to the garderobes were contained within them. The keep was protected by a ditch, some of which is still in evidence today. The old Roman fort provided a rampart around an outer bailey. Close by stood a mill, powered by the River Greta, which supplied flour to the garrison.

The most unusual feature at the time was the village of Bowes, which had been deliberately established alongside the castle. It included a market-place and a church and was planned rather than being the sort of piecemeal settlement that often grew up under the protection of a castle.

There does not appear to have been any further investment in Bowes Castle after 1187. The building changed hands a number of times, passing out of and back into royal control. Its last moment in the spotlight came in 1322 when Edward II wrested the somewhat dilapidated fortress from the Earl of Richmond and granted it to John de Scargill. This so enraged the local peasantry that they stormed the castle, set part of it on fire, liberated whatever took their fancy and reportedly downed four casks of wine for good measure.

It was the Scots who were to have the final say, though. They attacked repeatedly, making life at Bowes unsustainable. The castle was abandoned, and the inhabitants of the village sought safer fields to plough. Within 20 years of the binge-drinking episode, the castle was a wreck. Following the Civil War in the 17th century, a good deal of the stonework was appropriated for use in the construction of local buildings. So if you'd like to see more of Bowes Castle, you might try taking a look around the neighbourhood.

29 PRESTON TOWER
CHATHILL, NORTHUMBERLAND

An elegant refuge thrown up in a land of almost perpetual violence

LOCATION
Chathill, Northumberland
NE67 5DH

GRID REFERENCE
NU 183 254

PUBLIC TRANSPORT
The tower is just over a mile away from Chathill railway station, though sadly very few trains take the trouble to stop there. The nearest station with a frequent service is Alnmouth, 8 miles to the south, but that has no bus service to Chathill.

WHEN TO VISIT
Open all year, daily 10am–6pm or dusk, whichever is earlier.

ADMISSION CHARGE
Yes

WEBSITE
prestontower.co.uk

TELEPHONE
07966 150216

Northumbrian land is not the most productive in the nation. In the 14th century, as the rural population slowly expanded and family plots were divided up between sons on the death of their father, the chances of scraping a living by farming were often reduced to nil. With limited options when it came to surviving by honest means, it's hardly surprising that, in their desperation, people took to cattle rustling. And it is largely to this systemic fault in medieval English society – along with an interminable rivalry between England and Scotland – that we owe the presence of Preston Tower.

Pele or peel towers were a particular form of stronghold constructed in the border region on both sides of the divide. They were residences fortified sufficiently to hold out against all but the most determined and well-equipped attackers. In this respect they were a reflection of their times. In the 1300s, this region barely had a period of what might loosely be termed 'peace', and when the following centuries saw an end to the perpetual Anglo-Scottish warfare, it was riven with the violence of the reivers. The towers were thus characterised by their extremely thick walls (Preston's are 7ft thick), a vaulted ground floor – into which livestock and horses could be herded in an emergency – and an upper floor that was used as a living space/refuge. As is immediately apparent as soon as you enter the well-kept grounds at Preston, this pele tower was of some importance once upon a time, because it is three storeys high with twin turrets that rise higher still.

It was built between 1392 and 1399, when England and Scotland were still at each other's throats and northern England and the Scottish Marches were dangerous places to live. With cattle theft rife, vigilantism not only ruled the day but was officially sanctioned. Anyone who was the victim of a raid had the right to attempt to retrieve their stolen goods, even if the thieves had escaped over the border. But this right only extended as long as the injured party acted more or less immediately and the trail was 'hot'. This was called the 'hot trod' and it was usually aided by so-called 'sleugh' hounds who followed the scent of the captured livestock. Furthermore, you could press-gang your neighbours into joining your avenging party. If they refused, they could be tried and executed. It's no wonder that life hereabouts tended to be even poorer, nastier, more brutish and shorter than in other parts of the kingdom.

Although it is a magnificent example of a pele tower, sadly not a great deal appears to be known about its history. However, we know that one of its owners was Sir Guiscard Harbottle, who fought with an English army led by the Earl of Surrey at Flodden Field in 1513. Both Harbottle and the commander of the Scottish force, James IV, were killed (as was Duncan Campbell of Kilchurn Castle, page 259). When James VI of Scotland was crowned James I of England, the frontier between the two countries lost its significance and the border region was no longer ravaged by war. The king also moved decisively against the reivers, enacting draconian measures against them.

With the outbreak of peace and the reiver threat more or less extinguished, Preston Tower lost its *raison d'être*. Half of it was demolished and the stone was used for building works elsewhere, leaving the still-proud tower we see today. It has a ground floor partly taken up by small cell and a very modest guardroom. As a note next to the former explains, this is where prisoners would stew while hoping their fellow clansfolk would at some point arrive with whatever ransom money had been demanded for their release.

The most noticeable aspect of the ground-floor architecture is how very low the doors are. The stone door frames are about 4ft 8in high at the very apex of their arches. This gives the impression that people in the Middle Ages were exceedingly small but in reality they were not a great deal shorter than modern Britons. In the 14th century, the average adult female would have been about 5ft 2in tall, while her male counterpart would have measured a shade over 5ft 7in. One can only assume that at Preston Tower the occupants became quite adept at ducking.

A wooden staircase leads to the floors above. The first of these encompasses a bedroom and a living room, decked out as they might have been around the year 1400. The lack of a corporate touch with regard to the displays is rather heartening. There is nothing here that is truly 21st century or which could be described as slick. The bed looks not a little frayed and the amenities spartan, which gives them an air of verisimilitude. Meanwhile, handwritten notices hang in frames on the walls or are propped up wherever there's space. One shows a map of the English–Scottish border and the common surnames of reiver families that were once found along it, so that visitors can gauge the likelihood of having some of these ne'er-do-wells in their family tree. Another charts the fortresses in the border region that were extant at the time Henry V ordered a survey of them in 1415. Just in the area of northeast England between Newcastle and the frontier there were a staggering 37 castles and 78 towers, of which Preston was one.

On the second floor, one chamber has been designated the Flodden Room and is graced with an account of that battle. The same floor is home to the flat-bed mechanism of the tower's large and ornate clock, which has faces on both front and back walls. This is decidedly unmedieval. It is similar to that used in Big Ben's clock and was installed in 1864 by then owner Henry Baker Cresswell. A descendant of

Henry's, Gilfrid Baker Cresswell, is the tower's current owner.

Clamber up a final short flight of steps and you come at last onto the castellated roof. High above the canopy of trees, this was an excellent vantage point from which to scan the surrounding countryside and still proves so today.

Don't rush away from Preston Tower without first visiting the quiet gardens that surround it. Though the grounds are mostly laid to lawn, a circular pathway leads through a pleasant copse that includes walnut trees, tulip trees and a ginkgo. Even if we know little about them, one can readily imagine successive owners of the castle grabbing a few moments of peace in their unquiet lives by taking the air in a similar way in times gone by.

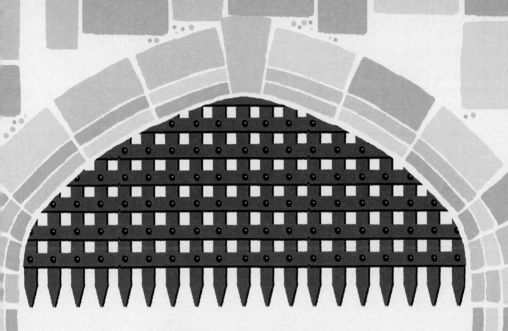

WALES

30 WISTON CASTLE
NR WISTON, PEMBROKESHIRE

One of Britain's best preserved motte-and-bailey castles may have been built by a Flemish immigrant called Wizo

LOCATION
Nr Wiston, Haverfordwest, Pembrokeshire SA62 4PN

GRID REFERENCE
SN 022 181

PUBLIC TRANSPORT
The 313 bus (Edwards Bros; edwards-tiers-cross.co.uk; 01437 890230) runs a few times a day from the bus station in Haverfordwest. This is a couple of minutes' walk from Haverfordwest railway station on the line between Carmarthen and Milford Haven. The bus takes just under half an hour to get to Wiston.

WHEN TO VISIT
Open daily 10am–4pm (last entry 3.30pm).

Closed 24–26 December and 1 January.

ADMISSION CHARGE
Free

WEBSITE
cadw.gov.wales

TELEPHONE
0300 025 6000

hough very small in comparison with most Welsh castles, Wiston is an immaculate little piece of ancient Welsh history. A classic motte-and-bailey castle, it sits on a hill in the midst of farmland with a ring of gorse embellishing its lower flanks. An impressive ditch encircles the motte, whose 40ft of height lifts the castle masonry comfortably above the surrounding terrain. The mound is 60ft wide at the top and still bears the stone wall of its shell keep.

That shell keep became a quintessential feature of motte-and-bailey castles once they had been converted from timber to stone. A 'normal' keep was a strong tower within a castle. A shell keep, on the other hand, comprised a thin stone circular wall that surrounded and protected all the other buildings on the top of the motte. It was usually constructed in place of timber fencing that served the same purpose.

The wooden buildings that would have been safeguarded by this particular shell keep have long since disappeared, of course, but the wall itself has one very interesting feature: although it's circular inside, it's not circular outside – it has no fewer than 18 sides. It wouldn't be until later in the 13th century, when those returning from the Crusades brought back with them tales of fortresses with round towers, that castle designers began to favour the circular form. Round towers were better at deflecting

cannonballs and other projectiles, and were less susceptible to toppling when undermined, and so proved very popular. Whenever it was that this wall was built, such qualities were of lesser value. Besides, an 18-sided wall must have looked very impressive, and giving the impression of strength was very much part of one's defence against attack.

What makes Wiston Castle so special and where it differs from most of its contemporaries is that it was neither altered nor enlarged in step with the improvements in castle design that occurred throughout the Middle Ages.

The vast majority of motte-and-bailey castles left in Britain today have been reduced to a motte (the sandcastle-shaped mound) and perhaps the odd ditch to show where the bailey (the outer wall) once was. Wiston, by contrast, is one of just half a dozen in Wales that have some remains of a stone keep. As one of the country's best preserved motte-and-bailey castles, it offers up not only a faithful representation of what they were like but also gives visitors some insight into the lives of those who inhabited it.

The origins of the castle are somewhat uncertain but, according to Welsh castles

enthusiast Jeffrey L Thomas, it was probably built, or at least started, by a Flemish colonist with the unlikely name of Wizo (or Gwys in Welsh). He was known to have settled in Pembrokeshire in the early 12th century, having corralled a band of fellow Flemish adventurers to take up the call of the Norman English King Henry I to colonise Celtic Wales.

Wizo had died by 1130 but not before he had selected the site of an Iron Age camp on which to build his castle. Such settlements were located on easily defendable land and often came with ready-made protective ditches so it is hardly surprising that Wizo's eye should have been caught by it when scoping out a locale for his castle. With a stockade thrown up as a bailey and a wooden fort on top, it would have sent a message to the dispossessed Welsh that there was a new power in the land. By 1112, Wizo is also credited with the construction of a church and the establishment of a small community.

The Welsh, undaunted, captured the motte-and-bailey fort in 1147 from Walter Fits Wizo ('fits', like the Irish 'fitz', simply meaning 'son of'). There are no existing documents that tell us the year Wiston Castle was built, so the 1147 seizure by prince and poet Hywel ab Owain is the earliest event we know of to have taken place there. The castle must have fallen back into the hands of the

Normans or their allies sometime later because the Welsh – this time led by one Hywel Sais ap Rhys – are recorded as capturing the castle again in 1193, only to lose it again two years later to the Flemish colonists.

Wiston Castle's real moment in the sun came in 1220 when it was seized by none other than Llywelyn ap Iorwerth, otherwise known as Llywelyn the Great, prince of Gwynedd. He was sweeping through south Wales, taking back territory that had been usurped by the English foe and their fellow travellers. Wiston's glory did not last long because Llywelyn ordered the castle to be destroyed, along with the settlement that had grown up alongside it.

However, it's possible that that did not signal the end of the castle. Henry III, still intent on securing Welsh land for his kingdom, commanded the Earl of Pembroke, William Marshal, to rebuild the castle. Marshal died in 1231, so any reconstruction on Henry's orders would presumably have taken place in the decade following Llywelyn the Great's destructive visit. Unfortunately, although there is archaeological evidence of two separate phases of rebuilding inside the keep, it's difficult to say whether the surviving wall is Marshal's work or simply the remains that were left after 1220. For instance, the grand archway that pierces the wall on the southern side of the keep does appear to date from before the early 13th century. It would once have framed the wooden entrance gate and it's still possible to see the holes that held the drawbars keeping it firmly shut against any intruders who had got past the large oval outer bailey and ditch.

The castle was still occupied in the 14th century – a family named Wogan had taken it over by then. A mansion house was built nearby and this rather eclipsed the castle, whose value as a fortified stronghold waned as the centuries progressed. However, it's possible that it did see one last flicker of action. During the Civil War, a small detachment of Royalists moved into Wiston and may well have used the castle as a headquarters. However, when the Parliamentarians passed through the area in force in 1644, the Cavaliers abandoned Wiston seemingly without a fight (assuming they were indeed using it). By the 1700s, the motte had been relegated to the role of a quaint attraction on the estate of the manor house. It's a humbling end for such a noble construction.

31 NEWCASTLE EMLYN CASTLE
NEWCASTLE EMLYN, CARMARTHENSHIRE

A rare Welsh-built stone castle that remained in the thick of the nation's politics for four centuries

LOCATION
Castle Street, Newcastle Emlyn, Carmarthenshire SA38 9AG

GRID REFERENCE
SN 311 407

PUBLIC TRANSPORT
Carmarthen is the closest railway station to Newcastle Emlyn (17 miles) but there is no bus service between the two. Travel to Fishguard or Aberystwyth by train and you can take the frequent T5 bus (richardsbros.co.uk; 01239 613756) to Cardigan, which is a mere 10 miles (16km) away, but still something of a hike.

WHEN TO VISIT
Open at any reasonable time during daylight hours.

ADMISSION CHARGE
Free

WEBSITE
n/a

TELEPHONE
n/a

I t's seen a bit of life, has Newcastle Emlyn Castle. If there was a rebellion going, you could be pretty sure that this fortress would be at the heart of it, changing hands seemingly every time the tide of fortune favoured one side or the other.

Although there's no absolute certainty about the identity of its founder, the most likely candidate is Maredudd ap Rhys, who is believed to have started work on the castle around 1240. Originally constructed of earth and timber, the fortress was soon rebuilt, making it one of the very few native Welsh castles in this region that were made of stone. However, it was not initially intended to be a military base but rather an administrative centre for the area.

This lack of emphasis on making the building defensible was reflected later that century during the revolt led by Rhys ap Maredudd, the son of Maredudd ap Rhys. The younger man felt that the English king, Edward I, had not remunerated him sufficiently for having taken no part in the First War of Welsh Independence and promptly rebelled against him in 1287. Roger Mortimer captured Newcastle Emlyn Castle for the king, only for Rhys to take it back soon afterwards. The following year, it was besieged and seized for Edward again by one Robert Tiptoft. However, that bald

summation hardly does justice to the efforts of Tiptoft. He had bearded his quarry at Dryslwyn Castle, besieging and finally capturing the fortress. However, Rhys managed to escape and flee to Newcastle Emlyn. Undeterred, Tiptoft employed 40 oxen to drag his siege engine from Dryslwyn to Cardigan – a distance of nearly 30 miles as the crow flies and considerably more as the ungulate plods. A further 60 oxen were then pressed into service to manoeuvre the engine another 10 miles up the Teifi Valley to Newcastle Emlyn.

Tiptoft's persistence was only partly rewarded. Though the castle fell, Rhys ap Maredudd managed to escape once more.

However, he was eventually arrested and his revolt extinguished once and for all with his execution in 1291.

Now in the hands of the Crown, the castle was periodically refurbished and improved by the first three Edwards of England. The gatehouse dates from this period, as does the (now missing) great hall and the small market town of Newcastle Emlyn. This last was badly hit by the Black Death in the mid-14th century. The rapid depopulation had an adverse effect on the castle, which had to be repaired when it came into the hands of Edward, the Black Prince, in 1343. It was one of a mere 26 castles under his control.

This long period of English domination was brought to an end briefly in 1403 with the coming of Welsh hero Owain Glyndŵr and his ultimately unsuccessful bid to deliver independence to his people. However, he managed to hold onto the castle for only a fortnight before Sir Thomas Carew seized it back for the Crown. The stronghold appears to have fared poorly during these engagements and it was not long before it had deteriorated to a mere ruin. However, that was by no means the end of the story. The castle was repaired once more and in the early 1500s converted into a luxurious residence by Sir Rhys ap Thomas.

Its death knell, in common with so many other fortresses around Britain, was rung by the Civil War. It started the conflict in the hands of supporters of King Charles. Captured by Parliamentarian forces in 1644, it was seized back soon after by Sir Charles Gerard. The Roundheads returned the following year and laid siege to the castle. This time they were seen off by Sir Charles after a bloody skirmish just outside the walls. It was only at the end of the war, with the defeat of the Royalists, that Newcastle Emlyn came back into the control of parliament. Cromwell's soldiers plundered the castle, set explosives and blew it up.

The remains of the castle you visit today are those left to us by those Roundhead troops. The most salient feature is the twin-towered polygonal

gatehouse. This was begun by Edward II sometime between 1307 and 1327 but not finished until 1349, during the long reign of his son Edward III. Its less-than-military-looking windows were installed by Rhys ap Thomas as part of his conversion works. A cellar with a fine vaulted ceiling lies below the north tower but access to this has been blocked off.

Pass to the right of the gatehouse and you'll come to the remnants of a tower which was once square in shape and defended the southern corner of the castle. A long curtain wall created a wedge-shaped ward to the east. At one point, this would have contained a great hall with an adjoining kitchen, above which was a chapel. A further defensive wall sealed another bailey that contained a watermill. Sadly, these features have all now disappeared.

However, one of the castle's main defensive features, the River Teifi, still flows on defiantly below. The castle was built on a peninsula of land almost entirely surrounded by a large loop of this important waterway, allowing it to be attacked only along a relatively narrow stretch of land to the west. The fact that the castle fell so often is an indicator that perhaps rather too much faith was placed in its advantageous location and not enough effort was put into making this diminutive stronghold defensible. It's a wonder really that the Parliamentarians felt the need to blow it up at all.

A 'weakhold' that was a comedy of errors ended not with a bang but a sandstorm

LOCATION
Pennard Golf Club,
Southgate Road, Southgate,
Swansea SA3 2BT

GRID REFERENCE
SS 544 885

PUBLIC TRANSPORT
From Swansea railway
station, make your way to
the nearby Christina Street
to pick up the 118 bus

(natgroup.co.uk) to Parkmill,
from where it's about a mile
(1.6km) across Pennard
Burrows to the castle, which
is on the western side of the
golf course.

WHEN TO VISIT
Open at any reasonable
time during daylight hours.
NB Do take care when
crossing the golf course.

ADMISSION CHARGE
Free

WEBSITE
n/a

TELEPHONE
n/a

Castles become ruined for all manner of reasons. Some are burnt down, others are blown up (we're looking at you, Roundheads), while many are simply abandoned. Falling prey to encroaching sand dunes, however, is an unusual way for a fortress to meet its end. In the case of Pennard Castle it was entirely predictable, having been built just above some spectacular dunes on the Gower Peninsula. Doubtless the lure of possessing a stronghold in such a strategically favourable location (and with such glorious views to boot) overcame the builder's qualms about what might happen when the sands moved.

In all likelihood, the builder in question was Henry de Beaumont, 1st Earl of Warwick, who held sway over the entire Gower. He had conquered the whole peninsula at the beginning of the 12th century in the name of Henry I, the Norman king of England and fourth son of William the Conqueror, who had granted him rights over the same. In order to safeguard this newly won territory, Beaumont founded manors across the Gower. At Pennard, he erected a simple castle comprising a ringwork of timber, a bank and a ditch. The ringwork was small – less than 40yds long and wide and in the shape of an oval. A timber hall was constructed in the middle of the ward. A similar castle at nearby Penmaen, presumably also built by Beaumont, has since all but disappeared.

James Maw 1965 - 2017

A brilliant mind

The reason why this very humble fortress has not sunk into the sand is that it is set on a limestone spur. High above the sea, it enjoys a sumptuous vista out over Three Cliffs Bay and guards the mouth of the Pennard Pill stream. With cliffs tumbling down on two sides, it was only vulnerable to attack from the south

(though any assailants would, perforce, have to haul themselves up a steep incline from the sea) and the east.

In the 13th century the castle received an upgrade. The de Braose family, then lords of Pennard, replaced the timber hall with one of stone. Local red sandstone rubble was used for the construction, with any fancy work being effected in limestone quarried from around the castle. Further improvements were made over the years, including the replacement of the timber wall with one of stone topped by battlements. However, it's fair to say that this was never a fine castle or even one that was particularly well constructed. Indeed, it rather seems the work of someone who has visited more cutting-edge castles, knows that it's probably a good idea to copy them, but has no real notion of what they're doing.

Thus, although there is a twin-towered gatehouse (see also Newcastle Emlyn Castle, page 151) on the eastern side, it has been thrown up in a manner that demonstrates that the builders had no grasp of how such a construction might best be used to defend the entrance to the castle. For example, if you examine the grooves down which the portcullis was raised and lowered, you'll notice that they do not reach the ground, which would have been something of a shortcoming. The arrow loops, such as they exist at all, have also been very poorly positioned and would hardly have stirred fear in the breast of an assailant. Perhaps the aim was to make would-be aggressors so helpless with mirth at the shambolic nature of the defences that they would be physically incapable of pressing home their attack.

A small square tower was built into the walls at the western end of the castle and seems to have been for the purpose of accommodation. The lower part of this has survived. Beside it there is a semicircular turret possessed of a single arrow loop looking out onto the west of the castle, presumably to counter anyone who had managed to climb up the cliff below.

But the sands of time were not so much running out for Pennard Castle as piling up against its walls. The substantial dunes, blown by the wind, began to encroach gradually on both the fortress and the small settlement that had sprung up beside it. By the end of the 14th century, the castle had been abandoned. By 1650, a surveyor described the place as 'desolate and ruinous' as well as being enclosed by sand. The romantic ruin in a picturesque setting became popular with artists in the 18th century but nothing was done to prevent its total collapse and disappearance until 1922. The Pennard Golf Club, on whose grounds the castle

now sits, got together with the Royal Institution and the Cambrian Archaeological Association to appeal for funds for essential repairs. Unfortunately, not much money seems to have been raised because the cheapest of solutions was put in train – that of using concrete to reinforce the walls that were in danger of falling down. Less intrusive repairs were made in the 1960s and the remains are in a more or less stable condition now.

If you approach the castle from the clubhouse (to the east) you'll pass close by the scant remains of a small church called St Mary's which was abandoned in 1532. This is all that is left above ground of the community that evolved beside the castle, which included a substantial warren in the dunes where rabbits were farmed. Any rabbits you might see playing in the sands today are very much wild.

33 CASTELL COCH

TONGWYNLAIS, CARDIFF

The sort of fortress that can be built when money is no object and your designer is probably a genius

LOCATION
Castle Road, Tongwynlais, Cardiff CF15 7JS

GRID REFERENCE
ST 130 826

PUBLIC TRANSPORT
Taffs Well railway station – which lies on both the Merthyr and Rhonda lines – is just over half a mile (0.8km) from the castle.

Conveniently, the Taff Trail leads past the station and goes all the way to Castell Coch.

WHEN TO VISIT
Open daily. Hours vary depending on the time of year but opening time is typically 9.30am and closing time between 4pm and 6pm – check website for precise times. Last admission 30 minutes before closing. Closed 24–26 December and New Year's Day.

ADMISSION CHARGE
Yes

WEBSITE
cadw.gov.wales

TELEPHONE
02920 810101

W hat do you do if you are absurdly rich and live in great luxury but have a hankering for a time when life was simpler, the air wasn't choked with industrial fumes, and people contracted good honest diseases like scrofula and plague while scratching around in the dirt and filth? Well, if you're the 3rd Marquess of Bute, you call up your favourite outré architect, ask him to build you a fairytale castle and tell him that money is no object. Hey presto! You're back in the Middle Ages.

And that is how we come to have Castell Coch: commissioned by John Crichton-Stuart, designed by William Burges, built between 1875 and 1891,

and used as a summer residence. But these bare facts are scant preparation for the experience of stepping inside the fortress. The interior of Castell Coch is a wonderland of 19th-century delights – a place where all the tiny details have their own tiny details. It's the apotheosis of Victorian decor, a maelstrom of overelaborate designs whose fussiness reflects the emotional repression of the times. It's a silent scream in castle form. It is not one, therefore, to be missed.

Furthermore, Castell Coch is not at all the fake fortress that it appears. Although it may not be easy to detect even by close examination, the palatial bolthole is actually built on the substantial remains

of a medieval castle. Its history goes all the way back to the Normans, who threw up a motte-and-bailey here in the late 11th century. The stronghold sealed off the narrow gorge through which the River Taff runs and was close enough to Cardiff to aid in its defence, although the castle does not appear to have been occupied for very long.

The first stone castle on the site was the work of Gilbert de Clare. Like the Normans before him, he was an invader keen to consolidate the local gains he had made from the Welsh. De Clare's more formidable structure made use of the motte (whose flanks he also made steeper) and took 10 years to build, starting in 1267.

It was the death of de Clare's son – another Gilbert – that was to cause the downfall of this second incarnation of the castle. In 1314, seven years after his father's death, the younger Gilbert was slain at Bannockburn while fighting for Edward II against the victorious Robert the Bruce. His demise was greeted with joy by his former Welsh neighbours who rose up in revolt. It's likely that it was around this time that the castle was sacked and partially destroyed.

The ruins came into the hands of the earls of Bute – and specifically the 3rd Earl, John Stuart – in 1760. A watercolour of the ruins painted just over 30 years later by the splendidly monikered Julius Caesar

Ibbetson indicates that the remains of the medieval castle were still quite extensive. They were inherited by John Stuart's great-grandson, the 3rd Marquess of Bute, in 1848 when he was only six months old. He was an excessively affluent baby. His great-grandfather had been prime minister under George III and had married the wealthy heiress Mary Wortley Montagu; his grandfather had married two heiresses; and his father's immense coal and iron interests had been boosted by his building of Cardiff docks.

Crichton-Smith became an orphan at the age of nine and eight years later met William Burges. Together they forged a powerful alliance. The marquess was one of the richest men in the world and his colossal fortune turned Burges' visions into reality. The two transformed Cardiff Castle, which is today one of the Welsh capital's major tourist attractions and a place of opulent splendour. A keen historian and lover of architecture, the 3rd Marquess also turned his attention to another of his ancient possessions, the ruins of a castle in a wood high above the village of Tongwynlais.

Known as Castrum Rubeum (Latin for Red Castle) on account of the red sandstone from which it is chiefly built, it was so smothered in ivy and debris that an antiquarian who had made a study of the remains in 1850 had failed to discover them all. Crichton-Smith ordered them to be completely uncovered. A later report by Burges concluded that the walls were in a fit state to be built upon should a summer residence be required. It was all the information the marquess needed.

Work began in 1875. Such was the lavishness of the castle that it took a decade to complete, using copious detailed drawings and models that Burges had made. The result was Castell Coch (Welsh for Red Castle). It's an exceptional example of Gothic Revival architecture, and with its high-pitched conical roofs it

more closely resembles a German *Schloss* or French *château* rather than a Welsh castle. Crichton-Smith rebuilt the three towers – named Kitchen, Well and Keep – along with the gatehouse, hall block and shell wall. There was even a nod to a romanticised Middle Ages in the form of a working drawbridge. The marquess also established a vineyard on the slopes. This was a bold move since commercial viticulture had long since died out in Britain. After a shaky start, Castell Coch produced wines that were reported to be quite palatable. Production ceased at the vineyard during World War I due to the sugar shortage and the vines were eventually grubbed up in 1920.

By the time the 5th Marquess of Bute succeeded to the title in 1947, the family fortunes had suffered a steep decline, due largely to the economic depression of the 1920s and the general downturn in coal production. In 1950 he presented the castle to the Ministry of Works, having first stripped out most of the original furnishings. Happily, these have since largely been recovered and are on display along with a fine selection of paintings, murals and sculptures.

In 1900, at the age of 53, the 3rd Marquess of Bute died from a kidney-based infection called Bright's disease. Though still relatively young, at least he had been able to enjoy the castle he and Burges had created. The architect himself was not so fortunate. He also died aged 53 (Oscar Wilde was among the many visitors to his deathbed). But that was in 1881, so he never saw his Gothic dream of the Middle Ages completed.

34 BRONLLYS CASTLE
BRONLLYS, POWYS

The stronghold that helped bring a war to an end before accidentally killing a rather important guest

LOCATION
A479, southeast of Bronllys,
Powys LD3 0HL

GRID REFERENCE
SO 149 346

PUBLIC TRANSPORT
The nearest railway station
to Bronllys is Abergavenny,
22 miles away, but the only
direct bus service runs from
Hereford. From the city's

bus station, the T14 bus
(stagecoachbus.com; 01633
485118) leaves passengers
with a five-minute walk to
the castle.

WHEN TO VISIT
Open daily 10am–4pm.
Last admission 30 minutes
before closing. Closed
24–26 December and New
Year's Day.

ADMISSION CHARGE
Free

WEBSITE
cadw.gov.wales

TELEPHONE
0300 025 6000

F or a castle seemingly lost in a wood, a lot went on at Bronllys. Indeed, for what was always a small castle, it punches above its weight when it comes to its historical significance. And yet it languishes in obscurity and suffers the further indignity of having had a modern house built on what used to be its inner bailey. Who would bear the whips and scorns of time?

The castle is the work of one Richard FitzPons. The baron of Clifford was a Norman knight based in Herefordshire who had served under Bernard de Neufmarché in a campaign that saw a good deal of Welsh land captured and Neufmarché himself become Lord of

Brecon (or Brecknock, as the English called it back then). One part of that land, Cantref Selyf, was apportioned to FitzPons in the 1080s along with permission to establish a manor there. The result was Bronllys Castle, which the baron built sometime around 1100 and from which he administered his newly acquired estate.

As might be supposed, given the castle's date and the heritage of the builder, this was a motte-and-bailey affair. It inhabits an obvious location for a stronghold in that it overlooks both the Llynfi and Dulais rivers at the point where they join forces and so controls what was and remains a major thoroughfare. As such, its mere presence at that spot played

a part in the subjugation of Wales by the Norman English. Generations of Cliffords would also have been obliged to supply both troops and finance to successive lords of Brecon in order that a firm grip be kept on the territory they had gained.

After Richard, the Clifford male line was sprinkled with occasional belligerent Walters. The first Walter's main claim to fame is that he was the father of 'The Fair Rosamund'. Lauded for her extraordinary beauty, she was known as 'The Rose of the World' and was the mistress of Henry II (who was married at the time to Eleanor of Aquitaine). She died a nun at Godstow in her twenties and became the focus of a

good many posthumous legends about her life, death and almost miraculous comeliness. Walter followed in his father's footsteps by going to war against the Welsh. This was a habit that was clearly ingrained in the men of the Clifford family that went by that name because Walters II and III did likewise. The last of these rose to some prominence in the area as lord of the so-called Three Castles – Grosmont (page 174), Skenfrith and White – and it was under his lordship that Bronllys experienced its most taxing times.

It was in 1233, during the rebellion against the English led by Llywelyn ap Iorwerth, that Walter III was moved to switch sides and take up arms alongside the Earl of Pembroke against Henry III. For his pains he lost both Bronllys and Clifford Castle – the two seized from him by the outraged English monarch. Seemingly unperturbed by this turn of events, he duly seized them back a few weeks later.

Some sources claim that Walter then installed around 10 knights and 100 men-in-arms here, while others put the latter figure as high as 200. Whichever is nearer the mark, a little castle like Bronllys would have been a very crowded place indeed. It was all in a good cause though, because this formidable show of strength succeeded in maintaining a tense peace in the area. Bronllys eventually hosted talks between envoys sent by Llywelyn and

Henry which would lead to the signing of the Peace of Middle on 21 June 1234. The truce held for the rest of Llywelyn's stint as leader of the Welsh.

But it's the castle's inadvertent involvement in the death of an unfortunate earl of Hereford nearly 70 years beforehand that is arguably the most memorable episode in its history. By then, the original timber keep had been torn down by Walter I, who replaced it with the stone round tower we see today. In 1163, the castle was inherited by his daughter, Maud, and two years later she and her husband are said to have received a visit from the earl. He was the youngest of five brothers, all of whom were to come to sticky ends and none of whom had produced an heir.

The historian Gerald of Wales includes the story of what happened next in *Journey through Wales*, his highly readable account of a lengthy trip he had embarked on in 1188. He writes that 'Mahel [Earl of Hereford] was being hospitably entertained by Walter de Clifford in the castle of Brendlais [Bronllys]' when the castle 'was by accident burned down, and he received a mortal blow by a stone falling from the principal tower on his head.' Gerald reports that Mahel lived long enough to repent of his persecution of the bishop of St David's, perceiving his accident as God dealing out retribution.

In many a history of Bronllys you'll find some version of this tale of the death of Mahel. This is all well and good but for the fact that he appears to have died in

1164 rather than 1165. Also, Gerald seems to be confused over which brother was the persecutor of the bishop of St David's (who happened to be the author's own uncle). He clearly intimates in the previous paragraph that it was the fourth sibling, William, who had taken against the cleric. Furthermore, if the host had been Walter I, as Gerald avers, that puts the date of the fire no later than 1163 (the year Walter died), which is earlier than is generally agreed.

Other sources claim that it was in fact William who died in the accident and that the fire took place not in 1165 but the following year. Whichever brother perished, the mishap put an end to a noble family line which their parents, Miles of Gloucester and Sybil de Neufmarché, must

have believed more than secure by the time their fifth boy was born.

The castle's final brush with history came in the 1320s. Local nobleman Rhys ap Hywel had aligned himself with the English throne and was handed Bronllys by Edward II as a result. However, he later joined his fellow Marcher Lords in rebelling against the king. He was captured, imprisoned and made to forfeit the castle. The tables turned with Edward's forced abdication in 1327, and Rhys ap Hywel claimed back his fortress above the Llynfi and Dulais.

The castle would go on to change hands many a time, but 200 years later it was reported to be in a hopelessly ruinous state, which makes its survival today all the more remarkable.

35 GROSMONT CASTLE
GROSMONT, MONMOUTHSHIRE

A highly attractive fortress that became one of an important axis of strongholds in the Monnow Valley

LOCATION
B4347, Grosmont,
Monmouthshire NP7 8EP

GRID REFERENCE
SO 405 244

PUBLIC TRANSPORT
From Abergavenny railway station walk to the corner of the A40 and Lion Street to take the X3 bus

(stagecoachbus.com; 01633 485118) to Llangua Terrace, Monmouth Cap. The bus stop is two miles (3.2km) from the castle.

WHEN TO VISIT
Open daily 10am–4pm. Last admission 30 minutes before closing. Closed 24–26 December and New Year's Day.

ADMISSION CHARGE
Free

WEBSITE
cadw.gov.wales

TELEPHONE
0300 025 6000

While some castles are foreboding, some romantic and some mysterious, there are others, such as Grosmont, that have such a lightness about them that they're a joy to be in. Perhaps it's the jaunty pink tinge that its red sandstone gives the castle walls or maybe it's the marvellous spiralling chimney that has somehow survived the ravages of time. Whatever the reason, a visit to Grosmont is almost guaranteed to lift the spirits, no matter what the sky above may be doing.

This is one of a trio of fortresses known, rather unimaginatively, as the Three Castles. Skenfrith and White Castle form the other two points of what was once a powerful defensive triangle in the

Welsh borderlands a little to the north of the important ancient settlements of Abergavenny and Monmouth. This location was to give them a particular significance in the wake of Welsh revolts against English domination in the 12th and 13th centuries.

Although Grosmont seems to have been intended as a fortified administrative base rather than as a purely military entity, no one is exactly sure when it came into being or even who was responsible for its construction. A stronghold may have been established here shortly after the Norman invasion of England in 1066, in which case the Earl of Hereford, William Fitz Osbern, is the most likely candidate as its founder. However, there's also

land at Archenfield, in southwest Herefordshire, in 1137. Shortly after his transaction with Stephen, Payn Fitz John was killed fighting against the native Celts.

It was during this revolt of the 1130s, when the Welsh rose up against Stephen, that the castle first came to prominence. Its strategic position made it a natural target for those hoping to overthrow the English yoke. However, in 1139, it was the Angevin revolt against the English king that saw Grosmont fall. It was captured by Brian Fitz Count of Abergavenny, the half-brother of the Duke of Brittany. Remarkably, the document in which Fitz Count grants the castle to Walter Hereford in 1142 is the first written record we have of the castle's existence.

It was under Hereford's lordship that Grosmont, Skenfrith and White Castle became the Three Castles – a powerful defensive bulwark against Welsh rebellion in the Monnow Valley.

Walter was killed on crusade in 1160, giving Henry II the opportunity to make the castle a royal stronghold once more. Some improvements to the building's defences were made in the 1180s in an attempt to counter further Welsh restiveness in the region.

The story of Grosmont during the first half of the 13th century reflects the chaotic nature of the politics of that era. The castle changed hands a dizzying number of times as the stars of the various

disagreement among historians and archaeologists as to whether the motte-and-bailey castle was first created out of timber, like a lot of its contemporaries, or built in stone at its very inception. If the latter, this would indicate that it came into being at a later date.

At the beginning of the 12th century we find the castle in the hands of the Marcher Lord Payn Fitz John. It had either been handed to him by the crown following the unsuccessful rebellion of Fitz Osbern's son Roger against the monarchy in 1075 or he had built it himself. Whichever is the case, he appears to have swapped it with King Stephen for *dramatis personae* on the stage at that time rose and dipped. In 1201, Grosmont was granted by King John to Hubert de Burgh, his one-time household chamberlain. Unfortunately for Hubert, four years later he was severely wounded and captured in France while fighting for the king. While John may have been grateful for his loyal nobleman's service, he didn't show it, promptly handing Grosmont to Hubert's rival William de Braose. It took just two years for John and William's friendly relations to deteriorate sufficiently for the king to take the castle back. William's son, also called William, seized the fortress during the First Barons' War, only to lose it in 1219 to Hubert, who had regained his freedom and recovered from his wounds. King John, in the meantime, had died unlamented and been replaced on the throne of England by the nine-year-old Henry III, whose reign would span a remarkable 56 years.

The resilient Hubert, who had become the 1st Earl of Kent by this point, took steps to improve Grosmont, transforming it from a fortified administrative building to a blood-and-thunder fortress that would prove more of a challenge to would-be attackers. This did not prevent him from falling from the king's good graces in 1232 and having

Grosmont and all his other castles wrested from his control. To make his humiliation complete, Henry handed them to a royal servant, Walerund Teutonicus.

Hubert was to have his revenge. The following year, when Henry sought to crush an Anglo-Welsh rebellion led by Richard Marshall, the Earl of Pembroke, his forces found themselves in an encampment in the shadow of Grosmont's walls. Marshall's surprise nocturnal assault sowed panic in the royal army and put it swiftly to flight. Hubert was one of those fighting with the rebels and this victory must have been sweet indeed, even though the castle itself was not captured

in the same action. He did not have to wait long to become its lord once more: in a bid to curry favour with Hubert, Henry handed him back the castle. There still remained one final twist in Hubert's relationship with Grosmont Castle. A few years before his death in 1243, he was at loggerheads with the king once more and was stripped of Grosmont for the final time, Walerund being the happy recipient again.

One thing today's visitor to the castle will note straightaway is that the motte is not exceptionally high (which is ironic given that the name Grosmont is derived from the Old French meaning 'great mound'). The extensive stonework that remains atop it is largely Hubert's doing (though his gatehouse has all but vanished now). The three D-shaped towers built into the castle walls are all his handiwork. Hubert's fourth tower was removed by Prince Edmund when he converted the castle into a fine residence in the latter part of the 13th century.

Edmund was also responsible for installing a large doorway on the eastern side of the castle. Any attacker foolhardy enough to break through the door would find that it only gave onto the ground floor and first floor. But the prince's lasting legacy with regard to Grosmont is the extraordinary chimney which still graces the castle and has understandably become its most famous feature.

36 DOLBADARN CASTLE
LLANBERIS, GWYNEDD

A symbol of vain Welsh defiance that was also prison to a solitary inmate for over two decades

LOCATION
Llanberis, Gwynedd
LL55 4UB
NB This postcode gives only an approximate idea of location.

GRID REFERENCE
SH 585 598

PUBLIC TRANSPORT
From Bangor railway station, on the line from Chester to Holyhead, take the 85 bus (arrivabus.co.uk; 0344 8004411) to Llanberis High Street from where it's a short distance to the castle. The entrance is on the right-hand side of the road that heads towards the National Slate Museum.

WHEN TO VISIT
Open all year daily 10am–4pm (last entry 3.30pm).
Closed 24–26 December and 1 January.

ADMISSION CHARGE
Free .

WEBSITE
cadw.gov.wales

TELEPHONE
0300 025 6000

The ruins of an ancient fortress overlook the western end of Llyn Peris in the Llanberis Pass. They belong to Dolbadarn Castle, built around 1230 by Llywelyn ap Iorwerth, better known outside Wales as Llywelyn the Great. It's an outstanding example of a castle constructed by native Celts, as opposed to the string of larger fortresses thrown up half a century later by the Norman English invader Edward I. And yet for two decades it was also the setting for an internecine episode that not only pitched one Welshman against another but one brother against his own sibling.

It's a shame that only the keep has survived the ravages of time more or less intact, but what a fine keep it is. It sits on a little knoll, guarding this strategically important pass through the mountains. Nearly 50ft high and with walls 8ft thick, the round stone tower lords it over the lake. With the Snowdonian mountains acting as a backdrop, it adds a splash of human drama to the scene.

The keep's only entrance, on the first floor, would originally have been accessible not via the stone staircase that stands there today but by wooden steps that could have been hacked away by the defenders in the event that enemy troops had penetrated the castle. A portcullis dropped down into the doorway gave further protection. Inside the keep, the

staircase to the second floor is still in situ and can be ascended by visitors. However, the battlements that ran along the top of the wall have long since disappeared.

Aside from the keep, there were once western and southern towers, and a further building on the eastern side. A hall at the northern end was probably a later addition constructed after the castle fell into English hands. Foundations and sections of low wall mark out the positions of the structures and can easily be traced. None of them were of any great size and all were crammed together inside a curtain wall, restricted by the comparatively small area of the mound's summit. What is not so evident is that they were built without mortar, using the dry-stone technique still employed in many parts of the country today to construct walls across farmland. Only the keep, the strongest and most defendable part of the castle, was afforded the luxury of mortar to hold its purple and green slate stones together. The inspiration for its design appears to have come from the round towers built by the English which were prevalent in the Welsh Marches. As Welsh round towers go, it is arguably the best surviving example we have.

Its builder, Llywelyn ap Iorwerth, began with a power base in Gwynedd, in the northwest of the country, and gradually expanded his princedom until, by the early 1200s, he had taken control

of the greater part of Wales. Dolbadarn was one of the castles he built in a bid to preserve his hold over the nation and ward against the increasing threat posed by the Norman English.

His grandson was Llywelyn ap Gruffydd, who became known (somewhat ominously for the Welsh) as Llywelyn the Last. He came to power as the result of winning the Battle of Bryn Derwin in June 1255. This settled a feud between Llywelyn and two of his three brothers, Owain Goch (an older brother) and Dafydd (who was his junior). Dafydd escaped but Llywelyn captured Owain and imprisoned him.

Although there is some debate about exactly where Llywelyn's older brother

was held, Dolbadarn is generally accepted as the fortress in question. It was the second time the unfortunate Owain had been held captive by a relative, having already spent time banged up in Criccieth Castle at the pleasure of his uncle (another Dafydd).

The 13th-century poet Hywel Foel ap Griffri wrote a lament for Owain, opening with the line: *Gŵr ysydd yn nhŵr yn hir westai* (A man who is in the tower, long a guest).

He would spend 22 years at Dolbadarn before his younger brother released him grudgingly in 1277, Owain's freedom being one of the terms of the Treaty of Aberconwy which Llywelyn signed with Edward I. The former inmate slunk off to his home in northwest Wales and troubled history no further.

Llywelyn ap Gruffydd had declared himself prince of Wales in 1258, a claim that was recognised by the English King Henry III seven years later. However, he fell foul of Henry's successor, his son Edward I, when he declined to pay homage to the English monarch. This led to Edward's invasion in 1277 and a savage war against the Welsh which took place over the next seven years.

Llywelyn ap Gruffydd was eventually killed near Builth in 1282. His brother Dafydd took up the cudgels but the following year his forces were pushed south from the coast into Snowdonia.

In May 1283 he made Dolbadarn his headquarters and administrative offices but by October he had been captured and executed after a manhunt that involved 7,000 English troops. The castle, too, fell into the hands of Edward's army.

The English king built his infamous chain of castles along the Welsh coast, with Caernarfon – six or seven miles away to the northwest – as the new centre of government. Dolbadarn became surplus to requirements and its days as a military stronghold were over. To rub salt into Welsh wounds, Edward had some of the timber and stones ripped out of Dolbadarn to be used in his castle at Caernarfon. He evidently hoped that the denuded Welsh fortress would stand as a reminder to the local population of the power of their new lord.

The castle was relegated to the status of a manor house but at some point it was abandoned and left to moulder. The picturesque ruins inspired J M W Turner to capture it in oils in 1800. His painting can be seen today at the National Library of Wales in Aberystwyth.

37 DOLWYDDELAN CASTLE
DOLWYDDELAN, CONWY

A stronghold of Llywelyn the Great whose revenge on the English was a dish served very cold indeed

LOCATION
A470, west of Dolwyddelan, Conwy LL25 0JD

GRID REFERENCE
SH 721 523

PUBLIC TRANSPORT
The castle is just over a mile (1.6km) away from Dolwyddelan railway station, on the pretty Conwy Valley line from Llandudno Junction up to Blaenau Ffestiniog. Unfortunately, that does entail walking along a stretch of the wide and busy A470. For a quieter stroll (1.25 miles; 2km), alight at the next station to the west, Pont Rufeinig (Roman Bridge), and take the minor road and track to the castle. Pont Rufeinig is a request stop so you'll have to advise the train guard that you wish to alight there in good time.

WHEN TO VISIT
Open April to September Monday to Saturday 10am–5pm; Sunday 11.30am–4pm; October to March Monday to Saturday 10am–4pm, Sunday 11.30am–4pm. Last admission 30 minutes before closing. Closed 24–26 December and New Year's Day.

ADMISSION CHARGE
Yes

WEBSITE
cadw.gov.wales

TELEPHONE
0300 025 6000

ravel through the Conwy Valley on the railway or along the A470 and just to the west of the village of Dolwyddelan you'll come across one of the most arresting scenes in all of Wales. Among the mountains a stern-looking rectangular keep sits on a slender ridge and glowers down on those who dare to scurry along below it. And Dolwyddelan Castle has been doing just that since it came into being in the early 13th century to guard this important pass through the peaks of Snowdonia. It's easy to overlook the fact that there's some sort of stump of masonry next to it, and that fact would certainly have caused joy to the castle's builder, Llywelyn ap Iorwerth.

The story is often put about that this towering figure in Welsh history – otherwise known as Llywelyn Fawr (Llywelyn the Great in English) – was not the builder of the castle at all but was born in it. However, there is nothing to suggest there was a structure on this site before around 1220, and Llywelyn was born c.1173. However, there is evidence of an earlier tower called Tomen Castell having existed on a nearby knoll (it's since disappeared). It's likely that he was born there instead, returning later in life to construct a new fortress in a more dominant position above the pass and the Afon Lledr that flows through it.

By the time he brought Dolwyddelan into being, Llywellyn had been Prince of Gwynedd, or at least large parts of Gwynedd (which at the time spread over northwest and most of mid-Wales), for a couple of decades or so. He had also got himself an advantageous marriage – his wife was Joan, the daughter of King John I of England. In order to protect his sprawling territory he ordered the construction of a string of castles, including Dolbadarn (see page 179), Criccieth and Deganwy.

But it was during the reign of his grandson Llywelyn ap Gruffydd (otherwise known as Llywelyn the Last) that the castle lived out its most dramatic years.

On 18 January 1283 it was taken by the English forces of Edward I. The circumstances of the Welsh defeat are obscure but it may have come about on account of the actions of a traitor in the midst of Llywelyn's ranks. Another theory is that it was simply a negotiated surrender. However the castle fell, the seizure of Dolwyddelan was a huge fillip to Edward's campaign, helping spur the king on to eventual victory in Wales.

As soon as the English troops took over, they began a programme of repairs to the castle and its nearby watermill. The garrison was also reportedly given white tunics so that they might be better camouflaged when fighting in the snow. Garbed in white or their summer wear (something the colour of rain would suit in these parts), they remained here for the next seven years. During that time the second tower at Dolwyddelan was raised. Not as strong or well fortified as the original keep, it would, nevertheless, have made the castle a more imposing place, sitting inside the curtain wall built by Llywelyn. The builders took the unusual step of importing sandstone for some of the door and window surrounds. This was a lot of trouble to

go to when grit and slate rubble – of which the remainder of the castle is made – was readily available.

However, despite these improvements, Edward's preference was to maintain his hold on the region through castles that could be supplied by sea and whose very size broadcast the message to the defeated Celts that resistance was futile. Thus, he constructed monoliths on the coast at Conwy, Caernarfon, Beaumaris and elsewhere. Smaller, more remote outposts such as at Dolwyddelan were discarded and abandoned.

Dolwyddelan was not to share the fate of so many small medieval castles whose military worth had run its course. It was granted a new lease of life when a nobleman named Maredudd ap Ieuan took up a lease on the building. In 1488, he added a further storey to the original keep. Since this upmost floor had no fireplace it would have provided somewhat spartan accommodation, particularly in winter. It's not clear at what point the castle fell out of use as a residence.

In the mid-19th century it was another nobleman, Baron Willoughby de Eresby, who repaired the castle at his own expense. Being a Victorian, mere restoration was not enough for the good lord, and he took it into his head to rebuild not only walls and floors but also the battlements that give the castle an appropriately combative look.

Back in the Middle Ages, visitors would cross a wooden bridge over a ditch to the entrance which, as now, is at the northeast corner of the keep. Inside, visitors can explore the castle thanks mainly to Willoughby's work. Before Maredudd ap Ieuan's additions, it would originally have been just two storeys high, with a cellar beneath reached through a trapdoor. The entrance doorway was on the first floor, accessed via an exterior wooden staircase that was fitted with a drawbridge at the top as an extra precaution. The main room of the keep sports a heavily restored fireplace and a small exhibition charting the history of the castle. Climb the stairs to the top of the keep to enjoy the ravishing views of the surrounding countryside, little changed from the days when Llywelyn's soldiers defended the outpost.

That view is no longer blocked on one side by the bulk of the English-built tower, which is said to have collapsed sometime around 1810. Dolwyddelan is thus once more a thoroughly Welsh stronghold, the reminder of its brief English interlude now all but withered away.

38 CASTELL DINAS BRÂN
LLANGOLLEN, DENBIGHSHIRE

One of the most dramatically sited castles in Britain has its roots in one of its oldest

LOCATION
Wern Road, nr Llangollen, Denbighshire LL20 8DU. NB The postcode will take you close-ish to the castle but not right to it

GRID REFERENCE
SJ 222 430

PUBLIC TRANSPORT
Take a number 5 bus (arrivabus.co.uk; 0344 800 4411) from Ruabon railway station to Llangollen. A footpath leads all the way for just over a mile (1.6km) from the town through Geufron and steeply up the hill to the castle.

WHEN TO VISIT
Open at any reasonable time duringdaylight hours.

ADMISSION CHARGE
Free

WEBSITE
cadw.gov.wales
Also, see the fascinating video showing a reconstruction of the castle and the hill fort that came before it at clwydianrangeanddee valleyaonb.org.uk.

TELEPHONE
n/a

or a castle as famous as Dinas Brân, it's surprising to find that the current ruins belong to a fortress that stood for less than 20 years over seven centuries ago. Furthermore, it was of no great size. While built upon a larger Iron Age hill fort, the later stronghold amounted to little more than three squat edifices with a high curtain wall joining them together. Inside the rectangular courtyard there were a few other ancillary buildings, and that was it. There was no great keep or gatehouse and even the tallest structures barely poked their castellated roofs above the height of the curtain wall. And yet Dinas Brân has managed to capture the imagination of generation after generation. It has become the focus for legends and has been endowed with an identity that is as enigmatic as it is fanciful.

There's no doubting that its spectacular location is at least partly responsible for this state of affairs. Perched on the top of a treeless and conspicuous hill, it exudes impregnability, an impression only heightened when one attempts to reach it. Only accessible on foot, the main route up from Llangollen sees the path obliged to take wild zig-zags in its final push up to the summit, so steep are the highest slopes. Mounting a frontal assault on such a place would seem an act of the sheerest folly. Which makes what happened there in 1277 all the more unexpected.

The best part of two millennia before that – around 600 BC – a fort was established on the crown of the hill. The inhabitants dug a ditch to protect its southern flank, threw up an earthen rampart all around it and in all likelihood constructed a wooden palisade on top. Inside the enclosure, they built the traditional Iron Age roundhouses, and presumably felt quite secure within them.

Fast-forward to the 1260s and we come to the building of the first and last stone castle here. It was the work of Prince

Gruffydd ap Madog, who died around 1270. He was the prince of Powys Fadog, the northern part of the former Kingdom of Powys (the southern part was called Powys Wenwynwyn). All we know about the history there, aside from what can be gleaned from the buildings he erected, is that two of his own sons (Gruffydd and Owain) set little store by the seemingly invulnerable location of the castle. In 1277 they ordered their men to set fire to it and flee at the approach of English troops, who were under the command of the Earl of Lincoln, Henry de Lacy.

The damage cannot have been excessive because de Lacy's men were able to repair the castle and garrisoned it for a while. Indeed, de Lacy himself waxed lyrical about his prize, claiming: 'There is no stronger castle in all Wales, nor has England a greater.'

In the end it was Dinas Brân's obscure location that did for it. It's all well and good being able to hold onto a hilltop but if that hilltop is miles from anywhere and of little strategic value, it becomes a drain on valuable resources. It's not known if the English still had a garrison there in 1282 when hostilities were resumed in the area or if the Welsh forces ever reclaimed it. However, it's clear that once the English had defeated their opponents in October that year the castle was handed over to the Earl of Surrey, John de Warenne. He preferred to establish a whole new fortress

at Holt in Flintshire and Dinas Brân was left to its own devices.

Over the years, much time has been spent agonising over the derivation of the castle's name. *Dinas* means 'city' in today's Welsh, but back in the Middle Ages it would have simply indicated a fortress or stronghold. That part at least is simple. It is the second half of the name that has sparked a whole cornucopia of suggestions as to its origins. The most common interpretation is that it should be translated as 'crow', since that is the meaning of the word *brân* in current Welsh. The English name 'Crow Castle' has been employed for hundreds of years but seems inappropriate for such an eminently Welsh site. Other possible sources for 'Brân' range from a nearby stream of that name (so called because its water ran as black as a crow); the word for hill (*bryn* in Welsh); a chieftain from Gaul named Brennus; a Celtic god called Brân Fendigaid; and a Cornish prince. According to legend, this last was called Brân and was at loggerheads with his brother Beli over the control of their kingdom in the wake of their father's death. Their mother, Queen Corwena, intervened before they went to war with each other. Beli wandered off east, eventually giving his name to London's Billingsgate, while Brân travelled north and built Dinas Brân. As legends go, it's pretty tame.

The Romance of Fulk FitzWarin is made of more stirring stuff. Written in the 12th century, it tells of curious happenings at 'Chastiel Bran' in the latter half of the 11th century (thus before Gruffydd had built his castle there). The yarn relates the story of a Norman knight called Payn Peveril who spent a night in the ruins with a small entourage in defiance of rumours that evil spirits inhabited the place during the hours of darkness. The party finds no evil spirits but they do encounter a dastardly giant called Gogmagog who attacks them. Peveril slays the colossus, ridding the countryside of a menace that had inconvenienced the locals thereabouts for years. In his death throes, Gogmagog plays tribute to King Brân, whose purpose in building the castle had apparently been to see off the giant but who had ended up running away.

Should you visit Dinas Brân on an early summer evening, you may see a green-ish unearthly looking light which you may take to be just the sort of luminescence that evil spirits or perhaps even giants might emit. However, it's more likely that you've simply been fortunate enough to chance upon the castle's latest inhabitants: a flourishing community of glow-worms. They almost certainly mean you no harm.

39 EWLOE CASTLE
EWLOE, FLINTSHIRE

Lost in a forest, all alone, this fortress has a pleasingly obscure history and a wonderful Welsh-style tower

LOCATION
Off the B5125, nr Ewloe, Flintshire CH5 3BZ

GRID REFERENCE
SJ 288 675

PUBLIC TRANSPORT
From Hawarden railway station on the Borderlands line north of Wrexham, take the X4 bus (arrivabus.co.uk; 0344 800 4411) to the Boar's Head on Ewloe Green. It's about a mile's walk along Holywell Road (B5125) and over the fields to the castle.

WHEN TO VISIT
Open all year daily 10am–4pm. Last admission 30 minutes before closing. Closed 24–26 December and 1 January.

ADMISSION CHARGE
Free

WEBSITE
cadw.gov.wales

TELEPHONE
0300 025 6000

wloe is an unusual castle in that it appears to have been craftily hidden in the woods. Indeed, visit it today and you might readily form the opinion that it is *still* very craftily hidden. As such, it's difficult to imagine how it might have presented a warlike front to anyone back in the Middle Ages. However, were you able to strip away the trees immediately outside its walls and see the castle as it was in the 13th century, you'd better appreciate its position on a significant promontory within a valley. The site's proximity to the English–Welsh border must also have recommended it as a location for a stronghold back in the day.

For all that, it is a castle that appears to have had an almost absurdly short lifespan. It may have been in service for perhaps no more than 20 years, following which it has notched up over seven centuries of quiet mouldering. Although this might not make a potential visit sound particularly promising, the castle's lack of utility has resulted in large parts of it remaining in an excellent state of preservation. It means that for anyone who wishes to see a fine example of the D-towers that were the signature design of native Welsh castles, a visit to Ewloe is a must. It's also an opportunity to see a rare castle built within a wood (albeit that some of the trees were no doubt cleared in order to prevent them from being used as cover by a potential enemy).

There's a deal of mystery regarding the genesis of Ewloe Castle. Although it's generally accepted that the Welsh prince Llywelyn ap Gruffydd began building the present edifice in or around 1257, there's some debate as to what stood here before that time or whether indeed there was anything at all. Some historians believe that Owain Gwynedd and Llywelyn ap Iorwerth (Llywelyn the Great) had strongholds on this site before Gruffydd came along. However, the archaeological evidence for this is somewhat ambiguous. What's more, there's just a single surviving contemporary document that mentions Ewloe, so no help can be found in that quarter either. On top of this, there's no record of how long Gruffydd spent on the building work, or even if he intended it as a military stronghold or merely a fortified hunting lodge.

So what *do* we know about this enigmatic castle in the woods? Well, that single contemporary record – a source known as the Chester Plea Rolls – does at least shed some light on the matter. At some point Edward II had clearly shown an interest in Ewloe because the Chester Plea Rolls mention that the justice of Chester had sent a potted history of the manor to the monarch in 1311 (in which year the castle was reported as being more

197

(it stands at the meeting of two streams, the New Inn and the Wepre).

The architectural highlight at Ewloe is no doubt the so-called Welsh Tower. This is a fine D-shaped construction favoured by the Welsh, though popular on both sides of the border for a hundred years or so from the late 12th century. Although it's likely that this tower was Gruffydd's doing, a study carried out in the 1940s posited the notion that it actually dated from around 1210 and was the work of Llywelyn ap Iorwerth, the builder of Dolwyddelan Castle (see page 184).

Whoever was responsible for its erection, it was enclosed by a curtain wall that formed an upper ward or courtyard. Below it to the west, a smaller circular tower defended a larger lower ward, also formed by a curtain wall. Though modest in size, the stronghold served to advertise Llywelyn ap Gruffydd's power. Having made his gains in North Wales during the ineffectual reign of Henry III, he cemented his hold on the region with the signing of the Treaty of Montgomery in 1267. It was simply his misfortune that the conceited yet faint-hearted Henry died in 1272 and the crown passed to his son Edward, who proved a much more astute military leader than his father.

or less intact). The writer maintained that Llywelyn ap Gruffudd had made gains in the area at the expense of the English and that by 1257 the land at Ewloe was in his hands.

We also know that, just two decades later, the sandstone structure was abandoned in the wake of Edward I's highly successful invasion of Wales. The monarch had no need for the fortress he'd captured – he preferred castles that were accessible by ship, on the grounds that they were much easier to maintain and supply. The castles he built at Flint and Rhuddlan thus served his purposes far better than the comparatively remote Ewloe, which was neither coastal nor could be reached by a navigable river

Ewloe's other claim to fame is as the site of an engagement that was fought here a century before the present castle came to be built. The Battle of Ewloe took place in 1157. That year Henry II had organised an invasion of North Wales in an attempt to claw back land lost to the monarchy during the 18-year civil war known as the Anarchy. His opponent was the Welsh prince Owain ap Gruffudd, a canny military strategist.

Henry was keen to recapture Rhuddlan Castle and was leading a vast army (of perhaps 30,000 men) up the narrow strip of lowland along the North Wales coast in order to effect this. However, on reaching Basingwerk he was held up by Gruffudd's far smaller force. In a bid to outflank the Welsh, he led a sizeable number of his troops back southeast towards Chester and then inland. He had only got as far as Ewloe Wood when his army was ambushed by Gruffudd's men, using the terrain as cover for a guerrilla-style attack. Although outnumbered considerably, they routed Henry's forces and would have killed the king himself had it not been for the swift thinking of the Earl of Hertford, Roger de Clare, who rescued the monarch when he became separated from his troops.

We may never know whether some sort of fortress existed in the wood when this battle took place. However, we can be thankful that the 13th-century castle that stands there today has been preserved for us by the same isolation that sealed its fate.

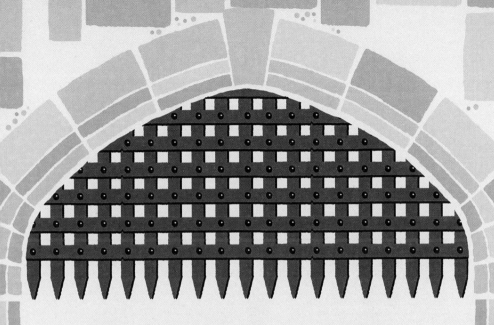

SCOTLAND

40 MACLELLAN'S CASTLE
KIRKCUDBRIGHT, DUMFRIES & GALLOWAY

A family's steady fall from grace is echoed by the castle they called home

LOCATION
Castle Street, Kirkcudbright,
Dumfries & Galloway
DG6 4JD

GRID REFERENCE
NX 682 510

PUBLIC TRANSPORT
From Dumfries railway
station (of *The Thirty-Nine*
Steps fame) take the 502 bus
to Castle Douglas, whence
a 502 bus (stagecoachbus.
com; 01387 253496) will
speed you to Kirkcudbright.

WHEN TO VISIT
Open April to September
daily 9.30am–5.30pm (last
entry 5pm). May close for
lunch 1pm–2pm.

ADMISSION CHARGE
Yes (free to HES members)

WEBSITE
historicenvironment.scot
(Historic Environment
Scotland)

TELEPHONE
01557 331856

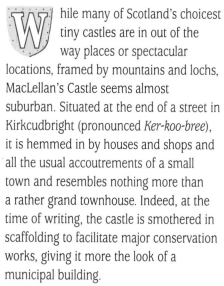

hile many of Scotland's choicest tiny castles are in out of the way places or spectacular locations, framed by mountains and lochs, MacLellan's Castle seems almost suburban. Situated at the end of a street in Kirkcudbright (pronounced *Ker-koo-bree*), it is hemmed in by houses and shops and all the usual accoutrements of a small town and resembles nothing more than a rather grand townhouse. Indeed, at the time of writing, the castle is smothered in scaffolding to facilitate major conservation works, giving it more the look of a municipal building.

The story of MacLellan's Castle (or Kirkcudbright Castle as it was known until the mid-19th century) is rather an unhappy one. Most castles experience peaks and troughs in their existence as they are blown about on the winds of fortune. Owners become richer or poorer; fall out of or into favour with the monarch of the day; or are supplanted by new owners. Meanwhile, enemies besiege, undermine, bombard, burn or slight them (many northern strongholds suffered this last fate during the War of Scottish Independence). In the case of MacLellan's Castle, the highpoint was arguably reached the day King James VI graced the castle with a visit in 1587. From then on, the decline of the MacLellan family was mirrored by the decline of their beautiful Jacobean tower house.

The future must have looked rosy for late medieval power couple Sir Thomas MacLellan and Grissel Maxwell back in the early 1580s. He was the Provost of Kirkcudbright and a rising political star

Reformation, during which Henry VIII dissolved scores of religious houses, and had been demolished. The well that sits in the castle grounds may be the convent's one surviving feature.

The four-storey tower house reflected the changing times. Although it is castellated and there are gun loops incorporated into the tower, the building is much less concerned with defence than tower houses had been up to that point, and much more inclined to luxury. The windows, for example, are large, numerous and even found on the ground floor, the section of the castle most vulnerable to attack.

Sir Thomas was the product of a powerful family line that probably traced its Scottish roots back to the Gaelic settlers who had arrived from Ireland nearly a thousand years beforehand. One persistent story has it that he was descended from the blacksmith who created Mons Meg, the enormous bombard now on show outside Edinburgh Castle. His own castle was not only intended to be a comfortable base of operations but also a statement to the world that he was on his way up. The provost may also have been involved in some illicit smuggling activities, in which case the location of his tower house (complete with vaulted cellars) right next to the harbour would have been convenient to say the least.

keen to ingratiate himself into royal circles. She held high status in her own right, being the daughter of Sir John Maxwell and Agnes Herries, Lady Herries of Terregles. Together they bought up the site of the town's Greyfriars Convent and proceeded to build themselves a fine tower house with a traditional L-plan layout. If the panels above the main entrance are to be believed, the work was completed in 1582 (though the couple only married two years later, which raises a question or two). The Franciscan convent had been founded by James II not all that long beforehand – sometime between 1449 and 1456 – but fell foul of the

The rot set in almost immediately, in the form of Thomas and Grissel's eldest child Robert, who seems to have been dangerously unhinged from a very early age. According to Historic Environment Scotland, the body entrusted with the care of the castle since 1912, Robert MacLellan 'was variously accused of attempting to assassinate his guardian, physically attacking the minister during a meeting of the parish council, casually taking pot-shots at local lairds while out riding around Kirkcudbright, and chasing a total stranger across Leith Links with a drawn sword'.

Robert took himself off to join in the colonisation of Ulster in 1610, built a (necessarily more defensible) castle near Derry/Londonderry, and became an MP, which led to him being raised to the peerage by Charles I as the 1st Lord Kirkcudbright. Since he was childless, his nephew Thomas succeeded him, followed swiftly by a cousin named John, both of whom poured huge amounts of the family wealth into the creation of Covenanter regiments to fight in the Civil War. Such was his passion for Presbyterianism, John MacLellan led a

minor uprising in 1663 when Greyfriars Church – next door to the castle – had the effrontery to appoint an Episcopalian vicar. He died in prison two years later. His son William became the 4th Lord Kirkcudbright briefly, dying in 1669. By this time, the family finances were in such dire straits that William's son James did not assume the title of 5th Lord until 1721. There has been no Lord Kirkcudbright since the last one died in 1832.

By then, the castle had long since become a ruin (albeit a well-preserved one). Indeed, it seems to have been abandoned around 1660, during the time of the warring vicar-hating 3rd Lord Kirkcudbright. It came into the Maxwell family of Orchardton (page 208) by marriage in the mid-18th century, and it's reported that he and his wife stripped it of its valuable roof and the best pieces of furniture. By the 1780s, fiscal difficulties

forced the sale of the castle to the Earl of Selkirk, who must have had some compelling motive for the purchase of the remnants of the once great tower house but he seems to have made no effort to repair it.

Despite the current and very necessary restoration project, there is still a great deal to explore at MacLellan's Castle, a building that once showed off Jacobean architecture to its best advantage. The ground floor, where the servants worked 'below stairs', as it were, is a succession of gloomy rooms (despite the windows) off low, narrow corridors. There can be no doubt as to this floor's occupants' place in the social order – it bears a resemblance to the tunnels and chambers of an ants' nest. The faint of heart should be warned that the two all-white ghosts in the kitchen carrying a slaughtered deer between them are in fact modern life-size models.

The uppermost floors once contained 15 private chambers and beneath them lay the great hall and other public rooms. However, you should be careful what you say while in the great hall. The fireplace hides a spyhole called the laird's lug. Sir Thomas (and doubtless his successors) would instal himself in a tiny secret room behind the fireplace where a hole would allow him to eavesdrop on conversations going on within. Knowledge, as they say, is power.

41 ORCHARDTON TOWER
NR PALNACKIE, DUMFRIES & GALLOWAY

A charmed existence has preserved the only round tower house in Scotland

LOCATION
Nr Palnackie, Dumfries and Galloway DG7 1QH

GRID REFERENCE
NX 817 551

PUBLIC TRANSPORT
From the Loreburne Centre in Dumfries, take the 501 (stagecoachbus.com; 01387 253496) to Dalbeattie, from where a 505 bus (houstonscoaches.co.uk; 01576 203874) will convey

you to Palnackie. Orchardton Tower is a little over a mile along a narrow country lane that heads south out of the village.

WHEN TO VISIT
Open April to September daily 9.30am–5.30pm (last entry 5pm); October to March Saturday to Wednesday 10am–4pm (last entry 3.30pm). Closed 25–26 December and 1–2 January.

ADMISSION CHARGE
Free (but donations welcome)

WEBSITE
historicenvironment.scot (Historic Environment Scotland)

TELEPHONE
0131 668 8600

Orchardton Tower owes its existence to the seemingly unceasing turmoil of medieval Scotland. When James II of Scotland won a hard-fought victory over the Douglas family (personally stabbing one of the earls to death in a frenzied attack), he took care to reward those who had supported him. One such was a minor laird named John Cairns who had been a tenant of the Earl of Douglas, paying him £6 rent per annum for a parcel of land around Orchardton (then known as Erysbutil). The king reduced the rent to a single penny. In or around 1456, Cairns seized this opportunity to build himself and his

family a tower house on the land. It was a fortified and all but free-standing dwelling in which the Cairns would have felt themselves reasonably secure. What makes it particularly interesting is that it is the only round tower house in Scotland and a puzzling anachronism in its day as well.

A visit to Orchardton provides not only an excuse for an excursion into the very pleasant Kirkcudbrightshire countryside but also gives a unique insight into the lifestyle of the upper echelons of society in southwestern Scotland in the late Middle Ages. We are so used to seeing circular keeps in Britain that the oddity of

house circular rather than square or rectangular, which were the floor plans favoured by his contemporaries. Living in the tower at Orchardton must have been akin to inhabiting a sail-less windmill, and the various owners down the years no doubt had all kinds of trouble acquiring furniture to fit its curved outer wall. The tower comprises a cellar (atypically for such buildings, there's no interior doorway to the house above); a first-floor hall reached from the outside by a set of stone steps; two floors of chambers above; and a wall-walk with a small caphouse (or shelter) at the top. Pleasingly, it's possible to climb right up to this wall-walk, which means that visitors can enjoy elevated views of the surrounding countryside once enjoyed by generations of former occupants. Before you attempt the ascent, though, have a look in the hall at the ornate aumbry – the sort of little cubbyhole more often associated with ancient churches – which gives the place an undeniably domestic feel.

the shape of this little fortress is easily overlooked. Castles in Scotland had changed a great deal since the heyday of the round tower in the 13th century. They had become more sophisticated as building technology developed and had incorporated a range of methods for combatting new offensive weapons. Thus, by the time John Cairns built Orchardton, the round tower was a period piece, a full two centuries out of date. No one rushed to imitate the laird's bold architectural move, and as a result there is nothing else quite like it in Scotland.

It's anyone's guess as to why Cairns settled upon the idea of making his tower

While the walls of the tower have survived pretty much intact, the structures that stood alongside it have fared less well. However, there are still extensive ruins of the great hall (this adjoined the tower), the kitchen and other ancillary buildings.

Once Cairns had experienced his welcome drop in rental outgoings and had had his anomalous circular tower

constructed, life appears to have pottered along rather peacefully. At least there is no evidence of any great upheavals and the next time Orchardton makes an appearance in the history books is in 1558, and even then the entry is hardly earth-shattering. We learn that in that year three sisters inherit it – the estate is broken up between them and the lairdship is lost. It's not until 1640 that Sir Robert Maxwell succeeds in completing his mission of buying up all the constituent parts of Orchardton and restoring the lairdship. The family name is made in 1663 when his son becomes the 1st baronet of Orchardton.

We have to wait another century for more news, but this time it is rather more remarkable. A later Sir Robert Maxwell, the 7th baronet, found himself in exile in France. He returned to Scotland in 1746 to lend his support to the Jacobite uprising that had erupted the year before. This led him to fighting at Culloden near Inverness where Bonnie Prince Charlie's forces were soundly defeated in battle by the Hanoverian redcoats, bringing the rebellion to an end. However, despite this setback, and the fact that Maxwell was now an outlaw, he contrived to regain the lairdship from which he had been disinherited by his cousins. The

precise means by which he did this have become embellished over the years but it's likely that a scene was played out at the very entrance to Orchardton Castle in which Maxwell had a showdown with his relatives.

This sort of success was not the usual outcome for a defeated Jacobite and one can only conclude that the 7th Baronet of Orchardton was a rather singular man (or that his story is largely fable). Sir Walter Scott certainly recognised that there was a good story to be made of his life, using it as a basis for his pacy 1815 novel *Guy Mannering*. However, Maxwell's luck was not to hold. In 1765, he began building an impressive home a couple of miles from what was by then his somewhat venerable tower house. Unfortunately, the costs of

this enterprise, along with an association with a bank that collapsed, led to his personal bankruptcy 20 years later and he was forced to sell Orchardton to a Liverpool merchant called James Douglas. The tower was eventually abandoned and handed over to the nation in 1912.

Although it doesn't make for a gripping history, we can be thankful that Orchardton Castle was never set on fire, slighted, undermined or subjected to bombardment by artillery. Indeed, there is no indication that it was ever attacked or even besieged. Its charmed existence has largely preserved this curio for posterity – to explore it is to step back in time to the late Middle Ages and experience a taste of the life a laird's family would have enjoyed.

42 CAERLAVEROCK CASTLE
GLENCAPLE, DUMFRIES & GALLOWAY

The triangular layout of this fortified stronghold is unique in Britain

LOCATION
Glencaple, Dumfries &
Galloway DG1 4RU

GRID REFERENCE
NY 025 656

PUBLIC TRANSPORT
From Dumfries railway
station, walk to Shakespeare
Street to pick up the 6A bus
(stagecoachbus.com; 01387
253496) to the end of Castle

Road, Caerlaverock. It's a
short stroll through the
grounds to the castle.

WHEN TO VISIT
Open April to September
daily 9.30am–5.30pm (last
entry 5pm); October to
March daily 10am–4pm
(last entry 3.30pm).

ADMISSION CHARGE
Yes

WEBSITE
historicenvironment.scot
(Historic Environment
Scotland)

TELEPHONE
01387 770244

T he word 'unique' is one of the English language's more ill-used words but when it comes to describing Caerlaverock it can be deployed without hesitation. There is quite simply no other castle like it in Britain. Built of red sandstone, its striking triangular geometry gives the fortress the look of something out of a fantasy rather than a stronghold created for the very practical purpose of defending territory at a highly contested frontier.

This spot by the coast just inside the Scottish border was a favoured location for a fortress long before the current Caerlaverock Castle was built. The Romans established a fort close by on Wardlaw Hill, and a later hill fort was garrisoned here in the 10th century. By the mid-12th century the land had passed to the monks of Holm Cultram Abbey but this brief interlude of non-military use was cut short around 1220, when King Alexander II granted the land to Sir John Maxwell. Making him Warden of the West March at the same time, the Scottish monarch put into Maxwell's hands the grave responsibility of both policing and shoring up the western end of the border with England against bandits and invaders.

Little remains of the square fortress Maxwell built to help achieve this end. The foundations now lie within a forest about

200yds south of the present castle (a trail takes visitors to the spot). It boasted a moat and was one of Scotland's first ever stone castles but seems never to have been completed. The work was abandoned in favour of a pioneering new project set in motion by John's brother Sir Aymer Maxwell around 1270.

It's not clear why Sir Aymer plumped for a triangular design. The rocky outcrop on which part of the castle is built is not triangular – only the gatehouse at the northern tip sits on it. Clay had to be used to create a platform for the remainder of the castle. The moat is not naturally that shape but was dug out (with some of the stone quarried from it used in the building process). The inspiration can hardly have come from abroad either. The only other triangular castle we know of – Fortezza di Sarzanello in Italy – was constructed in 1320, some 50 years later.

However it came about, there's a great deal to recommend it beyond the purely aesthetic. On two of the points of the triangle there are towers from which flanking fire could be ranged athwart the curtain walls, should attackers cross the moat. At the third point stood a double gatehouse which, aside from giving ample protection to the drawbridge, also provided much of the castle's accommodation.

Caerlaverock's first real test came in 1300, under the lordship of Aymer's nephew, Sir Herbert Maxwell. The year before, the garrison had taken part in an attack on the English-held Lochmaben Castle a little to the northeast. Now the English were coming for them. Edward I, the Hammer of the Scots, had pushed north of the border and Caerlaverock presented him with one of his first major obstacles. Bringing with him an army of 3,000 troops, including 87 knights, and a number of siege engines, he encircled Caerlaverock. It must have been a terrifying sight for the Scottish garrison.

'The Roll of Karlaverock' – a poem written in Old French by a herald in Edward's army – includes a blow-by-blow eye-witness account of the action, and as such is a most valuable source of information regarding castle warfare in the Middle Ages.

In C W Scott-Giles' translation of 1960, the herald sets the scene:

Mighty was Caerlaverock castle. Siege it
feared not, scorned surrender
Wherefore came the king in person.
Many a resolute defender,
Well supplied with stores and engine,
'gainst assault the fortress manned.
Shield-shaped, was it, corner-towered,
gate and draw-bridge barbican'd,
Strongly walled, and girt with ditches
filled with water brimmingly.

A series of brutal and bloody attacks on the castle takes place, led by one knight then another, with the defenders giving as good as they got. Arrows and great stones fill the air, battering the combatants.

Great the press, but the defenders
stubborn still the portway kept,
For as one fell out exhausted,
to his place another leapt;
Never thought they of surrender,
and the fray
Continued fierce day and night
and morn ensuing

Eventually the towers succumb to a 'mighty pounding' and the onslaught becomes too much for the garrison. However, their attempt to negotiate a surrender is rebuffed:

Now no longer could they suffer
and a pennon held aloft,
Sign that they for peace would parley;
but an archer sent a shaft
Piercing him who held the pennon
through the hand into the face

After two days of fighting the castle was captured. Many of the survivors from what had been a garrison of just 60 soldiers were hanged from the walls of the castle by the victors.

A few years later, Edward II returned the castle to the Maxwell family in the hope that they would hold it against those of their countrymen who were fighting for independence. Sir Eustace Maxwell switched his allegiance to Robert the Bruce, which brought about a second siege by the English, who this time did not prevail. However, in order to ensure that the castle was not captured by the Sassenach foe, Maxwell had it torn down.

It was reconstructed and over the following two centuries there were three further sieges – one by David II of Scotland and two by the English. The castle was variously damaged and rebuilt until a final siege occurred in 1640, during the Civil War. This time the aggressors were Parliamentarians, the Maxwells having thrown their lot in with King Charles. Caerlaverock withstood the siege for three months before capitulating. The Roundheads duly slighted the castle,

tearing down huge swathes of the curtain wall.

Thankfully, they left the wonderful double gatehouse intact, as well as the 17th-century Nithsdale Lodging, two luxurious residence ranges built within the courtyard by Robert, 10th Lord Maxwell, who became Earl of Nithsdale. He had had just six years to enjoy them before the Roundheads arrived.

A permanent exhibition at the castle introduces visitors to the sheer unpleasantness of siege warfare. There's also a cafe and an interactive app to download from the website. And if you have a particularly catholic taste in celluloid you might find you recognise Caerlaverock from the film *The Decoy Bride*, which, despite the talents of Kelly Macdonald and David Tennant, somehow failed to become a huge box office hit.

43 LOCHRANZA CASTLE
LOCHRANZA, ARRAN

This scourge of the MacDonalds was made famous by a Belgian cartoonist

LOCATION
Lochranza, Arran, North Ayrshire KA27 8HL
NB This postcode will get you only roughly to the right spot but the location of the castle itself will be fairly evident.

GRID REFERENCE
NR 933 506

PUBLIC TRANSPORT
There are two ways of sailing to Arran from the mainland (both calmac.co.uk; 0800 066 5000). You can either go from Ardrossan to Brodick or from Claonaig straight to Lochranza itself (in winter this becomes Tarbert to Lochranza, on a reduced timetable). The former leaves you midway down the east coast of the island of Arran, from where you can take the 324 bus (Western Buses; spt.co.uk; 0141 332 6811) to Lochranza at its northern end. The latter leaves you with a half-mile walk along the shore from the pier to the castle.

WHEN TO VISIT
Open April to September daily 9.30am–5.30pm (last entry 5pm).

ADMISSION CHARGE
Free

WEBSITE
historicenvironment.scot (Historic Environment Scotland)

TELEPHONE
0131 668 8600

rran, lying in the Firth of Clyde to the southwest of Glasgow, is one of Scotland's more accessible islands. Its importance today is underlined by the fact that it runs to two distinct ferry connections with the mainland. Near its northernmost tip, the diminutive Loch Ranza provides a useful haven for shipping (one of those ferries docks there today) and was thus a logical location for the building of a stronghold. Lochranza proved a great success as well. Over its lifespan it was far less sinned against than sinning and even went on to find unlikely fame in cartoon form long after it had been abandoned.

However, there is some debate over who actually built it. Lochranza was either the creation of the MacSween family, who were lords of Arran up until 1262 (but today have a name more familiarly linked with the production of haggis in both meat and vegan forms) or the Stewarts of Menteith, to whom Alexander III granted the island that year. If it was the latter, they were only able to hold onto it for a century or so before the lack of a male heir saw the castle fall into the hands of a

Despite this promotion, Lochranza's fate was to find itself forever being granted to this noble or that. In 1433 the Lord of Arran bestowed it upon Sir Duncan Campbell of Lochaw. Less than two decades later, James II handed it to Alexander, 1st Lord Montgomerie. But for all its role as perennial gift, Lochranza may be thought of as a lucky castle. Rather than being attacked, it was used as a headquarters from which to mount attacks on others, in particular the MacDonalds of the Isles. Both James IV and James VI took advantage of its location as a springboard for assaults on that large and powerful clan. Oliver Cromwell also saw the sense in holding an offshore base in southern Scotland and had the castle garrisoned in the 1650s.

Lochranza changed hands between aristocrats for the final time in 1705, when the Montgomery family (who had retrieved it after the Restoration) sold it to the Duchess of Hamilton. She ordered a chapel to be built nearby but it has since disappeared without trace.

Happily, enough of the castle itself has survived the ravages of time and neglect to make for a satisfying visit. Although there is just the one information board giving a few details of Lochranza's architectural development, the castle is dotted with little metal signs explaining which room is which and what to look out for. The modest hall house was a fortified two-

relative named John Stewart in 1371. Although born at least seven years before his parents took the trouble to get married, a disposition from Pope Clement VI gave his birth legitimacy, a fact that came in handy in 1390 because it smoothed the path to his crowning as king of Scotland (his father having acceded to the throne the same year John took possession of Lochranza). He assumed the title Robert III and became the second king in a Stuart dynasty that was to rule Scotland (and briefly Great Britain and Ireland) until 1714. This, of course, also saw Arran's little stronghold achieving the perhaps unlikely status of royal castle.

window) and you'll notice it was guarded by a *meurtrière* or 'murder hole' – the shaft through which rocks, missiles or boiling oil could be rained down on an attacker.

Another sobering feature of the 13th-century building was its prison, which is another survivor. The entranceway looks just as grim, dark and forbidding as doubtless it was when alleged criminals were held here pending trial. It cannot have been a healthy place to spend any length of time, given that the cell has no windows or any shafts allowing for the circulation of air. The generous hole in the wall where the end of the bar locking the door was inserted suggests there was little hope of escape either.

The Montgomery family gave the hall house a major overhaul in the 16th century, developing it into an L-shaped tower house. This involved adding two further storeys and, as might be surmised from the name, a tower. It's these features – the well-preserved square tower and the gable end on the main house leading up to a chimney – that give the castle its distinctive outline, particularly when viewed from the north. Note too the gun loops in the walls and a box machicolation – a structure overhanging the wall from which anyone attempting to gain entrance through the front door could be pelted with projectiles or liquids. The

storey affair, with a door on the first floor reached by an external wooden staircase adjoining the wall. That original entrance can still be seen today. It resembles a large blocked-off window but a sign tells of its lost purpose.

Inside, although the roof has obviously long since fallen in, the layout of the castle is still very much in evidence. Some of Lochranza's defences have survived too. Look above the former ground-floor entrance (in common with the other original entrance, this too became a

Montgomery family were clearly not complacent about the possible need to defend themselves.

By 1775, Lochranza had been abandoned and was reported by a visitor named Thomas Pennant to be in use by 'poor people who occasionally take refuge here'. The wall around the castle's courtyard – a feature incorporated in the designs of both the hall house and the tower house – has completely vanished, along with whatever buildings it protected. In 1892, there was also a major collapse of the remaining structure's northeastern section. However, the castle would have to endure another 60 years of decay before the Duke of Montrose handed it over to the authorities to save what was left for posterity. Nowadays, the pleasant greensward that surrounds it is a popular grazing area for red deer.

But that was not the end of the story for the ruined fortress because it had one more part to play: an unlikely starring role in a Tintin adventure. *The Black Island*, Belgian cartoonist Hergé's tale of derring-do in the Scottish islands, was published in 1937. Unfortunately, its author was not very clued up on things Hebridean and the book contained a number of mistakes that the publishers Methuen asked to have put right. Hergé packed off his right-hand man, Bob de Moor, to visit Arran and scout the island out for some more realistic settings. As a result, Lochranza Castle became the model for the book's fearsome (and haunted) Craig Dhui.

44 HERMITAGE CASTLE

NEWCASTLETON, ROXBURGHSHIRE

Arguably the most forbidding castle in all the land

LOCATION
Newcastleton, Roxburghshire
TD9 0LU

GRID REFERENCE
NY 496 960

PUBLIC TRANSPORT
Hermitage is famously in a lonely spot but it's just about accessible by public transport. From near Carlisle railway station take the X95

bus (bordersbuses.co.uk; 01896 754350) to Hawick, from where a 128 bus (telfordscoaches.com; 013873 75677) will transport you to the hamlet of Hermitage from where it's a mile's walk to the castle.

WHEN TO VISIT
Open April to September daily 9.30am–5.30pm (last entry 5pm).

ADMISSION CHARGE
Yes

WEBSITE
historicenvironment.scot (Historic Environment Scotland)

TELEPHONE
01387 376222

In Percy Bysshe Shelley's sonnet 'Ozymandias', the poet has the Egyptian pharaoh Ramesses II declare, 'Look on my works, ye Mighty, and despair!' One can readily imagine the builders of Hermitage Castle using precisely the same words, as the stronghold they created must have struck terror into the hearts of anyone who considered them an enemy, for it is an edifice that is not so much doom-laden as an embodiment of doom itself. If the castle allows us an accurate glimpse into the minds of its creators, we can only be thankful we ourselves were never around to incur their wrath.

Hermitage was never a large castle. Although its walls are high, it's an

extraordinarily compact affair and there is no evidence it ever possessed curtain walls, a bailey or ancillary buildings. However, what it lacks in stature it makes up for in gothic horror without actually appearing all that gothic in style, which is quite the trick. Here you will find no fancy stone tracery or ornamentation of any kind. This is a brutish hulk of a thing, its gargantuan flying arches, assemblage of stark right angles and high expanses of windowless wall giving it an air of utter impregnability. Within its walls, Beauty has been sacrificed on the altar of the god of Utility. It is a castle intended to dominate, oppress and subject – a place where the best one could hope for would be the very coldest of comforts. The fact

that it is located in a rather lonely backwater only exacerbates its dubious qualities.

There's doubt over the exact year in which building began on this site in the Liddesdale Valley, a handful of miles from the English border. A hunting lodge was constructed near here by the de Sules (or Soules) family in 1240 but they may not have started on a castle on this spot until sometime around 1327–32. The Englishman Sir Hugh de Dacre replaced the de Sules' modest wooden structure with a luxurious fortified manor house around 1360. However, it was not until the formidable William Douglas, 1st Earl of

Douglas, took over Hermitage in 1371 that it began the metamorphosis into the extraordinary building we see today. By then, William had already shown his mettle by killing his own godfather – also called William Douglas – in a fight in Ettrick Forest. The crux of the dispute was the ownership of Hermitage. Despite his victory he had to wait another 18 years before he got his hands on it. Since the older William had been responsible for the starving to death in a dungeon at Hermitage of a newly minted sheriff he had kidnapped solely because he was furious at not obtaining the post himself, his demise might not have been considered a great loss to humanity.

The younger William put Hermitage into the keeping of his son James and between them they converted the residence into a mighty stone tower house. This is now known as the central tower. Among other rooms, it contains an upper hall which has an unidentified face carved into the stone around one of the windows. Three other towers were added – the well tower, the prison tower and the Douglas tower. These are believed to have been the work of George Douglas, William's illegitimate son, who became 1st Earl of Angus when his half-brother James was killed at the Battle of Otterburn in 1388. If George was responsible for the towers' construction, they are a young man's doing, for the founder of

the lengthy dynasty known as the Red Line died of plague as a prisoner of war in his early 20s.

With the creation of all four towers, Hermitage became a castle to be reckoned with. It had to be, too – the borderlands between England and Scotland were notorious for cattle raiding and more violent crimes carried out by lawless reivers. Whoever held Hermitage had the responsibility of attempting to bring order from the chaos. An imposing castle certainly helped in this regard, as did the fact that the holder of this particular poisoned chalice was considered by the authorities to be above the law himself.

Throughout its life, Hermitage Castle was used as a political pawn – there are no fewer than four instances of Scottish kings (Robert the Bruce, James IV, V and VI) wresting it from its owner on account of their treasonous behaviour (in the middle two cases for conspiring with the Sassenachs) and handing it to a favoured underling who had proved himself more loyal.

It's fitting, therefore, that the most famous event to have occurred at the castle involved a woman who was forever at the heart of political intrigue: Mary, Queen of Scots. On 15 October 1566, Mary rode 25 miles on horseback to

Hermitage to visit the then owner James Hepburn, 4th Earl of Bothwell. The nobleman had been wounded while arresting infamous reivers, the Elliots of Liddesdale. Mary's cross-country dash was spun by her enemies as an adulterous lovers' tryst, but this seems far-fetched since she was accompanied by an entourage and had legitimate matters of state to discuss with the earl. It almost cost the queen her life, though – immediately after her return journey (during which she was reputed to have fallen from her horse into a bog), she contracted a fever from which she nearly died.

Bothwell recovered from his wounds and, four months later, would be accused (but later acquitted) of involvement in the murder of Mary's second husband, Lord Darnley. Later that year, he abducted, allegedly raped, and then married the queen (who may or may not have been a willing victim). The alliance proved controversial, and Bothwell's opponents were victorious over his own forces at the Battle of Carberry Hill. The earl fled to Scandinavia, where he spent the rest of his life in prison, seeing neither Mary nor Hermitage ever again.

The castle's significance as a frontier stronghold came to an end in 1603 when James VI ascended to the English throne (becoming James I of England) and the border between the two countries became less politically important. Hermitage was

abandoned and was only rescued from dilapidation by two Sir Walter Scotts. The author of that name brought the castle to national attention with his anthology of ballads *Minstrelsy of the Scottish Border*; while Sir Walter Scott, 5th Duke of Buccleuch, funded a major restoration of Hermitage in the 1830s.

After visiting, do take time to seek out the ruined chapel that lies a short walk from the main entrance to the castle grounds. This probably served the hunting lodge that the de Sules family built before they started the nearby castle and so provides a pleasing link back to the very first owners of Hermitage.

45 PORTENCROSS CASTLE

PORTENCROSS, NORTH AYRSHIRE

The proud venue of royal charter signings ended life as a glorified fisherman's hut

LOCATION

Portencross, nr West Kilbride, North Ayrshire KA23 9QA

GRID REFERENCE

NS 175 489

PUBLIC TRANSPORT

West Kilbride railway station is just over 2 miles from Portencross Castle. Simply head west out of town along the B7048.

WHEN TO VISIT

Open daily for first half of April and the whole of July and August, also weekends and holiday Mondays from April to September, 11am–4pm (last entry 3.45pm). Check website for events and exceptional closed days. It is possible to arrange access outwith these dates. Anyone interested in a private visit, group visit

or other event should contact Ann on the phone number below.

ADMISSION CHARGE

Free (but donations gratefully received)

WEBSITE

portencrosscastle.org.uk

TELEPHONE

01294 823799

W hen first encountering Portencross Castle it's almost impossible not to be won over by its delightful setting. The squat tower stands on the rocks of a short and low headland between a long beach and a tiny natural harbour. Behind are the few vulnerable-looking houses that make up the coastal hamlet of Portencross, seemingly putting their faith in the castle to protect them from the wrath of the sea. Close by, across the water, lies the island known as Little Cumbrae. It's all very picturesque. However, this was no castellated residence built for the aesthetic enjoyment of its surroundings, for the apparently insignificant point on which Portencross Castle holds sway is Farland

Head, North Ayrshire's westerly extremity. It guards the eastern side of the mouth of the Firth of Clyde, the major sea route into the Central Lowlands, Scotland's most populous region.

Old though it be, Portencross Castle wasn't the first stronghold hereabouts (nor Portencross its first name – the area used to be known as Arnele). Iron Age settlers constructed themselves a fort on Auld Hill, which rises up behind the current castle. A stone fort was built on the site of the Iron Age camp in the 12th century. This served to defend against incursions from Viking settlements on the neighbouring islands of Great and Little Cumbrae and Bute until the Battle of Largs in 1263 put paid to the Norse threat.

In 1315, Robert the Bruce, still buoyed by a significant victory over the English at Bannockburn the previous year, gave the lands at Arnele to a steadfast supporter from Kilmarnock named Robert Boyd. It appears that, at some point in the middle of the century, tired of the inconvenience of the fort's lofty position when using the little harbour down below, a later Robert Boyd descended from the timeworn eerie to build himself a stronghold by the shore. However, it's possible that an earlier Boyd made such a decision beforehand, constructing a wooden building where the later Robert's stone structure now stands. Whichever is true, the move was an unqualified success and Arnele Castle very quickly assumed an important role out of proportion to its size and relatively isolated location. It became a favoured venue for the signing of royal charters, and King Robert II – grandson of Robert the Bruce – made frequent working visits during his reign. Photographs of extracts of a couple of the charters – which sought to extend the king's power and influence – are on display in the castle's vaulted cellar.

At its conception, the castle was what is known as a hall house: a defensible cube-like two-storey building with battlements and a garret. This was probably enhanced by a barmkin – a wall protecting its landward side with a smaller structure or two in the courtyard formed between wall and castle. The

diminutive castle later evolved into something more like a tower house. At different times the Boyds added an east and west wing to the original building. In the 15th century, further storeys and attics added some height, while sometime later came larger windows and an internal staircase (both of which must have been absolute boons to the occupiers). Though still very much on the small side, it's possible that the castle had two kitchens, the grander of which would have serviced any royal party that happened to be in situ. There was also a small and unpleasant pit prison, or 'bottle dungeon', for holding alleged miscreants in such a degree of discomfort that on occasion a stay there proved a death sentence.

Back in the time when Portencross functioned as a castle, entry was gained by climbing a wooden staircase up to a door that gave onto the vaulted great hall. Today the entrance used is a storey below the erstwhile front door and is rather more prosaic, leading into the cellar, a surviving feature of the original structure. However, the exhibition here is far from commonplace: it's a fascinating little trove of stories and objects relating to the castle. These include some first-rate cut-away illustrations of the various phases of the castle's life; evidence of the unlikely later use of the cellar; and a matchstick model of the castle made by a gentleman from Kilwinning. As part of the recent restoration undertaken by the Friends of

Portencross Castle, stairs lead all the way up to the roof, allowing access to each of the storeys, though the floors of the upper ones have long since disappeared. Even so, the climb is well worthwhile because many details of the private chambers are still visible, and the sea views from the roof, in what used to be an attic room, are quite a treat. Dioramas there help visitors identify points in the seascape.

After Robert II, the castle played a less prominent role in political life. However, its pocket-sized harbour remained an important staging post for vessels on their way up and down the coast, the Hebridean single-masted square-sailed birlinn being the transport of choice throughout the Middle Ages.

A ship of a different kind produced a few days of excitement at the castle in 1588. One of the Spanish escapees from the ill-fated Armada sank just offshore. The wreck's 19 survivors were allowed to settle in Scotland or return home. In 1740, divers descended and retrieved 20 cannons from the ship, 10 of which were found to have been made in England and exported to Spain despite a ban on arms sales to that nation being in place. No such thing could happen today, of course.

The Boyd family were still masters of Portencross in 1660, when Charles II was restored to the throne, at which time they moved to a nearby mansion. The castle was abandoned the following century. It was then put to use in a very unlikely way: as a base for fishermen. Fishing out of Portencross was a thriving industry in the 1700s but had dwindled to just one family, the Sheddens, by the 20th century. When brothers Jack and Ronald Shedden retired in 1980 after 50 years plying the waters for salmon, commercial fishing here finally petered out. Their going closed a chapter in the life of the castle's cellar, which had been used for storage and as a mending and drying area for fishing nets. The dangerously dilapidated castle may have been lost entirely but for the timely intervention of the Friends. Restoration work began in 2009 and now this tiny treasure on the North Ayrshire coast is open to the public.

46 CRICHTON CASTLE
CRICHTON, MIDLOTHIAN

A place of continual intrigues and plotting sports a visually stunning interior

LOCATION
Pathhead EH37 5XA

GRID REFERENCE
NT 380 611

PUBLIC TRANSPORT
At just 4 miles away,
Gorebridge is the nearest
railway station to Crichton
Castle. However, you can get
a little closer to the fortress
by getting out of the train at

Eskbank and walking to
the Old Edinburgh Road
at Dalkeith from where a
51 or 52 bus (bordersbuses.
co.uk; 01896 754350) will
take you to Pathhead, which
is just over 2 miles from
the castle.

WHEN TO VISIT
Open April to September
daily 9.30am–5.30pm
(last entry 5pm).

ADMISSION CHARGE
Yes (free to HES members)

WEBSITE
historicenvironment.scot
(Historic Environment
Scotland)

TELEPHONE
01875 320017

Some castles are proud of being architecturally interesting. Some revel in the part they played in history. Still others bask in the reflected glory of their beautiful location. Crichton Castle is one of those rare instances of a fortress that can boast of all three. Not only does it possess an extraordinary studded façade that has to be seen to be believed, it also attracted historical events with the same enthusiasm that a child collects football stickers, and sits in a gloriously scenic location above Tyne Water. One can safely say that it's a castle with a bit of pizzazz.

Crichton began life as a tower house, erected sometime in the latter part of the 14th century, which makes it one of

Scotland's oldest surviving examples. It was a tangible symbol of the growing power of the Crichton family and was built by one John Crichton and then expanded, and its distinctive courtyard established, by his son William c.1430–50. William Crichton is a little-known name nowadays but he was a formidable presence in 15th-century Scotland. Royal envoy, governor of Edinburgh castle, Master of the Royal Household, sheriff of Edinburgh, guardian to the infant James II of Scotland, and finally Lord Chancellor of Scotland, his political rise was inexorable and his influence considerable. He was also a murderer: responsible with two co-conspirators for the cold-blooded slaughter of the teenage Earl of Douglas

and his brother after a state banquet at Edinburgh Castle, having first wined and dined the boys at Crichton for two days. The great hall William had built at his castle a few years before his own death remains a testament to his power.

The castle was the focus of a plot against James III; was taken from the Crichtons and eventually handed to Sir Patrick Hepburn, 1st Earl of Bothwell; and was later presented to Agnes Stewart, a former lover of James IV and mother to one of his many illegitimate daughters. Countess Agnes lived at Crichton for nearly five decades, marrying and outliving three of the most powerful men in Scotland and bearing at least eight further children, and yet still found time to involve herself in political intrigues at the highest level.

Another great intriguer, Mary, Queen of Scots, came to Crichton to attend the wedding of her half-brother in 1562 but the castle's connection with the monarch by no means ends there. Crichton was one of the castles that belonged to James Hepburn, a grandson of the redoubtable Countess Agnes. He was the 4th Earl of Bothwell and happened to become the third husband of Mary in 1567 (see page 231). He wound up spending the last 10 years of his life held in chains in a prison in Denmark after fleeing Scotland for his own safety.

Francis Stewart, 5th Earl of Bothwell, was the nephew of the 4th earl, grandson of an illegitimate son of James V, and Mary, Queen of Scots' godson. He was also the last nobleman to reside at Crichton and, like his predecessor, ended up being obliged to make haste from the country in order to save his skin before eventually dying abroad. In his case, he had made the unwise move of attempting – and, crucially, failing – to kidnap his cousin and former friend James VI as part of an unsuccessful rebellion. Somewhat more bizarrely, before this occurred Francis was charged with trying to bring about the king's death at sea by causing storms through witchcraft – an accusation he vehemently denied.

One of those initially accused, Agnes Sampson, was questioned under torture. After initial resistance, she claimed that the king would be 'consumed at the instance of a nobleman Francis, Erle Bodowell'. Bothwell was duly arrested in 1591 and held in Edinburgh Castle. Two months later he escaped. After being declared an outlaw and dramatically pursued twice across the country by the king and his retinue, he raised a force of 300 men and tried to capture Falkland Palace, inside which stronghold was the king. Forewarned, James and his wife Queen Anne bolted themselves inside the palace's tower. Bothwell withdrew and a further month-long pursuit ensued. Three days after he was stripped of his earldom, Francis Stewart and some of his supporters forced their way into the king's

presence to wring a pardon from the monarch. This was later revoked and Stewart sought exile in France, Spain and finally Italy. He died impoverished in Naples in 1612.

Nowadays, the castle could hardly be more peaceful. Situated in an isolated spot a little to the southwest of the hamlet of Crichton, it is reached by a pleasant walk through open fields past the Collegiate Church of St Mary and St Kentigern. There are views across a lush valley through which flows the upper waters of the River Tyne (not to be confused with its more famous namesake to the south). However, despite its compactness, the castle has maintained its power to impress, even from a distance. Extremely well preserved and standing four-square on a grassy terrace commanding the gentle glen below, even the colour of its stone is out of the ordinary: a wash of pinks, corals and dusky orange. Crichton can claim to be a reflection of the landscape itself since that stone was hewn from quarries located right beside the castle.

Inside, the central courtyard is surrounded by four ranges, including a truly magnificent diamond-studded façade supported by an elegant arcade. The design was influenced by the 5th Earl of Bothwell's early travels in Renaissance Italy and incorporated around 1580. At its zenith, the southwest tower was six storeys high, with each of the upper four floors comprising a private bed chamber with en-suite toilet, which would have been quite the luxury in its day.

But it's the many smaller details that bring this castle back to life, such as the drain for the slops in the kitchen. Even the stairs are worthy of note. We are so used to conventional staircases that it is perhaps surprising to learn that they were once revolutionary. The straight, so-called 'scale-and-platt' staircase at Crichton is believed to be the first of its type in Scotland. Beforehand, staircases had been circular, which meant they took up the minimum of space, were relatively simple to build, and easy to defend against an aggressor mounting them.

Venture back outside the castle and you'll notice a building that looks for all the world like a large chapel. This may actually have been a stables – look out for the horseshoe-shaped window light above the north entrance.

The castle grew and developed as the respective owners' fortunes waxed and architectural predilections changed but, unusually, the castle's previous incarnations were not obliterated. Alterations had ceased altogether by the turn of the 17th century, which means visitors can enjoy a feast of evolving medieval architectural styles almost unrivalled in Scotland.

Crichton's last owner, Lord Humbie, was imprisoned in the Tower of London by

Oliver Cromwell's forces and the castle was thenceforth abandoned. Sir Walter Scott put it on the map as a tourist destination by using it as a central feature of his epic poem 'Marmion' in 1808 but little is known of the castle's history after Lord Humbie's capture.

Because it is so well preserved, Crichton is a great castle for firing the imagination of children – if you're taking youngsters along, you might want to print off the fun quiz on the HES website before you go. The nearby Collegiate Church that William Crichton founded in 1449 also repays a visit – it's administered by a private trust and is open on Sunday afternoons from May to September.

47 HUME CASTLE

HUME, BERWICKSHIRE

Despite appearances, this is not a desert fortress come to a Scottish border hill

LOCATION
Hume, Berwickshire
TD5 7TR

GRID REFERENCE
NT 705 414

PUBLIC TRANSPORT
From Tweedbank railway
station, walk to the B6374
from where you can catch

the 60 bus (bordersbuses.
co.uk; 01896 754350) to
Greenlaw, less than four
miles from the castle.
The occasional B01 bus
(E & A J Robertson; 07969
043874) heads out from
there to Hume.

WHEN TO VISIT
Open all the time.

ADMISSION CHARGE
Free, but there's a box
for donations

WEBSITE
humecastle.org

TELEPHONE
n/a

There's no denying it, there's something remarkably odd about Hume Castle. A common first reaction from visitors on observing it from afar is that it must be some Saharan fort belonging to the French Foreign Legion that has been air-lifted from the desert and lowered onto this grassy southern Scottish hillock. And yet as medieval castle designs go, Hume was a relatively conventional L-plan tower house. The answer to this riddle from the sands lies in the 18th century and what today we would call an act of extraordinary cultural vandalism.

Hume Castle takes its name from the Old English word *hôm*, meaning 'a place on a high outcrop'. The outcrop in question is only 742ft above sea level but such is the flatness of the surrounding countryside that for hundreds of years the fortress proved a vital vantage point from which to observe advancing foes and generally keep an eye on who was doing what at the eastern end of the border. Indeed, Hume was in such a strategically significant position – looking south and east into England, north to the Lammermuir Hills and west towards the important town of Galashiels – that for centuries it was the key stronghold in the region, a citadel that simply could not be ignored. Its importance was further magnified by the fact of it being just 35 miles – perhaps a two-day march – from the Scottish capital. It's little wonder then that it was the scene of many a violent struggle and changed hands several times before it met its final destruction.

The castle gave its name to the clan who built it in the 13th century. There's some confusion over the name – the family name was traditionally spelled Home but pronounced 'Hume' and both spellings are now in circulation. However, the castle itself is said to have gone through eight different spellings in its history, which rather puts things into perspective. Of the Home clan, the best known today is the 14th earl, otherwise known as Sir Alec Douglas-Home, who had a long political career and was prime minister for a year in 1963–64.

The fortress slowly grew and developed as one Lord Home after another – in their role as Warden of the Eastern

Marches – attempted to keep order in the generally lawless border region. By 1460, James II himself began using Hume as a military headquarters while pressing an attack on nearby Roxburgh Castle, one of the few strongholds in the region held by the English at the time. He did not live to see it taken, however, because one of his own cannons blew up while he was standing near it. The king was struck in the thigh and died shortly afterwards.

The castle left the custody of the Home family near the start of the following century. A falling out occurred between Alexander, the 3rd Lord Home, and John Stewart, Duke of Albany, after the latter was installed as regent for the infant James V in 1513 (the king's father having been killed at Flodden – the last monarch in British history to die in battle). The 3rd Lord refused to acknowledge Albany's regency and sought English help to thwart it. In response, the duke captured Hume Castle in 1515. Home himself was imprisoned in Edinburgh Castle (a perennially leaky prison – see page 235). This began a rather exciting period of his life. He escaped with his brother-in-law, the Earl of Arran, and together with the Earl of Angus openly rebelled against Albany. They intercepted ammunition sent by the French and destroyed it, then Home led a force against Dunbar Castle and kidnapped a high official in order to demand his mother's release in return (she was being held prisoner on Albany's instructions).

Eventually, Albany offered to pardon Home, the duke tricking him and his brother into coming for a meeting at Holyroodhouse in Edinburgh. The siblings were arrested and held on the fortified island of Inchgarvie on the Firth of Forth. They were charged with various crimes – some more credible than others – and beheaded.

This meant that there was suddenly a vacancy as owner of Hume Castle. Albany attempted to fill it with a French ambassador named Antoines d'Arces. A distant cousin of the late 3rd Lord Home, disgusted by the turn of events, murdered the newcomer, cutting off his head and sticking it on a pole in the village of Duns.

The 4th Lord Home was mortally wounded in a skirmish on 9 September 1547, the day before the Battle of Pinkie Cleugh near Musselburgh. This was to be the last pitched battle between the English and the Scots (to date, at least). After coming away victorious, the English commander, the Duke of Somerset, set about trying to capture Hume Castle. The late 4th Lord's daughter-in-law, Mariota, was in charge of the defence, her husband having been captured at Pinkie Cleugh. She was compelled to surrender 12 days later when Somerset threatened to have her son executed. The new English overlords at Hume splashed £700 on

improvements to the castle – a not insignificant sum in those days. It would be to no avail. Two years later, under cover of night and with the help of inside informants who knew the stronghold's defensive deficiencies, the castle was taken back by Mariota's husband, the 5th Lord Home. Avenging his father's death, he slew every single member of the garrison.

The English were back again in 1569, this time occupying Hume for three years. The death knell was to sound nearly a century later, in 1651. During the Civil War, a Parliamentarian force led by Colonels George Fenwick and Edmund Syler bombarded and captured the stronghold. On Cromwell's orders, with no further ado, they blew it up.

However, that wasn't quite the end of the story for Hume. First the ruins were occupied by government troops during the 1745 Jacobite uprising. Then, in January 1804, with an invasion by the French apparently imminent, a watchman at Hume Castle erroneously believed he spied a warning beacon in the distance and consequently lit his own. This started what is now called the Great Alarm – 3,000 local volunteers were rushed out to defend the nation from the non-existent invaders.

Today, the village of Hume, to the north of the castle, lies at peace. In the Middle Ages a clutch of houses clung precariously onto the southern slope of the outcrop. All have vanished now and it takes an eagle-eyed archaeologist to identify the odd ripple in the ground that betrays remains below the surface. Pass through the curtain wall via the suspiciously small gate and you enter an undulating grassy courtyard in which you can appreciate just what a good job those Roundhead sappers did when they set explosives to it. There is very little left of the castle building beyond a fragment of wall roughly in the middle of the enclosure and a good many humps and lumps. A grate covers the opening of a well where, in the 19th century, a skeleton wearing a chain of office is said to have been found.

This was believed to be the remains of James IV, there being a persistent myth that his body had been rescued from the battlefield and hidden by four Hume cavalrymen. If a skeleton was indeed discovered here, it has long since disappeared again, so we'll never know.

Look out for a stone panel dated 1829 and blotched with lichen. It records the latitude, longitude and height above sea level of the erstwhile building. A more modern addition is a roundel indicating the very many points on the landscape that can be viewed from the castle. And encircling everything are those gloriously outsize crenellations.

Which brings us to our late 18th-century act of vandalism. The perpetrator was Sir Hugh Hume-Campbell, 3rd Earl of Marchmont, who decided that the southwesterly view from his house at Marchmont, about five miles away, needed spicing up. His solution was to buy the scant remains of Hume Castle and build a new curtain wall, topping it with outlandish crenellations. Nowadays, the good folk at the Hume Castle Preservation Trust are there to save the site from any further desecration.

48 DUNADD FORT
NR KILMARTIN, ARGYLL & BUTE

An ineffably ancient stronghold brought low by Viking raiders

LOCATION
Off the A816, 2 miles south of Kilmartin, Argyll & Bute

GRID REFERENCE
NR 837 936

PUBLIC TRANSPORT
Take a 926 coach (citylink. co.uk; 0141 352 4444) from Glasgow's Buchanan bus station to Lochgilphead, from where you can pick up a 423 bus (westcoastmotors.co.uk; 01586 552319) for the short journey to Dunadd Castle.

WHEN TO VISIT
Open all the time.

ADMISSION CHARGE
Free

WEBSITE
historicenvironment.scot (Historic Environment Scotland)

TELEPHONE
0131 668 8600

L ook left as you head along the main road from Lochgilphead to Kilmartin Glen and you may notice a small outcrop about 600yds away, rising out of some flat boggy fields. Should you give the mound a second glance you might take in the farm buildings huddled in its lee, protected from the westerly winds blowing in off the Sound of Jura. Unless you happened to know what you were looking at, it's unlikely that you would give the scene a moment's further thought. However, what you would have just observed is not only one of the most important ancient historical sites in Scotland but in the whole of Europe.

To reach this much overlooked treasure, you must walk along a track that leads past the gorse, bracken and low grasses of the knoll's lower slopes. Then, all of a sudden, a tricky climb begins. The path takes the easiest way up but this still requires it to pick its way steeply between rocks, heading this way and that (with little arrows near the ground guiding visitors onwards). It passes through a dramatic rocky cleft, heads across a sloping enclosure and takes one last leap precipitously upwards to reach the summit. All this serves to reinforce just how difficult this fortress would have been to conquer by a conventional assault, and why it became a royal capital for many hundreds of years.

Successive occupants of the fort employed the massif's four natural terraces as ready-made defensive rings, enhancing them from time to time with boulders that filled in any gaps. (In essence, the fortress foreshadowed the

Norman motte-and-bailey castles that were to become such a common sight in Britain hundreds of years later.) Before potential attackers could even think about how to overcome these formidable barriers, they would first have had to negotiate the wide expanse of bog – Moine Mhòr ('great moss') – that surrounds the knoll like an immense swampy moat. If these attributes were not enough to recommend the outcrop as a prime site for a fort, it is also served by a river, the Add, and is located just a few miles from the coast. These were hugely important considerations in an age when the sea and rivers formed the major transport routes. It is also likely that when the outcrop was first occupied it was an island surrounded by the sea, which receded to leave a bog and river.

The first people to make Dunadd their base of operations did so roughly 2,000 years ago, during the Iron Age. However, the stronghold's golden age was to come much later, from the early 6th to the early 9th century (some historians add a century to this latter date). That is the period in which Gaelic monarchs made this otherwise insignificant mound their capital, ruling the kingdom of Dalriada (*Dál Riata* in Gaelic) by fair means or foul from its lofty-ish heights (about 180ft) and gradually overwhelming the region's indigenous Picts. St Columba is also reputed to have dropped by in the late 6th

century, apparently bumping into a trader from Gaul here.

As it happens, it was not surprising that the saint should have come across a merchant from overseas at Dunadd because the stronghold was also an important trading post. Excavations have uncovered not only locally made weapons and tools but also glass receptacles brought from Germany and pottery imported from Gaul (roughly the equivalent to today's France). Historic Environment Scotland, the government agency that looks after the site, goes so far as to claim that Dunadd has 'yielded the largest and most diverse range of pottery of any site in northwest Europe'. There is also evidence that Dunadd was one of

Europe's most important metalworking centres. Doubtless many of the products made in the workshops here – intricate brooches appear to have been a speciality – were exchanged for fancy goods brought by the numerous traders who braved the difficult sea voyage from the Continent.

This is an area rich with prehistoric rock art (the information board at the car park serves as a handy guide to local sites) and it is a fascinating carved stone that provides the highlight of a visit to Dunadd. On a terrace just below the summit lie two exposed rocks separated by a few feet of grass. On the shorter one a small round basin has been carved out – this was probably used for ceremonial purposes. The longer rock (now protected beneath a replica) is called the Inauguration Stone and offers up much to enthuse fans of

ancient British history. Inscribed upon it is a rough rendering of a boar, a Pictish motif thought to express some idea of sovereignty. There are also some letters in Ogham script, a Gaelic language used up until the 11th century. Its meaning is obscure but one section has been translated as 'Men of the Moss', which ties in with Dunadd's location within Moine Mhòr.

But the most impressive features of the rock are two hollow footprints, both human and both quite separate. The most obvious footprint is the one into which the prospective king may have placed his own foot during whatever passed for an inauguration ceremony in the days of the kingdom of Dalriada. The act of planting one's foot in the footprint is believed to have symbolised the new king's oath of

fidelity to the land that would sustain his subjects. Legend has it that the footprint was created by Ossian – son of mythical warrior Fionn mac Cumhaill – when he landed here after leaping from Rhudle Hill, a jump of over half a mile. The basin on the other rock was formed where he hit his knee against it, while his trailing hands somehow traced the Ogham words onto the surface.

Once you have examined the rock, Dunadd offers up various other points of interest to look out for. An impressive section of wall, a small cell in the angle of a wall, and a well have all made it into the 21st century. Though precious little is left of the summit enclosure – the citadel and the most heavily fortified section of the fortress – with a bit of imagination it is not difficult to bring into being a picture of the mighty defences that must once have stood here.

It was the Vikings who proved the downfall of Dunadd. In 850, their continual raids led to what had then become the Kingdom of Alba (an amalgamation of the kingdoms of the Scots of Dalriada and the Picts) upping sticks and moving their capital to the safer precincts of Scone, far away to the east by Perth.

Today, a trip to Dunadd not only provides the visitor with a glimpse into the past, but also affords cracking views of the mountains of Jura and Arran, a panorama once enjoyed by kings and chieftains of yore. To date only a very small proportion of this exceedingly venerable fortress has been excavated. Who knows what secrets Dunadd has yet to reveal?

49 CARNASSERIE CASTLE
NR KILMARTIN, ARGYLL & BUTE

An opulent castle and homestead built by a giant bishop keen to fool passers-by

LOCATION
A816, 2 miles north of
Kilmartin, Argyll and Bute

GRID REFERENCE
NM 838 009

PUBLIC TRANSPORT
Board the 926 coach
(citylink.co.uk; 0141 352
4444) from Glasgow's

Buchanan bus station to
Lochgilphead. From
there, take the 423 bus
(westcoastmotors.co.uk;
01586 552319) to
Carnasserie Castle.

WHEN TO VISIT
Open all the time.

ADMISSION CHARGE
Free

WEBSITE
historicenvironment.scot
(Historic Environment
Scotland)

TELEPHONE
0131 668 8600

hough there's barely five miles between Carnasserie Castle and Dunadd Fort (page 249), the two strongholds are as alike as haggis and tweed. While Dunadd has its origins in prehistoric times, Carnasserie is a confection raised into being in the latter half of the 16th century. Whereas Dunadd has been reduced to mere isolated fragments of its former self, much of Carnasserie still remains for us to enjoy. And most strikingly of all, the ancient fortress down the road was very much a working stronghold built to withstand the onslaught of enemy forces. Carnasserie, though equipped with proper defences, is a clever fake.

1565 was a red-letter year in the life of Séon Carsuel (often anglicised to John Carswell or Carsewell), a giant of a man

said to have been over 7ft tall. The former rector of Kilmartin and tutor to the son of the 5th Earl of Argyll had done very well out of his service to his noble lord. Six years earlier, the earl had put into his safekeeping a parcel of land at Carnasserie on which lay the remains of a broch or small castle. Carsuel's enhanced status in society doubtless aided his advancement within the Church of Scotland, for whom he became the Protestant Superintendent of Argyll and the Isles. But his name was made in 1565, when Mary, Queen of Scots made him Bishop of the Isles (the Church of Scotland, not being keen on bishops, refused to recognise him as such but he took the title anyway).

Carsuel began work on a castle at Carnasserie the same year, using funds from his new bishopric. The work was

ostensibly carried out on behalf of his benefactor, the earl, and would take seven years to complete. By a happy coincidence, as ward of the castle, Carsuel was also its principal occupant. He thus furnished himself with a home on the grand scale without dipping too much into his own purse. Two years into the construction, Edinburgh publisher Robert Lekprevik launched *Foirm na n-Urrnuidheadh*, Carsuel's rendering of John Knox's Book of Common Order. It was the first book ever printed in Gaelic and was written at Carnasserie.

The edifice Carsuel built is set a little way off a road that snakes along the bottom of Kilmartin Glen. A track leads to a swiftly climbing zig-zag path and steps that ascend through increasingly well-tended grass until the castle is gained. It gives every impression of being a very ancient square keep to whose western side a much later hall has been attached. And that's just what John Carsuel wanted people to think. In reality, the whole castle was built at the same time, probably recycling some of the stone from the ruined stronghold (of whose existence evidence can be seen about 20yds to the north).

Though a *trompe l'oeil* on a grand scale, it would be wrong to say that the building was in any sense a folly. Its Scottish Renaissance architecture was

extremely fashionable at the time, and the apparent blend of ancient and modern would have been thought rather clever. Furthermore, although principally designed as a luxurious home – one of the finest in Scotland in its day – and to demonstrate what a powerful lord the Earl of Argyll was, Carnasserie did function as a stronghold as well. It boasted gun loops, corbelled angle turrets and a high walkway protected by a parapet, while the entrance was defended by five gun ports and a guard chamber.

Carsuel died in 1572, the same year his castle was completed. The bishop's journey into the afterlife was not without its complications. His body was being transported by boat to Ardchattan Priory for burial when a storm blew up, whisking his coffin into the sea, with his mortal remains inside it. It was retrieved four days later and its occupant was laid to rest in the priory chapel.

The castle survived for not much more than a century after its builder's demise. The most notable event during that time was the imprisonment there of John Campbell of Ardkinglas in 1594. He was held for questioning about the murder of his namesake, John Campbell of Cawdor, three years previously.

And it is Campbells who feature right at the start of any tour of the castle. On a panel above the entrance are the words 'DIA LE UA NDUIBHNE' (God be with Ó Duibhne). This is a reference to Diarmuid Ua Duibhne, the demi-god who is said to have founded the Campbell clan. Duibhne is also the name given to the clan chief. On the ground floor of the range there is a

Auchinbreck in 1643 and by 1681 it had been inherited by a descendant, Sir Duncan Campbell of Auchinbreck, who undertook some largely superficial changes. However, his tenure over the smartest address in the district was to be brief. Carnasserie's weaknesses as a defensible stronghold were demonstrated in 1685 during the Argyll's Rising against James VII of Scotland. Allied to the Monmouth Rebellion against the king, which took place in the southwest of England, the rising was championed by Archibald Campbell, the Earl of Argyll, and was a cause to which Sir Duncan Campbell of Auchinbreck had pinned his colours.

A force loyal to the king led by Maclean of Torloisk duly laid siege to Carnasserie, murdering Sir Duncan's uncle in the process. On capturing the fortress, Torloisk had his men employ explosives to blow up enough of the structure to make it unserviceable – this was no mean job given that the walls of the keep were over 5ft thick – before setting fire to it. Auchinbreck never recovered from the loss and the castle was left as a ruin.

And so it remains today, largely unchanged since that fateful day in 1685. As such, it provides us with a rare unadulterated view of the domestic life of Scottish nobility and their favoured followers during the 16th and 17th centuries and of the wonders of the Scottish Renaissance.

whole array of rooms including a kitchen complete with oven and water inlet, and a vaulted chamber that was possibly used as a wine cellar and contains a well. A stairway from there leads to what was probably the main reception room, given the magnificence of its Renaissance-style fireplace. Indeed, there's a satisfying amount to explore at Carnasserie – narrow spiral staircases lead to upper floors where platforms have been created to view the layout of the castle itself, and three-quarters of a walkway near the top of the 'medieval keep' is accessible.

Until its downfall, the castle does not appear to have known any lean times, even when it passed out of the hands of the Marquis of Argyll. He handed Carnasserie to Dugald Campbell of

50 KILCHURN CASTLE
LOCH AWE, ARGYLL AND BUTE

This picturesque ruin was once Scotland's first purpose-built barracks

LOCATION
Loch Awe, Dalmally,
Argyll & Bute PA33 1AF

GRID REFERENCE
NN 132 275

PUBLIC TRANSPORT
Both Loch Awe and Dalmally
railway stations are about
two miles from the castle.
Unfortunately, most of that
distance is along the busy
A85 road. However, two
infrequent buses run
between both stations and
the castle. The 976 bus
(citylink.co.uk; 0141 352
4444) runs thrice daily in
each direction, while the 403
(Awe service station) does
the school run in the
morning and afternoon.

WHEN TO VISIT
April to September daily
9.30am–5.30pm (last
entry 5pm).

ADMISSION CHARGE
Free

WEBSITE
historicenvironment.scot
(Historic Environment
Scotland)

TELEPHONE
0131 668 8600

There are some places in
Scotland that so cry out for a
castle that, even if warfare were
a concept alien to our species, it would be
only right and proper to build one there.
Such is the case at Loch Awe's far
northeastern shore. Here you'll find a
small hummock cradled by mountains
and flattered by a looking glass that
doubles as one of Scotland's most scenic
lochs. The tower house that sits there
now is so perfect it appears to have been
deliberately left to ruin *à la picturesque*
for the benefit of artists. It's therefore
something of a bonus to discover that
Kilchurn also happens to be the British
mainland's oldest surviving barracks and
is thus a historical, as well as a
visual, treat.

From the main road (the castle
is unsignposted), visitors dip beneath
the Oban branch of the West Highland
railway line on a well-made path over
the wide, flat and rather marshy
peninsula that drives its way into Loch
Awe, rising to a low mound at the far
end. As you walk out to the castle, it's
easy to imagine it sitting on its own tiny
island in the loch, as it did in medieval
times. The island became part of the
mainland only in 1817 when works on
the loch's outflow were carried out,
with a consequent drop in the
water level.

However, it was only by an unexpected misfortune that the castle was built at all. Colin's older half-brother Archibald 'Gillespic' Campbell died suddenly in 1440 in his mid-30s (his grave can be seen at Kilmun parish church, which his parents founded). Their father, fearing that Colin might see the death as an opportunity to seize the leadership of the clan, kept him sweet by giving him this parcel of land around the end of Loch Awe. Colin clearly didn't let the grass grow under his feet because there was already a mention of Kilchurn Castle by 1449, when its name appeared in a charter.

Sir Colin Campbell was the first person to both recognise the excellence of this particular spot of the Highlands as a location for a stronghold and have the means to do something about it. Kilchurn Castle was the result. Commanding one end of Scotland's longest freshwater loch (at 25 miles, it's even longer than Loch Ness) and protected from the vicissitudes of the Highland winter by a semicircle of low mountains and from the attentions of enemies by the loch waters that surrounded it, it's little wonder that Kilchurn Castle became the headquarters of the Campbells of Glenorchy from its construction in the mid-1400s to the end of the 16th century.

The fortress constituted the first step on the way to a massive expansion of the clan's territory and influence, and as such played an important role in the medieval history of the Highlands. For all that it had five storeys, Colin Campbell's original tower house offered little more than the most basic necessities for a stronghold of its day: a hall, sleeping quarters, kitchens, a cellar and a courtyard protected by a high wall. Its only indulgence as such was that it boasted its own prison cell. Colin's son, Duncan, added a range and hall in the courtyard before meeting his end at the disastrous Battle of Flodden in 1513. A later Duncan, the gloriously monikered Black Duncan of the Seven Castles, fortified the castle to some extent at the end of the 16th century following attacks by the Macgregors, former allies and the previous owners of the land. A later Colin finessed the tower house with the addition of four angle turrets. However, construction work was restricted by the smallness of the island on which the building stood, so the castle never outgrew its original footprint.

Happily, a great deal of what was thrown up here is still in existence. Enter the castle today and you'll pass beneath an imposing lintel and into a dark barrel-vaulted basement at the bottom of the tower (in wet weather you'll need to avoid a cascade or two of water). The original prison cell is off to the left. It's usually possible to climb two flights of stairs to a platform (closed at time of writing due to conservation works) which affords a grandstand view of the layout of the castle and its courtyard. Much of this is very well preserved, though the cellars, chapel and sundry other buildings have long since disappeared.

It was the 6th lord, Colin Campbell (he of the four angle turrets), who moved the headquarters of the Campbells of Glenorchy to distant Balloch (now Taymouth) in Perthshire in the 1570s. Though suddenly diminished in importance, Kilchurn remained in Campbell hands, and was even able to withstand a brief siege by General Middleton in 1654. Middleton had been handpicked by the exiled Charles II to lead

a Royalist uprising in his native Scotland. However, his siege of Kilchurn Castle was emblematic of the fiasco that the rebellion became. The blockade lasted just two days before Middleton and his army scurried off at the approach of Roundhead forces led by General Monck.

The castle would doubtless have continued as a pleasant enough outpost of the Campbell territory but the turbulent nature of Scottish politics – and in particular the first Jacobite Rising of 1688 – had a different future in store for it. At this point, that lintel over the entrance is worth a second look, because it marks a key turning point in the life of the castle. It bears the date '1693' along with three crowns, a coat of arms and the initials EIB and CMC, denoting the 1st Earl of

Breadalbane and Countess Mary Campbell. (The lintel also bears two masons' marks left by stonemasons who worked on the castle.) The nobleman referred to here is Sir John Campbell of Glenorchy. A man given to conquest and double-dealing (he was known as 'Slippery John'), he led his clan in a hugely successful and notably bloody campaign against the Sinclairs of Caithness in 1680, becoming the 1st Earl of Breadalbane the following year. In 1689, he not only made Kilchurn his retirement home (a long retirement as it turned out – he died 28 years later) but converted the castle into Scotland's very first purpose-built barracks.

Around 200 government soldiers could be garrisoned at Kilchurn. The barracks thus came in very useful during the major Jacobite Rebellions of 1715 (when John predictably hedged his bets by pledging allegiance to both government and rebels) and 1745. Officers were lodged in the tower house while other ranks had to make do with a barrack block built alongside the courtyard's northern wall. There were some home comforts though: the barracks were heated and had kitchens, as well as latrines that were flushed by rainwater, of which there was rarely a shortage.

When there were no further insurgencies to put down, Kilchurn fell out of use almost immediately. Within 30 years it was a ruin, its roof taken out by a lightning strike sometime before 1769. A quarter of a millennium later, it's astonishing that so much of the barracks is still intact.

As is so often the case with ancient castles, Kilchurn is said to harbour a resident ghost. Legend has it that a child was immured in some high part of the tower and that the unfortunate victim's plaintive cries can sometimes be heard. Given the castle's history, it would be rather more fitting if the phantom noises were those of a contented Campbell whistling a jig or of a Redcoat gently snoring, but the spirit world clearly abides by its own rules.

51 BURLEIGH CASTLE
MILNATHORT, PERTH & KINROSS

A castle whose romantic appearance is at odds with the love story connected with it

LOCATION
Burleigh Road, Milnathort, Perth & Kinross KY13 9SR

GRID REFERENCE
NO 128 045

PUBLIC TRANSPORT
For a relatively small place, Milnathort is well served by buses, with direct routes to and from Edinburgh, St Andrews, Perth, Dunfermline, Kinross, Abernethy and even

Inverness. The quickest direct bus from a railway station town runs from Dunfermline. The 56 (stagecoachbus.com; 01383 660880) takes 45 minutes to get to Milnathort. The castle is on the Burleigh Road, on the eastern outskirts of the small town.

WHEN TO VISIT
External access is open all year round. Internal access is permitted from April to

September daily 9.30am– 5.30pm (last entry 5pm) but please ring the phone number below in advance.

ADMISSION CHARGE
Free

WEBSITE
historicenvironment.scot (Historic Environment Scotland)

TELEPHONE
01241 878756

U sing the word 'romantic' is a deeply hackneyed way of describing castle ruins, but it must be said that some remnants of former strongholds *do* have more romance about them than others. In the case of Burleigh Castle, the romance shines out despite the uninspiring setting in which it now finds itself: a little grassy field on a kink of the A911 just outside a (sorry, good people of Milnathort) rather nondescript small town. But there may be something fitting in that, because the story with which Burleigh Castle is most closely associated is that of a romance gone very badly wrong.

The castle's story begins prosaically enough. The land on which the building stands came into the possession of Sir John Balfour of Balgarvie around 1445, having been granted to him by James II of Scotland. Balfour may have built a house here soon afterwards but it's not altogether certain. However, we do know that the current four-storey tower house was constructed by a later Balfour a good deal after that, in the late 15th or very early 16th century, either incorporating an earlier house or not, depending on whether Sir John got around to building himself a residence. It also had a garret floor (now mostly lost) at the top. This is known as the north tower and is the oldest part of the existing remains. The roofless edifice shares the same warm russet stone as the rest of the castle but is a no-nonsense rectangular affair, unadorned but for corbelling near the top and rounded bartizans (turrets overhanging the wall) at three corners, with a caphouse at the fourth. The wall-walk supported by the corbelling has long since disappeared.

Although nowadays access to the castle is from a gate to the east, if you want to travel back in time you'll have to imagine approaching from the western (Milnathort) side along a handsome avenue of trees. Beyond, on the castle's eastern and southern sides, you'll also have to conjure up a quadrangular courtyard within which were further smaller buildings protected by a perimeter barmkin wall (*barmkin* being an old Scots word for medieval defensive enclosures). If you look closely to the west of the tower

you'll notice a dip in the ground – this may be all that remains of a ditch or moat.

The castle's romance stems from the southwest tower, built in 1582. An inscription on the tower's north skew putt (a supporting stone at the foot of a gable) helpfully includes this date as well as the initials 'S.I.B. & M.B', a reference to husband and wife Sir James Balfour of Pittendreich and Margaret Balfour (who inherited Burleigh). The tower they constructed – which today almost bursts out onto the road – begins on a circular plan and is pierced with occasional gun loops. However, on the second floor, by some artful overhanging stonework at each corner, the tower becomes square. This gives it a rather playful look, as if someone has whimsically plopped a Wendy house on top of a small medieval keep. The tower is roofed and it's possible to explore it on requesting the entrance door's rather splendid key (see page 267).

There was once a whole range between the towers, probably three storeys high, but all that is left of these buildings now is the front wall and the fine arched entrance through it. The wall connects the two mismatched towers, which look rather awkward together. Indeed, if it weren't for the continuity of stone, one might be tempted to believe that they had originated from two completely different castles and had been fused together in an ill-judged experiment. But there's little

doubt that this odd-couple arrangement is also the source of the romance of Burleigh.

The castle passed peacefully down generations of Balfours for over two centuries, the main event during this time being the raising to the peerage of James and Margaret's son Michael, who became Lord Balfour of Burleigh and served as ambassador to the Duke of Tuscany and Lorraine. However, in 1707, the family's fortunes took an abrupt turn for the worse. Young Robert Balfour, son of the 4th Lord Balfour, had fallen in love with a servant girl. His horror-stricken father swiftly intervened, sending his son abroad in a bid to cure him of this inappropriate attachment. Robert swore that if his sweetheart married another in his absence he would smite the man down. The young woman in question (for reasons probably to do with the patriarchy, we don't know her name) married a schoolteacher from

Inverkeithing named Henry Stenhouse, apparently giving him fair warning of Robert Balfour's vow. Good to his word, when he came back from his travels, the young nobleman enquired after his beloved and, on discovering that she had married, rode over to Inverkeithing and calmly shot Stenhouse through the shoulder. On 21 April 1707, 12 days after the shooting, the schoolmaster died.

Balfour was arrested and tried for murder. Although he pleaded that he had not intended to kill Stenhouse but merely frighten him, he was found guilty. He would have been beheaded but for the success of a simple escape plan by which many a prisoner down through the ages has outwitted their gaoler. A few days before he was due to be executed, Robert's sister went to see him in his cell in Edinburgh Tolbooth. The two switched clothing and the condemned man slipped out disguised as his visitor. He is said to have returned to Burleigh for a while, hiding out in the hollow of an ash tree, before judiciously making off for the Continent.

When his father died in 1713, Robert became the 5th Lord Balfour. He returned to Scotland the following year. Now a keen Jacobite, he was an enthusiastic participant in the 1715 uprising. When this failed, he was attainted by parliament, an action that deprived him of his title, his property and his estates. He died in exile in France in 1757. He had neither paid with his life for the crime he had committed 50 years previously nor ever married. It wasn't until 1869 that the attainder was revoked and

Alexander Bruce became the 6th Lord Balfour of Burleigh.

The castle, meanwhile, was sold to a family by the name of Irwin and later to the Grahams of Kinross. It was partially dismantled – which accounts for those missing range buildings and others in the courtyard – and the stone taken away to build the nearby Burleigh House.

The ruins of the castle reputedly harbour a ghost. It's not, as one might think, the spectre of the raging lovelorn Robert Balfour but an apparition known as Grey Mary. If she does loiter about the castle precincts, nobody takes a great deal of notice, which seems a sage approach to such matters.

52 BROUGHTY CASTLE
BROUGHTY FERRY, DUNDEE

A spruce sentinel fit to guard the mouth of Scotland's longest river

LOCATION
Castle Approach, Broughty Ferry, Dundee DD5 2TF

GRID REFERENCE
NO 464 304

PUBLIC TRANSPORT
This is one of Scotland's more accessible castles. From Broughty Ferry railway station, just along the coast on the line from Dundee, it's less than a half-mile walk along suburban streets to the castle, which is on the waterfront.

WHEN TO VISIT
April to September Monday to Saturday 10am–4pm; Sunday 12.30–4pm; October to March Tuesday to Saturday 10am–4pm; Sunday 12.30–4pm.

ADMISSION CHARGE
Free

WEBSITE
historicenvironment.scot (Historic Environment Scotland)

TELEPHONE
01382 436916

roughty Castle is a rather unexpected treat. Travel out from the centre of Dundee along the main road that follows the broad River Tay towards its mouth and you'll pass mile after mile of the sort of suburban houses you might find in a hundred other towns around the country. Then, all of sudden, peering over the water beside the harbour at Broughty Ferry, you'll see a very neat and trim castle. As an added bonus, Broughty is no ruinous hulk but one of those rare fortresses that began life in the Middle Ages and was still active in defending its particular locality in the 20th century.

Five storeys high (including the garret at the top), the tower house that became Broughty Castle was constructed by Andrew Gray, the 2nd Lord Gray, between 1490 and 1496. However, the genesis of the stronghold can be traced back a little further, to 1454, when George Douglas, the 4th Earl of Angus, saw the makings of a good defensible position in this rocky promontory where the Tay meets the sea and had some fortifications built upon it.

It was in the following century that Gray's castle came to prominence. South of the border, Henry VIII had broken away from the Catholic Church in order to obtain a divorce from Catherine of Aragon. However, Scotland's James V had defied his uncle and kept faith with Rome. Henry duly organised a huge raid into Scotland in 1542 in a bid to change James's mind.

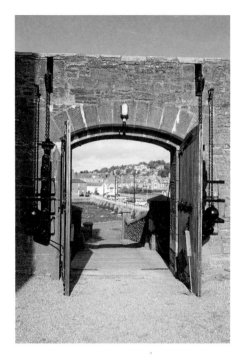

This led to what became known as the Rough Wooing (1543–51), one of the most notorious euphemisms invented for one country's attempt to impose its will on another by outright warfare. The English army arrived at the Tay in 1547 and rather than take the strategically important Broughty Castle by force or siege, simply purchased it from its owner, Lord Gray of Foulis. The Tay gave access not only to Dundee but also to the important city of St John's Toun (now Perth), the town of Dunkeld and a host of other settlements. To have possession of Broughty Castle was to control shipping between all the Tay communities and the sea. It was the

English garrison that improved the defences of the fortress by digging a ditch on its landward side. Foulis was later pardoned for what some understandably interpreted as treason.

On 22 November 1547, the Earl of Argyll attempted to wrest control of the castle, but the garrison held firm. He failed again in January the following year, the Scottish force of 150 men led by Duncan Dundas proving incapable of dislodging the 100 or so soldiers and three gun ships defending Broughty. It was only in 1550 that the castle finally succumbed. Following a siege, on 6 February an assault on the fortress by the French (Scotland's ally in the war) was led by Paul de Thermes. He lost 50 men, with another 240 wounded, yet still the castle did not fall until six days later when its defenders surrendered and its commander, John Luttrell, was taken hostage.

In stark contrast to this testament to Broughty's merit as a stronghold, the castle's role in the Wars of the Three Kingdoms (the conflict formerly known as the English Civil War) can be justifiably characterised as ignominious. When General Monck and his Roundhead army approached in 1651, the Royalist garrison took to their heels and fled, apparently without firing a shot.

The castle was sold off in 1666, an event that heralded a long hiatus in its history. For 180 years it gently mouldered

until, in 1846, it was taken on by some very unlikely buyers. The year before, the Edinburgh and Northern Railway Company had been given the go-ahead to establish a line from Edinburgh to Perth and Dundee. They bought Broughty Castle and the land around it in order to build a harbour for their revolutionary railway/ferry service. Their ferries had rails on them, allowing wagons to roll straight onto them and then back onto the railway once the far shore of the Tay had been reached, a system that worked very well. Though it no longer operates, there's still a railway station (Broughty Ferry) nearby and the harbour itself still exists.

In 1855, the castle was sold off to the War Office, which was getting jittery about a possible invasion up the Tay by the Russians. However, no guns were installed and, with the Crimean War ending the

following year, these fears melted away. By 1860 a new threat had surfaced: this time it was the possibility of a French invasion by Napoleon III. This was clearly perceived as a more probable event (the French would certainly have had a shorter distance to come) because this time the castle was greatly strengthened. Evidence of the re-fortification can be seen outside: three 40-pounder rifled breach-loading guns made sometime around 1859–66 and rare survivors of their type. They had actually been half buried in the ground at Broughty Ferry pier to serve as bollards and it was only when an astute visitor came by in 1989 and recognised them for what they were that they were unearthed and put on display.

The castle was further adapted in 1186–87, with a range built to the east providing accommodation for volunteer submarine miners. These were men charged with laying mines in the River Tay in the event of an enemy attack over the water. A couple of years later, a magazine was added and the gun emplacements remodelled. In World War I, further adaptations were made as the castle stood guard against German naval vessels. The most recent tweak was made in World War II, when a defence post was installed at the top of the tower.

Today, when the sun shines, the castle gleams in hues of burnished gold. The tower stands aloft, protected still by the

Tay, a walled courtyard, gun emplacements and a series of gun loops in the walls. In 1969, however, Broughty Castle was given a well-deserved retirement from its defence of Scotland's longest river and was converted into a museum. A narrow spiral staircase leads up to a ticket office, shop and galleries. The opening room offers scale models and locally sourced artefacts that tell the story of the Broughty area. In other galleries visitors can marvel at a fragment of a mammoth's tusk; a range of taxidermically preserved wild animals; and a good deal of local weaponry, including muskets from different periods and a fine early medieval battle axe. Space has also been found for a selection from the Orchar Collection which comprises more than 300 artworks accumulated by 19th-century Dundee businessman James Guthrie Orchar.

An added bonus for the visitor who makes it up to the top floor is a small white room – the World War II defence post – from whose high windows views can be enjoyed to the southeast across the mouth of the Tay to Tentsmuir Forest; to the west towards Dundee and the famous Tay bridges; and to the east along the sandy beach that comes right up to the castle mound – this last making for an excellent post-visit saunter.

53 EDZELL CASTLE

EDZELL, ANGUS

A fortified residence with formal gardens that are a joy to visit

LOCATION
Edzell, by Brechin, Angus
DD9 7UE

GRID REFERENCE
NO 584 691

PUBLIC TRANSPORT
Laurencekirk in
Aberdeenshire is the nearest
railway station to Edzell but
unless you want to walk or
cycle the 11 miles, you'll
have to travel instead to
Montrose on the line
between Dundee and
Aberdeen. From Montrose
High Street take the 39 bus

to Stracathro Hospital (by
the porter's lodge) where
you can change to the 21
bus (both stagecoachbus.
com; 01382 313700) which
will take you to the Tuck Inn
(ho ho) on Edzell High
Street. Stroll back along the
High Street and turn left into
Lethnot Road. Walk for
about 0.8 miles and you'll
come to the entrance to
Edzell Castle on your right.

WHEN TO VISIT
April to September daily
9.30am–5.30pm;
October daily 10am–4pm.

NB Children under the age
of 16 must be accompanied
by an adult.

ADMISSION CHARGE
Yes

WEBSITE
historicenvironment.scot
(Historic Environment
Scotland)

TELEPHONE
01356 648631

 to have been a Lindsay of
Edzell. The family has gone
down in history as being
lichtsome, a word perhaps best translated
in English as 'carefree' or 'blithe'. This
is all the more remarkable because they
lived at a time and place when to be free
of care was an almost unknown pleasure.
Scotland in the Middle Ages was a place
of feuds, upheaval, uncertainty and
violence, which are not the most
promising conditions in which to nurture
peace of mind, a full stomach or a long
life. Sadly, the times eventually took

their toll on the lichtsome Lindsays.
The potted history of the family provided
by Historic Environment Scotland, in
whose care Edzell Castle now rests, goes
on to describe them as also 'turbulent
and tragic'.

It's ironic then that their lasting legacy
has been a wonderful formal garden
known as the Pleasance, a monument
far more impressive than the fragment
of their modest castle that remains. And
yet without the castle there would be no
garden, so it's only right to celebrate
them both.

Edzell Castle stands at the foot of the Hill of Edzell, between the rivers West Water and North Esk. Little remains of the first fortress built to defend this potential gateway into the Highlands. That was thrown up in the 1100s as a motte-and-bailey affair and was made of timber. The Crawford Lindsays bought it up around the middle of the 14th century but it wasn't until the 1520s that they started work on a stone castle close by to replace it. They built what is known as the Tower House, with extensions to it coming along in later decades. The fabulous walled garden was added in 1604 by David, Lord Edzell. Though called a castle, it never amounted

to much more than a fortified residence, though it was considered grand enough for Mary, Queen of Scots to pay a visit in 1562 (when David would have been just 11 or 12, though by then he had already been laird of Edzell for four years). Her son, James VI of Scotland (later also James I of England), stayed twice. Such visits, while a great honour, were a burden financially – putting up a monarch and entourage was not something one could do on the cheap.

Should you pay a visit yourself (the cost is now borne by the guest rather than the host but is rather more reasonable than of old), you'll first notice the simple L-shaped Tower House, the vivid pink of its

red sandstone walls providing a contrast to the lush parkland and verdant farmland by which the castle is surrounded. Further rooms for the family are ranged along a courtyard in a less imposing building built on Sir David's orders.

Do have a look at the Summer House too. It was created at the same time as the garden so that the family and their guests might enjoy a banquet and perhaps some *al fresco* entertainment away from the confines of the main house. Behind there lies the large sumptuous garden with its 12ft-high walls on three sides and a lower wall on the other, forming an enclosed space full of the geometrical joys of a formal parterre garden.

Unique joys as it happens, since the three high walls are ornamented with a combination of stone reliefs you'll not see in another garden anywhere. One wall is devoted to depictions of the seven cardinal virtues, another shows the seven planetary deities, while the third is concerned with the seven liberal arts. They were copied from prints that Sir David had brought back from Germany, one of the many countries he visited on educational tours.

This last wall is a celebration of the Renaissance – the arts in question being Arithmetica, Astronomia, Dialectica, Geometria, Grammatica, Musica and Rhetorica. These encompass the whole gamut of liberal education in the great universities of Europe in the early 17th century. The panel portraying Astronomia has sadly vanished, but the other six are still in situ. The seven planetary deities can be viewed in the Summer House (where they are kept to protect them from the damaging effects of the weather).

The seven virtues – rather less well known than the seven deadly sins – are Charity, Faith, Fortitude, Hope, Justice, Prudence and Temperance. If they do not seem quite as well executed as the other panels, that may be because David Lindsay had rather overstretched himself, fiscally speaking, what with the garden and the Summer House (and a bath house too). There's every chance he had commissioned a lesser craftsman to knock these seven off at a bargain rate just so he could get the garden finished. He died in 1610, so did not have long to enjoy the fruits of his expenditure. It's said that in the midst of life we are in debt and that was certainly true of his surviving family, who were bequeathed a wonderful garden and attendant buildings, but were plunged deep into the red at the same time.

It's surprising that the Lindsays managed to hold things together for another century or so. Eventually, though, their fortunes took a fatal turn for the worse and they were forced to sell Edzell Castle in 1715, that most momentous of dates in Scottish history. The man they sold it to, the Earl of Panmure, joined the first Jacobite Rebellion that year and before he had even had time to change the wallpaper, Edzell had been confiscated from him as a punishment for his supposed treachery. It was to be the undoing of the castle and marked the beginning of its decline into ruination. The estate fell into the hands of the York Buildings Company, a sort of 18th-century asset stripper which went bankrupt about 50 years later. Pretty much everything of value was then ripped out and sold on behalf of the company's creditors.

Thankfully, the property was handed to His Majesty's Office of Works in the 1930s and the Pleasance was returned to the splendour it enjoyed under the lichtsome family that created it. To see it at its best, drop by in early July, when the bedding plants are in full bloom. Listen closely and perhaps you'll even hear a spectral Lindsay give an approving sniff of the floral scents wafting through the air.

54 BRAEMAR CASTLE
BRAEMAR, ABERDEENSHIRE

A tower house that became a homely residence caught up in a 20th-century scandal

LOCATION
Braemar, Aberdeenshire
AB35 5XR

GRID REFERENCE
NO 156 923

PUBLIC TRANSPORT
Braemar is pretty much
equidistant from Perth,
Dundee, Aberdeen and
Inverness, all of which are
around 45–50 miles away as
the crow flies. Pitch up at
Aberdeen and you can pick
up a direct bus to Braemar
– the bi-hourly 201
(stagecoachbus.com; 01224
591381) from Union Square
bus station takes just under
two and a half hours. The
castle is about 0.75 miles
northeast of the town on
the A93.

WHEN TO VISIT
April to June and September
and October Wednesday
to Sunday 10am–5pm;
July and August daily
10am–5pm. Guided tours
can be organised for
groups up to 40 on any
day from April to October.
NB All rooms accessed by a
steep spiral staircase with a
rope handrail.

ADMISSION CHARGE
Yes

WEBSITE
braemarcastle.co.uk

TELEPHONE
013397 41219

As infants go, there can be few in Scottish history as divisive as wee James VI. He'd only just made his first birthday when he became king, splitting Scotland decisively into two camps: those who supported the mewling monarch and those who pledged themselves to his rival, Mary, Queen of Scots. As can be seen in the case of Sir Adam Gordon at Auchindoun Castle (page 294), the rift caused endless trouble and not a few violent deaths. And the man who had Braemar Castle built had been right at the epicentre of the conflict.

As a very young man, John Erskine, the 2nd Earl of Mar, had been the guardian of the young King James. At least, the king had been his nominal ward, the real power lying with the regent, James Douglas, 4th Earl of Morton. When Morton was arrested, Erskine's star fell with him. The construction of Braemar Castle came at the other end of the Earl of Mar's life. In 1628, he would have been around 70 (the precise year of his birth is unknown) and he had just six years to live. By then he had been Lord High Treasurer of Scotland for 13 years and was by no means a pauper. Desirous of a stronghold (and a handy hunting lodge), he ordered what was then called Mar Castle to be erected on high ground above the River Dee, just

outside the twin hamlets of Auchendryne and Castleton – now the village of Braemar. This effectively kept an eye on a number of key transport routes and today it guards another, the A93 (the Old Military Road).

This version of Mar Castle did not last long. In 1689, just 61 years after its construction, John Farquharson of Inverey (otherwise known as the Black Colonel) set fire to the fortress, severely damaging it. The cause was a dispute over another king called James. Farquharson was a Jacobite – a backer of the deposed James VII, who was a Catholic. Charles Erskine, the 5th Earl of Mar and then owner of the castle, had thrown in his lot with the Protestant William III, who had gained the English throne in the so-called Glorious Revolution the year before. What particularly provoked Farquharson's ire was that the Earl of Mar had given his assent to the castle being used to garrison government troops sent north to deal with the 1689 Jacobite Uprising. The destruction of the stronghold stopped this plan in its tracks.

Two Jacobite Rebellions (1715 and 1745) later, Mar Castle was still a ruin, though by now it had been bought by the Farquharson family who had previously destroyed it. John Farquharson leased the derelict building to the government in 1748. In a bid to forestall future rebellions by the restless Highlanders, the army set about reconstruction work and soon had it

fitted out as a barracks with its own protective star-like curtain wall. Step into the dining room or drawing room of the current castle and you'll be able to see graffiti from this period etched in wonderful copperplate lettering.

In 1831, with the threat of further uprising a receding memory, the castle was returned to the Farquharson family, who set about transforming it into a family home. Various innovations came and went, including a ballroom which was attached to the side of the castle and had disappeared by the end of the 19th century. It was only relatively recently, in the early years of the 20th century, that the building became known as Braemar Castle. By then its association with the Earls of Mar had long since ceased and the castle was being leased out again. However, this was not such a downturn in fortunes as might be supposed, because one of its tenants was a member of the Russian royal family, Princess Alexis Dolgouthi. A later occupant of somewhat greater notoriety was John Profumo, who lived in the castle in 1960, along with his wife Valerie. A year later he would embark on the ill-fated affair with the 19-year-old Christine Keeler that would end in scandal and the abrupt termination of his political career.

The castle closed to visitors in 2005 but two years later was leased to the people of Braemar for 50 years and is now not only open again but is the sole community-run castle in Scotland. An enterprising million-pound fundraising effort to carry out the restoration and conservation of the castle is currently afoot. Various repairs have already been made and a 19th-century wing that was something of an eyesore has been removed.

The castle you can visit today is an amalgam of an exterior that largely harks back to the original tower built by John Erskine in 1628 and the remodelling carried out by the army after 1748, combined with an interior that reflects the comfortable home the castle became in later years. The many small domestic objects that adorn the dozen or so rooms that are open to the public give the place an undeniably homely feel that is rare in such tower houses. One can easily imagine the occupants leaving their four-poster beds in the morning to take breakfast in the dining room before seeing to the morning's correspondence in the laird's day room. Indeed, the kitchen, with its very small range on which to cook and little table shoved in a corner, seems suspiciously humble for its setting.

There's also an attempt to bathe in the reflected glory emanating from Robert Louis Stevenson: a small display centres on his bestseller *Treasure Island*, whose early chapters were written while the author was holidaying in Braemar.

Meanwhile, aspiring geologists may find the exhibition of the Farquharson mineral collection to be of interest.

Only one interior feature harks back to the more troubled times in the castle's history. Visitors can still see the entrance to the dungeon which, in the *oubliette* style, is a shaft down which prisoners were dumped. The tiny space below is said to have held 17 inmates at one point in the stronghold's first incarnation, which cannot have been anything but unpleasant. Still, every good castle should have *something* to send a shiver up the spine.

55 CRAIGIEVAR CASTLE
NR ALFORD, ABERDEENSHIRE

A flight of fancy that went on to become seriously engaged in warfare

LOCATION
Alford, Aberdeenshire
AB33 8JF

GRID REFERENCE
NJ 566 095

PUBLIC TRANSPORT
Unfortunately, Craigievar is not well served by public transport. From Aberdeen, it's possible to take the hourly 202 bus (stagecoachbus.com; 01224 591381) to the village of Lumphanan from where it's just under 5 miles to the castle but with no onward bus. The small town of Alford, which is served by half a dozen bus routes, is about 7 miles from Craigievar.

WHEN TO VISIT
April to June Friday to Tuesday 10.30am–5pm (last entry/tour 4pm); July to September daily 10.30am–5pm (last entry/tour 4pm); October to March access by (non-bookable) guided tour only, maximum of 10 people per tour. Tours run approximately every 30 minutes. Grounds open daily all year from dawn to dusk.

ADMISSION CHARGE
Yes (free to National Trust for Scotland members)

WEBSITE
nts.org.uk (National Trust for Scotland)

TELEPHONE
01339 883635

There's something thrilling about a castle that can dress itself in a hue that, depending on the light, might be coral or might simply be pastel pink, and just brazen it out. After all, these are not generally the colours associated with warfare in Britain or likely to fill an enemy with dread. But this is not a castle in the usual sense of the word. Sitting at the end of a long tree-lined drive, and many miles from a town of any size at all, Craigievar is not only a splendid fairytale-like fortress in the best traditions of Disney, it's also a tranquil retreat, the sort of place you wouldn't mind holing up in for the winter with a plentiful supply of firewood and stock of good books.

It also happens to be the best preserved and arguably the most important tower house in the whole of Scotland. And although it was never intended for military use (despite the impression given by the weaponry on display), in later life its owners did play their part in both World Wars, including raising an entire battalion of the Black Watch at the personal request of Lord Kitchener.

No one knows exactly when John Mortimer of Craigievar built his castle in

the wilds of Aberdeenshire but it would have been sometime between 1575 and 1595. He had been elevated to the title of baron, and doubtless he felt that a grand tower house was just what he needed to cement his new-found status. He evidently didn't stint on the building work because the majority of Craigievar that exists today – the first four storeys – was his doing. Only the turrets and the other fancy trimmings of the upper storeys were built by a later hand.

But it's something you can't see from the outside that perhaps tells us most about the times in which John Mortimer lived. A Catholic living after the Reformation, he had a chapel installed at one end of the castle's main hall but ensured that there should be no exterior indication of its existence.

In the early 1600s, Craigievar was purchased by one William Forbes, a wealthy merchant and son of the bishop of Aberdeen. His work had allowed him to see something of the Continent – particularly the lands abutting the Baltic Sea – and inspired by the architecture he had seen, he tore down the castle's uppermost storeys and replaced them with the confection of conicle-roofed turrets and viewing platforms that give Craigievar its other-worldly character. Henceforth the

tower house would carry off a pleasing impersonation of a defensible castle without ever imagining itself to be so.

Forbes was also responsible for introducing moulded plaster ceilings – making them among the earliest examples in Scotland – and decorating one with the images of Roman emperors, a knowing nod to the Renaissance. It was his grandson, 'Red' Sir John, who endowed the castle with his rather curious if eminently sensible motto: 'Doe not vaken sleiping dogs.' An oak roundel carved with this appeal to caution and his coat of arms can be seen in the hall.

The castle passed down through the Forbes family for generations, with the exterior of the building remaining relatively unchanged but for the blocking up of some windows to reduce the amount of window tax levied. Another William Forbes, who inherited the castle in 1773, found his meagre income did not stretch to the upkeep of such a fine residence and, on his death, handed on a mountain of debt to his son Arthur, who had already managed to accrue even larger debts himself, imagining he could pay them off with his inheritance. The castle suffered as a result, with maintenance kept to a bare minimum or foregone altogether.

Arthur had the good sense to die young, in 1823, leaving his younger brother John to clear up the mess. John Forbes returned to Aberdeenshire from

India, where he had been a judge, and employed a local architect called John Smith to undertake a thorough review of the castle and what needed to be done to put matters back on an even keel. Smith was something of a visionary and was instrumental in changing the way Scottish baronial houses were viewed. The mark he made on Craigievar can still be seen to this day: he recommended that the building's harl (the Scottish term for a lime-based plaster), which was then off-white, should instead 'match the colour of the granite mouldings'. These were a very pale pink, so two pigments were added to the harl to replicate their colour.

Queen Victoria clearly approved, because when staying at Balmoral she visited the castle twice, bringing with her a clutch of European monarchs (the Craigievar visitors' book for 1848–1908 is quite the document). The queen wrote about her first excursion in a journal entry for 18 June 1879:

> ...*Craigievar is a strange and curious old castle, consisting of one large square tower with small turrets at the corners, and is very old indeed. It is still inhabited, but there is no one there just now. Got out and went into some of the curious small low rooms with old furniture in them, as well as the Dining Hall which has a vaulted roof. There is only one steep cork screw staircase. At first no one knew who we were, but it gradually dawned upon them.*

Her description of the castle stands as true today as it did then. A visit to Craigievar is a trip into the past, but a past that is wont to slide endearingly about from one era to another as you go from room to room. The over-arching impression, however, is of a real home. By usual stately home standards, one could describe most rooms as being on the pokey side. Even the high-ceilinged hall, the largest public room, feels relatively cosy with its long fireplace and unaffected (albeit tartan-upholstered) sofa and chairs. Each floor is connected to the next by the same narrow spiral staircase climbed by Victoria and which evidently made the movement of furniture in or out of the castle a nightmare.

The fact that Craigievar is now in the hands of the National Trust for Scotland (NTS) tells a story about 20th-century Britain. The last of the Forbes dynasty – yet another William (and also the 19th Lord Sempill) – was prohibited by the terms of his inheritance to pass the castle on to a daughter. His first wife gave birth to two girls but no boys before she died. His second wife produced three further daughters but no sons. With the castle's future in jeopardy, three years before her husband's death in 1965, Lady Sempill approached the NTS. Happily, she was able to persuade the organisation to buy the castle and thus ensure that the building, along with its contents and grounds, could be enjoyed by the public in perpetuity.

56 AUCHINDOUN CASTLE
NR DUFFTOWN, MORAY

A dark and grim castle associated with an even darker grimmer deed

LOCATION
2 miles south of
Dufftown on the A941,
Moray AB55 4DR

GRID REFERENCE
NJ 348 374

PUBLIC TRANSPORT
From the mainline railway
station at Keith, you can
walk into town to take

Britain's most northerly
heritage railway line, the
Keith & Dufftown Railway
(keith-dufftown-railway.
co.uk; 01542 882123 –
operating days only) to
Dufftown. The castle is
then about 2 miles to
the southeast

WHEN TO VISIT
Open at any reasonable time

ADMISSION CHARGE
Free

WEBSITE
historicenvironment.scot
(Historic Environment
Scotland)

TELEPHONE
0131 668 8600

here's something rather
ghoulish about the ruins of
Auchindoun Castle. They stand
alone on a low grassy knoll, surrounded by
a high stone wall, and though there is a
great deal left of the stronghold's single
tower, one side appears to have melted
away as if it had been made of plastic and
set on fire, leaving all the innards on show.
As a result, a visit to the castle feels not
unlike entering a coffin in which a skinless
corpse lies mouldering with all its entrails
visible. It's all rather unsettling.

As it happens, the reason why
Auchindoun ended up in its current
sorry state may well be more macabre
still. And as is so often the case with
Scottish clans, it involves a bitter and
senseless feud.

But we're getting ahead of ourselves.
First we much reach the castle, which
guards an obscure stretch of the River
Fiddich, two miles from the nearest
settlement of any note, the small
community at Dufftown. The track to the
stronghold from the A941 dwindles to a
pathway by a farmhouse (evidently built
with stone filched from the castle), before
at last disappearing into a field. The visitor
must climb a slope, first passing a spring.
The castle had its own well, which one
assumes drew water from the same
subterranean source that surfaces here.

The wall towering above you at this
point almost entirely encircles the castle
and is held upright by a series of stout
buttresses. However, before you arrive at
them, you must first pass through an

impressive defensive ditch. This is all that remains of an Iron Age fort raised up about 2,000 years ago, taking advantage of a position that is both high above the river and also controls one of the major routes between Aberdeenshire and Speyside. An archway in the wall gives access to the grim ruins within.

The current state of the castle constitutes quite a fall from grace. In its heyday it would have served not only as a safe haven but also as a comfortable residence. It was built around 1470, probably by one Thomas Cochrane, for John Stewart, the youngest son of James II of Scotland. Cochrane was a highly skilled mason who found himself much in demand and the subject of a good deal of royal patronage.

By the early 16th century, the castle was in the hands of the Ogilvy family but, in 1567, Auchindoun was bought by Sir Adam Gordon. It was this transaction that would eventually be the castle's undoing.

Gordon was keen for Mary, Queen of Scots to accede to the throne, a view that put him at loggerheads with supporters of James VI. At the grand old age of 13 months, James had become king of Scotland in the same year Gordon purchased Auchindoun, and he would go on to be crowned James I of England. Notable backers of the infant monarch

included John Forbes of Towie, who lived at Corgarff Castle, about 20 miles from Auchindoun. Aside from this difference of opinion, the Forbes and the Gordons had sustained a long-running feud over more personal matters.

One November day, four years after moving into Auchindoun, Gordon and his men paid the Forbes family a visit. The male adults in the household were away (it's not clear whether Gordon knew this in advance or not) but Margaret Forbes, John's wife, responded to Gordon's demand for her to surrender Corgarff by aiming a shot at the aggressors with a pistol, hitting one of them in the knee. Gordon duly had his men light faggots of wood and place them at the foot of the garderobe (toilet) shafts. This was either to smoke the occupants out, or to set fire to the building. Whatever his intentions were, the modest tower house burnt down, killing all 24 women and children within its walls. Not for nothing did Sir Adam Gordon of Auchindoun gain the moniker 'the Herod of the North'.

Depending on whose version of events you choose to believe, the sacking and burning of Auchindoun Castle in 1591 was either a delayed act of vengeance against Sir Adam for this heinous crime or on account of an entirely unrelated dispute. Feuds being what they were in those days, there was never any shortage

of resentments, so the latter is certainly a possibility. What is known is that William Mackintosh and his entourage attacked and set fire to Auchindoun, badly damaging it.

The following year, Mackintosh is said to have been seized with remorse for his deed and to have presented himself at Gordon's residence at Gight to make amends. Sir Adam was not at home but his wife, Henrietta, admitted the penitent. In a show of contrition, Mackintosh laid his head down on a block on which cattle were butchered. Henrietta apparently surprised him by ordering her cook to chop his head off there and then. The tale is told in a ballad entitled *Turn Willie Mackintosh*, while the Corgarff massacre is commemorated by the ballad *Edom O'Gordon*.

That was not quite the end of the story for Auchindoun. Three years after the attack, the castle passed back into the hands of the Ogilvy family. The damage was made good and Auchindoun became habitable once more. It is not clear when its final demise came about but we do know that by 1725 it had been abandoned. Given the length of time that has passed since, it's remarkable how much of the castle remains. The scars it bears today also seem to convey an essence of the deeply unpleasant episode with which it will be forever associated.

57 DUNSCAITH CASTLE
NR TOKAVAIG, ISLE OF SKYE

A once important clan seat that became the epicentre of a MacDonald vs MacLeod feud

LOCATION
Nr Tokavaig, Isle of Skye,
Highland IV44 8QL

GRID REFERENCE
NG 595 120

PUBLIC TRANSPORT
Dunscaith Castle is
refreshingly tricky to get at.
The simplest way is by
taking the ferry (calmac.co.
uk; 0800 066 5000) from

Mallaig (at the end of the
very fetching West Highland
railway line) to Armadale
then hopping on the
somewhat infrequent 52 bus
(stagecoachbus.com; 01478
613671) to Tokavaig Road
End just past Teangue. From
there, it's 7 miles up the
Tokavaig road to where a
signed farm track heads off
towards the castle about
600yds away.

WHEN TO VISIT
Open at any reasonable time

ADMISSION CHARGE
Free

WEBSITE
n/a

TELEPHONE
n/a

O n the northern coast of the
Sleat Peninsula in southwest
Skye lie the scant but
unarguably dramatic remains of a very
ancient castle. In its day, Dunscaith
(pronounced Dun-scath) must have been
quite the place. Filling a diminutive
headland that eons of battering by the
wind and the sea had begun to wrench
away from the mainland, it is protected
by a stony man-made gully on the
landward side and by low but hazardous
cliffs dropping into the water everywhere
else. This must have given some sense
of security to anyone harboured within
its walls, though history informs us that
its location by no means made the castle
impregnable. There's no denying that its

occupiers enjoyed a glorious view
though (at least in those seemingly rare
moments when the clouds allow it).
From Dunscaith it's possible to gaze
across Loch Eishort all the way to Skye's
magnificent Cuillin mountains.

The advantages of this site were
apparent before even Clan MacDonald of
Sleat got around to building a castle here
in the 1300s, for there is evidence of an
earlier fort of unknown antiquity on the
same spot. Norse rule over the island had
ended as recently as 1266 and the tectonic
plates of power had yet to settle down.
Dunscaith (*Dun Sgathaich* in Gaelic) did not
stay in MacDonald hands for long. Before
the 14th century was over, it had been
snatched from them by the MacLeods and

then held for a short time by the MacAskills, the so-called clan sept or junior partner in an alliance with the MacLeods. The MacAskills had aided in the capture of Dunscaith and had been rewarded by the MacLeods with a large swathe of land.

In 1395 and 1401, the MacDonalds made unsuccessful attempts to wrest control of Dunscaith from their foes. Channelling the spirit of Robert the Bruce, they tried again a few years later and regained their lost possession at last. It would become one of their principal seats, along with Armadale Castle, on Sleat's southern coast, and Duntulm Castle (page 303), far away on Skye's northern shore. That's not to say it was a particularly safe

seat, though. In 1431, the castle caught the gimlet eye of James I of Scotland. In order to assert his authority as monarch, he had engaged in a number of pre-emptive actions against the nation's more dominant clans. Now it was the turn of the powerful MacDonalds to be sent a message and the king's forces besieged then captured Dunscaith. However, in order to show that he could be a magnanimous ruler, he allowed the clan to hold onto the castle.

Dunscaith successfully resisted a further siege by the MacLeods in 1515 and from then on appears to have lived a more or less peaceful existence before eventually being abandoned a century later. By then, its major shortcoming had

become problematic: by dint of its location it was simply impossible to enlarge or improve in any substantive way. The MacDonalds took themselves off, finding lodgings in more commodious accommodation at Duntulm.

It should be said that crossing the gully to enter the castle itself is a precarious business and not to be recommended. The central portion of the drawbridge has disappeared (only its pivot holes remain), leaving only narrow stone ledges both sides and a drop between them that is long enough to break bones. Beyond it, a short set of steps leads up and into the remains of the castle. The sheep that make the perilous journey across the bridge have grazed the greater parts of the compact space inside the perimeter of the fortress but elsewhere Nature has had her way, mostly in the form of nettles. Below, in the sea loch, lies Eilean Ruairidh Mòr, a narrow island where, in antiquity, stood a very small fort.

An artist's impression of the castle in its heyday shows it high-walled and battlemented with a small gatehouse at the top of the steps that lead from the bridge. If accurate, then Dunscaith was a tidy little fortress that utilised more or less every square inch of serviceable ground on the summit of its pocket-sized promontory. Nowadays, a good deal of imagination has to be exercised to bring that vision back to life.

Some of the most intact sections can be found at the entrance to the castle where the bridge, for all its deficiencies, is quite remarkably well preserved. Dunscaith's curtain wall was around 5ft thick and some small stretches of this are also in evidence beyond the entrance. They seem of very rough and ready construction but must actually have been built with some care because they constitute some of Skye's oldest surviving lime-mortared walls. To create them, workers fashioned a hollow wall with large unfinished stones, filling in the gap with small pieces of whatever bits of rubble were available nearby. A mortar made from lime was then used to fix the stones together, thus strengthening the wall.

In one corner of the castle, a few steps from a spiral staircase are still in situ. These would have led up a tower to a defensive walkway along a parapet. Meanwhile, in the courtyard, there is a very obvious well – a crucial feature in times of siege. The rest is an assortment of lumps and mounds which are all that remain of the castle's interior buildings. Despite the beauty of the surroundings, there's a certain sadness to the scene – a once important stronghold reduced to a few pitiful stumps that no self-respecting ghost would bring itself to haunt.

Of course, it wouldn't be a proper Scottish castle without having some legend or other attached to it. In Dunscaith's case, there are several. The two most oft-recounted are that a witch enabled builders to construct the castle in just one night; and that it was the site of the fabled School for Heroes. This unorthodox academy was said to be run by a Celtic queen called Scáthach ('Shadow' in English) who was an expert warrior and trained would-be heroes in the martial arts. Her most famous alumnus was the Irishman Cú Chulainn, after whom the Cuillin Hills may or may not be named (there's some debate about it). Cú Chulainn was the god Lugh in human form, and also his own father, so probably made for quite an interesting pupil. The name of his teacher, Scáthach, lives on in the name of the castle: Dun Sgathaich (Fortress of Shadows).

58 DUNTULM CASTLE
DUNTULM, ISLE OF SKYE

The sister castle to Dunscaith has proved a popular haunt for wailing apparitions

LOCATION
Kilmaluag, Isle of Skye,
Highland IV51 9UF

GRID REFERENCE
NG 409 743

PUBLIC TRANSPORT
After arriving at Kyle of
Lochalsh railway station, the
eponymous terminus of an
extremely picturesque line,
make your way to the
nearby harbour slipway to
pick up the 916 coach
(citylink.co.uk; 0141 352
4444) to Uig Pier. From
there, a 57C bus
(stagecoachbus.com; 01478
613671) will take you all the
way to Duntulm at the far
end of Skye.

WHEN TO VISIT
Open at any reasonable hour

ADMISSION CHARGE
Free

WEBSITE
n/a

TELEPHONE
n/a

here are several similarities between sister castles Duntulm and Dunscaith (page 298). The two former seats of the chiefs of the MacDonalds of Sleat may be divided by the Cuillin mountains and the best part of 50 miles of rugged Skye countryside (and rather more than that by road) but the two share more kinship than is rendered to them by their clan bond alone. For instance, they both came into being during the 14th century; they both occupy exposed promontories overlooking a tiny island; they were both heavily involved in the interminable feud between the MacDonalds and the MacLeods; they're both defended by cliffs on three sides and a deep ditch on the landward side; and they're both the subject of a plethora of unlikely tales. Where the two diverge

rather dramatically is on the question of remains: while Dunscaith has crumbled away to a few scattered fragments, enough endures of Duntulm to envisage the proud fortress it once was.

Situated on the Trotternish Peninsula's northwestern edge, just a few miles from the most northerly point of Skye, Duntulm is slightly closer to the Western Isles than it is to the Scottish mainland. It was constructed in the 1300s – probably by the MacLeods while they were at loggerheads with the MacDonalds of Sleat. Although no evidence has been found for an earlier building, it is thought that there had previously been a broch – a very basic prehistoric stone tower – on this site. The first written evidence of the current castle is a record of a visit by James V. He dropped by in 1540 and evidently enjoyed himself because he spoke favourably of the reception he had received and the robustness of the castle's defences.

An attempt to put an end to the MacLeod/MacDonald feud was made in 1618 when the Privy Council drew up a charter confirming that the latter clan had the rights to the castle and land around it. The document also reveals that the castle was in some state of disrepair because it compelled Donald Gorm Og MacDonald to make the fortress good again (and to agree to live in it – his seat at the time was at Dunscaith). The 1st Baronet of Sleat and 9th chief of the Donald clan added a second tower for good measure. Around 30 years later some sort of house or great hall was constructed in the courtyard. This and other improvements ushered in a golden age for the castle.

The MacDonalds' uncontested dominance in Trotternish proved to be Duntulm's downfall. It was only around 80 years later, in 1730, that the castle was abandoned. Sir Alexander MacDonald built himself a fine new mansion called Monkstadt House about five miles to the southwest (incidentally very close to the spot where Bonnie Prince Charlie would land in 1746 when he sailed 'over the sea to Skye'). Monkstadt was reputedly Skye's first residence to sport a slate roof. It was also built with a great deal of stone taken from Duntulm. The mansion is a ruin nowadays, though some of the estate has

survived, with one of the original barns now being let as a holiday cottage.

From the road at Duntulm, it's a very pleasant stroll across pasture to the castle, with views across the Minch towards the Western Isles. Just in front of the ruin stands a modern cairn dedicated to the memory of the MacArthur clan, who served as pipers to the MacDonalds during the 18th century. As for the castle itself, its courtyard is surprisingly undulating. The majority of what can be seen dates from the 15th century, including vaults at the foot of what was once the main four-storey tower and some large sections of outer wall. From the 17th century, there are the remnants of the second tower as well as the rectangular house.

Until relatively recently, there used to be a good deal more of Duntulm than this. In a photograph taken of the castle in the late 19th century, a substantial amount of the main tower is still standing. Time and the elements have done their worst, with major collapses occurring in the 1980s, followed by Donald Gorm Og MacDonald's tower falling down in 1990. Of which, it should be noted that there are two signs on the path to the castle that state: 'This site is structurally unstable. For your safety you are requested not to proceed beyond the castle fence line' – so a visit is very much at your own risk. Furthermore, the cliffs at Duntulm are a great deal higher than those at Dunscaith

and great care should be taken not to wander too close to the edge, particularly in or after wet weather.

Apparently, the cliffs aren't the only scary things at Duntulm – there are tales of at least three ghosts haunting the ruins. One is that of Hugh MacDonald who, in life, plotted to murder his cousin (the tower-building Donald Gorm Og MacDonald) in order to become chief of the clan. He was arrested in 1601 before he could carry out his scheme and tossed into the Duntulm Castle dungeon. Evidently deciding that a swift execution was too good for his would-be assassin, Donald left his cousin to die of thirst in the prison, having first supplied him with a serving of salted beef and an empty pitcher. Hugh MacDonald is said to have gone mad before he finally expired, which explains why his ghost is apt to emit manic screams.

At least he doesn't want for company, and what company it is, for one of the other wraiths reported to lurk around the place is none other than Donald Gorm Og MacDonald himself. He is said to go about in a belligerent manner fighting his fellow phantoms, which, as ghost stories go, at least has the benefit of novelty.

The third of Duntulm's most noteworthy spirits belongs to a nursemaid. She is said to have had charge of an infant son of a MacDonald chief but carelessly allowed him to topple out of a castle window to fall to his death on the rocks. Her punishment was to be set adrift on the open seas in a tiny boat. The tragic accident has been quoted as the real reason why the castle was abandoned in 1730, but there's no evidence to suggest it ever happened. Like that of Hugh MacDonald, the nursemaid's ghost is also a screamer, so what with those two and Donald's perpetual bouts of fisticuffs with all and sundry, it's a wonder anyone in the nearby hamlet of Duntulm gets any sleep at night at all.

59 ARDVRECK CASTLE

LOCH ASSYNT, SUTHERLAND

A place of dark deeds that brought a fanatical monarchist to a grisly end

LOCATION
A837, Loch Assynt, nr
Inchnadamph, Sutherland
IV27 4HN

GRID REFERENCE
NC 239 236

PUBLIC TRANSPORT
Ardvreck may be miles from
anywhere but its location on
the A837 means it's far from
inaccessible. Take the train

to Inverness and, from the
railway station, the 61 bus
(decoaches.co.uk; 01463
222444) to Ullapool. From
there, the 809 bus
(georgerapsontravel.com;
01463 242649) will
transport you to the castle.

WHEN TO VISIT
Open at any reasonable time
during daylight hours.

ADMISSION CHARGE
Free

WEBSITE
n/a

TELEPHONE
n/a

owards the southern end of the six-mile long Loch Assynt, a low promontory juts out into the waters. It's a naturally defensible position, particularly on those occasions when the loch has risen high enough to flow over the lower parts of the peninsula, so creating an island. It's no surprise then to find that the past owners of this corner of Assynt, the MacLeod clan, saw fit to raise up a castle here to defend their land.

By all accounts the original building was a modest affair: a three- or possibly four-storey rectangular box, a miniature Brutalist monument thrown up nearly half a millennium before the Brutalists would have their day. Dwarfed by the conical Glas Bheinn behind it to the north,

Ardvreck (*Aird Bhreac* in Gaelic) is now reduced to what appears to be a fist of stone with a single finger pointing accusingly up at the sky. As you approach the castle from the main road that runs alongside the loch, traces of a ditch and the remnants of a dry-stone wall can also be seen, ghosts of a once more formidable defensive barrier.

The castle was built by Angus Mor ('the Great') III sometime in the second half of the 15th century. Several modern sources, probably copying an error made by one of them, claim the date of construction as 1590 or 1591. This was in fact around the time that enlargements were made to the fortress by Donald Ban IX. A datestone recording the

improvements, showing either 1591 or 1597, was recorded in 1794 but has since disappeared. However, such was the diminutive size of the original castle that, even after a slim circular tower topped by a square caphouse had been added by Ban, Ardvreck was still not even big enough to run to kitchens – these were housed in a building of their own. The servants too were forced to live in quarters outside the castle, as were the horses, whose stables occupied a separate plot on the peninsula.

Small it may have been, but Ardvreck has a reputation as a castle within whose walls many violent and bloody atrocities occurred. Its owners, the MacLeod family, were certainly a boisterous lot, much given to feuding – often within the clan itself – and renowned for being swifter in employing the claymore and dirk

to resolve disputes than was perhaps healthy. However, many of the details of the abominable acts that are said to have taken place in the castle appear to have been lost in the fog of time, and perhaps that's as well. What we do know is that Ardvreck has one claim, if not to fame, then to a solid footnote in the annals of history. It arises from an event that took place in 1650. Though it could hardly have been known at the time, the incident was to sow the seed of the castle's ultimate destruction.

The story begins with the execution of King Charles I in January 1649. The regicide did not stop certain avid royalists from continuing to fight for the cause – indeed, for many the act inflamed their desire to see the monarchy restored. One such devotee was James Graham, Marquess of Montrose. The dashing

nobleman, soldier and poet had been an extremely successful champion of King Charles in Scotland during what is now known as the Wars of the Three Kingdoms (formerly the English Civil Wars). During a campaign waged in 1644–5, he knitted together a fine army from various disparate Highland elements and Confederate Irish forces. He secured victories at the Battles of Tippermuir and Aberdeen, sacking the latter and slaughtering many of its inhabitants. He led his men in winter through thick snow to the slopes of Ben Nevis in a bold flanking move that resulted in his triumph at the Battle of Inverlochy. Further victories were gained over the pro-Parliamentarian Covenanters at Auldearn, Alford and Kilsyth. This last battle put the marquess in control of more or less the whole of Scotland.

However, it all went badly wrong shortly afterwards, when Graham's forces were soundly defeated at the Battle of Philiphaugh in September 1645. A period of exile in Norway ensued, before he returned to Scotland, landing in Orkney in the spring of 1650. With Charles I dead and the Commonwealth declared, Graham took up the cudgels on behalf of Charles II. On 27 April 1650, he led a Royalist army into battle at Carbisdale, and suffered the embarrassment of defeat to a far less numerous but more organised Covenanter force.

Fleeing from the field, he eventually sought sanctuary at Ardvreck, a 30-mile ride to the northwest of Carbisdale, though Graham's journey appears to have been somewhat more circuitous. The owner of the castle at that time was Neil MacLeod but he happened to be away when his unexpected visitor arrived. Graham was thus welcomed in by MacLeod's wife, Christine Munro. Unfortunately for the marquess, the couple were no friends to the Royalist cause. Seizing her chance at glory, Munro cannily inveigled Graham into entering the castle's dungeon. No sooner had he stepped inside than the door was slammed, the key turned and his fate sealed. Covenanter troops were called. They took Graham to Edinburgh where he was hanged, drawn and quartered. His

head was put on a spike outside St Giles' Cathedral, where it remained for the next 11 years.

The restoration of the monarchy in 1660 saw the tables turned on the MacLeods, whom Charles II naturally blamed for the death of the ill-starred Marquess of Montrose. Debts began to pile up, some of which were bought up by one of the MacLeod clan's Highland foes, the Mackenzies of Wester Ross. In 1672, the Mackenzies came calling at Ardvreck, claiming the castle as part-payment for the debts. The owner, by that time one John MacLeod, refused to hand it over. For a fortnight, the fortress was besieged, with MacLeod surrendering only when the Mackenzies took delivery of some siege engines.

If you look east along the A837 from Ardvreck, you'll see another ruin not far off. This was once Calda House, now a melancholy skeleton whose history is intertwined with that of the castle. Just over half a century after his family had taken over the lochside fortress, Kenneth Mackenzie (and more particularly his wife Frances) tired of its rather spartan living quarters and made the decision to build something rather more comfortable. Calda House was the result. It was constructed partially of stone taken from Ardvreck, which helps to explain the diminished state of the castle today. Unfortunately, the creation of this 14-bedroom luxury mansion led to the clan's financial meltdown and, just 10 years after its completion, the Mackenzies found themselves having to sell up. The Earl of Sutherland bought the house. In a fit of pique, the Mackenzies (who hated the Sutherlands) duly burnt it down.

As might be expected from a castle with a reputedly violent past, its remains are said to be haunted. The myriad ghosts who wander its precincts include an unnamed daughter of a MacLeod chief. She unwisely agreed to marry the devil in a (vain, as it turned out) bid to keep the castle in MacLeod hands. Regretting her decision, she drowned herself in Loch Assynt, and it is said that she can sometimes be seen on the beach, weeping. The information board at the castle also mentions the shade of a 'tall man in grey' who 'seems to be an altogether happier ghost', so perhaps not everything at Ardvreck was perpetual doom and gloom after all.

60 CUBBIE ROO'S CASTLE
WYRE, ORKNEY

Once part of Norway, this castle was known as 'a very unhandy place to attack'

LOCATION
Half a mile from pier, Island of Wyre, Orkney KW17 2QA

GRID REFERENCE
HY 441 263

PUBLIC TRANSPORT
A trip to see Cubbie Roo's Castle is one for the dedicated (or those who happen to be Orcadian). The simplest way is to leave mainland Scotland by taking the Pentland Ferries vessel (pentlandferries.co.uk; 0800 688 8998) from Gills Bay to St Margaret's Hope on

Orkney. From there, the X1 bus will convey you to the bus station at Kirkwall, whence a number 6 bus (both stagecoachbus.com; 01856 870555) will speed you further northwards to Tingwall Ferry. As the name suggests, a ferry (orkneyferries.co.uk; 01856 878014) sails from the dock there to the island of Wyre. Cubbie Roo's Castle is a half-mile walk along the road from the pier, turning right along a track by the (somewhat anonymous-looking) heritage centre,

where you'll find tea- and coffee-making facilities and some information boards about the castle and the natural history of the island.

WHEN TO VISIT
Open all the time

ADMISSION CHARGE
Free

WEBSITE
historicenvironment.scot (Historic Environment Scotland)

TELEPHONE
0131 668 8600

There's something exhilarating about standing not merely on an island but on an island off an island. The isle of Wyre is just over a mile square in area, making it one of the smallest inhabited islands in the Orcadian archipelago. With a population that does not even run to double figures, it is obliged to share a ferry service with neighbouring Rousay and Egilsay for the short hop to Orkney Mainland. It means that a trip to the island's premier attraction, Cubbie Roo's Castle, can be something of an odyssey, but one well worth making. It is,

after all, the earliest known medieval castle in Scotland. And furthermore, for over six centuries, it was part of Norway, so you get to do some international time travelling as well.

Had you come here in 1145 – the most probable year of the castle's construction – you'd have found yourself under the rule of a powerful Norse chieftain named Kolbein Hrúga. It was he who ordered the construction of Cubbie Roo and he who has lent his name to it, albeit that it has been passed down to us in a somewhat adulterated form. Although

none of the walls that remain of his stronghold are very high, the main outlines of the castle buildings and fortifications are surprisingly well preserved and, along with the defensive ditches and ramparts, give the feel of a labyrinth.

The mound on which the venerable fortress is located is of no vast elevation but Cubbie Roo still affords excellent views from the top of the tower across the waters surrounding Wyre. This would have allowed Hrúga and later holders of the castle to keep a good watch on shipping moving about this central part of the archipelago. The Orkneyinga Saga – a lengthy history of the area written in the early 13th century – describes the stronghold as a 'fine stone castle'. A later chronicle, King Haakon's Saga, notes that 'it was a very unhandy place to attack', an observation that doubtless arose from the siege of Cubbie Roo that took place in 1231. Earlier that year, Jon Haraldsson had been murdered in Thurso, on mainland Scotland. His assailants were Snaekoll Gunnisson and a man named Hanef who slew him during a drunken confrontation over the rights to the Earldom of Orkney. The killers and their retinue fled across the sea to Cubbie Roo with the murdered earl's kinsmen in hot pursuit. A siege ensued but such was the strength of the little castle that the avenging party could find no way of breaching its defences. In time, the two sides agreed to seek out King

Haakon of Norway to have him arbitrate in the matter.

Norse rule over Wyre ended in 1468, when Orkney and Shetland were ceded to Scotland by Christian I of Denmark and Norway. The islands were offered in lieu of a dowry settled on the king's daughter Margaret on her marriage to James III of Scotland. The history of Cubbie Roo from that point becomes rather obscure but we do know that by the late 18th century the castle was a ruin. It was subjected to unfortunately amateurish excavations in the 1920s and 1930s, first by its then owner and then after it had been taken into the guardianship of the state. Most of the records and finds from those digs have been lost.

There are very few Norse castles in Britain that we know of, and none at all in Scandinavia, since no one there felt the need to build them during that epoch. Cubbie Roo is one of only two that have been excavated (the other is the slightly later Castle of Old Wick in Caithness), which makes it a very special place indeed. But for all its historical significance, it's the domestic details that have survived that bring the past into focus for visitors today. In particular, the very fine subterranean rock-cut water tank at the foot of the tower and the stone oven in the kitchen next door give a taste of what it would have been like to live in the castle. The farmstead that sustained the inhabitants was established alongside and is still a farm nearly 900 years later. It's called the Bu and you can see it from the castle – the farm buildings are to the left and beyond the ruined church.

Of which, since it's likely you'll have travelled some distance in order to visit Cubbie Roo's Castle, it would be an act of folly not to drop in on St Mary's chapel (which you would have to pass on your way to the castle in any case). This Romanesque place of worship was probably constructed by Kolbein Hrúga at the same time as the castle and would have been an important part of the estate. In 1933, the remnants of some iron mail armour adorned with brass rings were discovered in the nave. The item appears to have been placed there not long after the chapel was built, which means that, rather excitingly, it may have belonged to the great chieftain himself. Just like Cubbie Roo, it's a little piece of Norway left on Scottish soil.

AUTHOR'S ACKNOWLEDGEMENTS

'Silent gratitude,' wrote Gertrude Stein, 'isn't very much use to anyone.'

I would thus like to offer some very loud gratitude to the following people, organisations and companies:

Pentland Ferries for their kind assistance and safe passage over to Orkney and back (if you haven't been to Orkney, do go, it really is a smashing place and the sailing from Gills Bay is a glorious one).

Anyone who gave me a free ticket or a tour or simply the wisdom of their experience.

Camilla Nichol, who not only gave me a lift to the excellent Pengersick Castle from Penzance station on a Sunday morning, but who made me coffee to take around with me while I was exploring it.

Peter Marquis, who is one of a team who have done a great job of saving Hopton Castle.

The very nice woman on the desk (it pains me that I have forgotten your name but you know who you are) at Edzell Castle who made me a lovely cafetière of coffee and cheered me up when the clouds refused to budge.

Everyone at Historic Environment Scotland who assisted me, with special thanks to Michelle Andersson. You all carried out your work with professionalism and a can-do attitude even though I lobbed things your way at the last minute. It's much appreciated.

Anyone who turned up with a key to let me into a castle and then locked up afterwards without locking me in.

Shuna Williams at Cadw, the Welsh historic environment service, for your help and advice.

Particular thanks go to Mark Woolley for the excellent photographs of Pendragon Castle and to Gerald Strother for the fine images of Caerlaverock.

James Tims at AA Publishing for agreeing that this would make a ripping book and for sifting through all the many thousands of photographs I subsequently took.

Donna Wood for wielding the magic blue pencil with such aplomb (that semicolon on page 127 is all her work, you know). By rights, she should really get a co-author billing.

Judith Forshaw for proofreading the book and ensuring that it contains absolutely no misprunts. (This is my standard 'thanking the proofreader' joke but until I stop enjoying it I'll keep using it.)

Anyone who aided me in some way, large or small, but who has found themselves unaccountably left off this list. This is self-evidently more a reflection on

my feebly functioning brain than on the value of the service you provided. Write to me and I'll include you in the next reprunt.

Before I go, let us keep in mind those immortal words of the 17th-century French belletrist, François de La Rochefoucauld:

'Gratitude is merely the secret hope of further favours.'

PICTURE CREDITS

AA Media wishes to thank the following illustrators, photographers and organisations for their assistance in the preparation of this book.

Abbreviations for the picture credits are as follows –
(t) top; (b) bottom; (l) left; (r) right; (c) centre

Map illustrations by David Wardle

Endpaper courtesy of The Heraldry Society, theheraldrysociety.com

23; 24; 25; 27; 28-29; 34; 38; 45; 47; 49; 52; 53; 99; 100; 101tl; 101tr; 101b; 106; 119; 120; 129; 136-137 © Historic England Archive; 78 © Skyscan Balloon Photography. Historic England Archive; 215 mauritius images GmbH/Alamy Stock Photo

All other photographs taken by Dixe Wills.

Every effort has been made to trace the copyright holders, and we apologise in advance for any unintentional omissions or errors. We would be pleased to apply any corrections in a following edition of this publication.

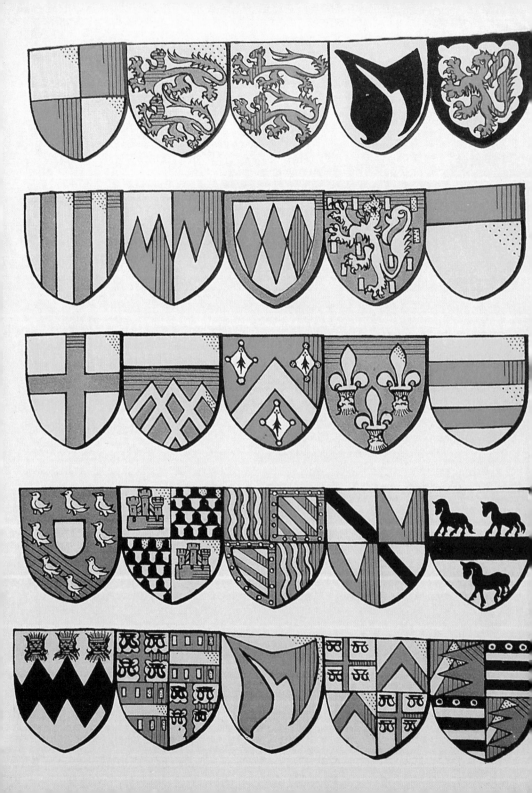